Learning to Read in a New Language

Learning to Read in a New Language

Making Sense of Words and Worlds

Second Edition

Eve Gregory

Los Angeles • London • New Delhi • Singapore

SAGE Publications Ltd
1 Oliver's Yard
55 City Road
London
EC1Y 1SP

SAGE Publications Inc
2455 Teller Road
Thousand Oaks, California 91320

SAGE Publications India Pvt Ltd
B1/I1 Mohan Cooperative Industrial Area
Mathura Road
New Delhi 110 044

SAGE Publications Asia-Pacific Pte Ltd
33 Pekin Street #02-01
Far East Square
Singapore 048763

Library of Congress Control Number 2007935305

British Library Cataloguing in Publication data
A catalogue record for this book is available from the British Library

ISBN 978-1-4129-2856-4
ISBN 978-1-4129-2857-1 (pbk)

Typeset by Dorwyn, Wells, Somerset
Printed in Great Britain by Cromwell Press Trowbridge Wiltshire
Printed on paper from sustainable resources

To Elsie, George and Klara and to all the children,
past and present, who appear in this book

Contents

List of figures

Foreword

While the issues of literacy and culture continue to be the focus of attention – and matters of contention – for many teachers, education students, parents, researchers, interested citizens and politicians, there is currently limited understanding of the teaching and learning processes through which young children become literate in a new language. As a consequence, teachers around the world in this 'post-monolingual' age (Soto and Kharem, 2006) often struggle to teach reading and writing to the increasing numbers of children in their classrooms who are learning in a language new to them. Most use models that presuppose a 'monolingual mind' based on children learning to read in their home language. *Learning to Read in a New Language* synthesizes research, models and practice, and provides a way forward, that is, a way of working with new language learners that is responsive to a range of children, approaches, contexts and languages.

Gregory begins this important, useful book with a carefully detailed, theoretical analysis of new language learners, describing the complexity of what they *can* do as well as their learning needs, their expertise as creative and active learners and teachers, and the valuable but often ignored literacy experiences with a range of adult and child teachers that they bring with them from their homes and communities. Her analysis draws on the concept drawn from sociocultural theory of the integration of mind and culture and, thus, the synthesis of intra-personal, interpersonal and cultural processes of becoming literate. Interwoven throughout this discussion are excerpts from literacy interactions with real children from a variety of cultural and language backgrounds, bringing the concepts to life and adding children's voices to the mix. Throughout, she argues that literacy tuition involves explicit teaching that takes full account of the sociocultural context within which children live and learn.

Building on this analysis, Gregory provides a critique of current approaches to literacy instruction and then shares her innovative and teacher-friendly inside-out/outside-in model which 'puts meaning in the middle', integrating decoding and meaning-making in personal interactions and attending to the specific language strengths and weaknesses of each child. This model of literacy as 'making sense of words and worlds' includes a clearly explained graphic organizer that synthesizes different kinds of literacy and language clues, a discussion of the unique ways that individual new language learners may use such clues, and detailed plans – including activities, materials and books – that build on that model.

This book is a terrific resource that stands as an example of the finely tuned teaching recommended for use with new language learners. It scaffolds the reader's developing understanding and moves the reader from theory to practice, from insights to implementation. Gregory has carefully designed this progress, building slowly with ideas and images, examples, questions and summaries used in combination with a well-developed argument. Her book makes an important contribution and challenges us to address this critical educational and social need with the tools she provides. It urges us to ask ourselves: with whom will we share this book and our new-found knowledge? Teachers? Colleagues? Teacher education students? Parents? A local politician? How will we use it in our courses and our classrooms? How will we change our understandings and our practice? How can we make sure that the insights, expertise and energy generated by this book are used to improve radically the literacy teaching of new language learners? How can we build on the remarkable strengths and abilities of children like Annie who at 7 years of age can speak Thai, is learning to read it and simultaneously is learning to both speak and read in English?

Soto, L.D. and Kharem, H. (2006) A post-monolingual education, *International Journal of Educational Policy, Research, and Practice*, 7: 21–34.

Dinah Volk
Early Childhood Program, College of Education
Cleveland State University

Preface

I concluded the Preface to *Making Sense of a New World: Learning to Read in a Second Language*, written in 1996, by saying: 'In Britain, it is still easy to feel "cocooned" within a monolingual world. Yet … there is every reason to believe that the age of the emergent bilingual has scarcely yet begun'. Those words were written as the twentieth century drew to a close. Scarcely a decade later, that statement would have been impossible. Yet few could have predicted the speed with which this change would happen. In 2008, most large cities in the world are abuzz with different languages being spoken and different scripts being written or read. In many parts of London, monolingual children are exceptional and classrooms are able to draw on the wealth of numerous languages offered by families and their communities. Although a proportion of newcomers to cities are still, like their predecessors, fleeing persecution or economic poverty, important new factors have emerged that were not fully envisaged a decade ago. New technologies, and especially the Internet, have transformed people's ability to conduct their work anywhere in the world and informed their choice of residence. Students are spending time at institutions thousands of miles from home and often taking their children with them. Families are deciding to relocate to more pleasant climates and their children immediately switch languages in school. Additionally, the development of new technologies and resulting globalization have led to the dominance of certain languages which have become a lingua franca across the world. At present, English has attained this status. By the end, or perhaps even the middle, of the twenty-first century a different language may prevail. The status of English means that many young children across the world, not just in private but in state schools, are becoming bilingual and using two or more scripts. Of course, this has always happened in community contexts as the children in the first edition of this book revealed. However, it is now the norm as primary schools in many Asian and African countries show.

All this has led to a surge of interest in the field of language, culture and identity, and to a growing sophistication and change in the terminology used. Researchers and teachers are now distinguishing between the multilingualism and multiculturalism of communities and societies and the plurilingualism and pluriculturalism within individuals themselves. Others focus on the syncretism as young children blend cultures and languages to create new practices and forms. In recognition of the increasing scope and changing role of language learning in the lives of young children, I adopt the term 'new language learner' instead of 'emergent bilingual' in this book. The term recognizes the fact that, although many children may go on to become fully bilingual, others will stop before that point and will step in and out of different languages at different ages or stages of their school career.

In contrast with the growing sophistication in work on languages, cultures and identities, studies in early literacy learning have not kept up with the burgeoning research in this field. This is ironic, since all children will need to learn to *read* in the new language they learn. However, although we have always had plurilingual children, studies into how children learn to read have generally assumed a *monolingual mind*. Instead of drawing upon the skills and knowledge (as well as recognizing the weaknesses) of children who are able simultaneously to deal with more than one, or even two, languages and scripts, we often try to squash them into a monolingual mould. The tragedy of this is that we are in danger of suppressing the creativity of young children as they play and experiment, not just with words, but with future worlds. It is this creativity which, in this book, I try to reveal.

Eve Gregory
London, November 2007

Acknowledgements

This book owes its existence to a number of people. First and foremost, I thank the families, teachers and community teachers who invited me into their classrooms and homes and gave their time generously. I should especially like to thank Alan, Dabir and Nicole, who spared me time in their busy lives now they are no longer children, and Joy and Paul Stanton, who searched out Alan and Dabir for me. I also thank the teachers of Canon Barnett School in the London Borough of Tower Hamlets, Military Road School, Northampton and Sir John Heron School in the London Borough of Newham and, particularly, Rani Karim who facilitated much of my recent school work. Early episodes owe much to the patience of Nasima Rashid who worked with me for some years visiting families and community classes and teaching the children in school. Episodes with siblings were collected and analysed by Ann Williams and Ali Asghar who worked with me on an Economic and Social Research Council (ESRC)-funded project on Siblings as Mediators of Literacy in East London. Episodes with grandparents were collected by Mahera Ruby and Tahera Arju and analysed by Charmian Kenner and John Jessel, who worked with me on the project Intergenerational Learning between Grandparents and Young Children in East London, also funded by the ESRC and I am grateful to all these colleagues for their ongoing support. Episodes with peers were collected and analysed by Yangguang Chen and I should like to thank her for these. I also owe other examples of peer learning to Susi Long and her colleagues, Dinah Volk and Charmian Kenner. I should also like to thank Dinah Volk for contributing the Foreword to this book. I should especially like to thank my co-authors in Chapter 2; Dinah Volk, Joan Bursch, Pippa Stein, Lynne Slonimsky, Keang Vong, Yu-chiao Chung, Mukhlis Abu Bakar, Allan Luke, Joan Kale and Mahera Ruby who generously offered their work and, of course, the families who worked with them. I should like to thank Pashamon Prabpal and Annie Gregory for their contribution to Chapter 1, Roy Gregory for writing the music for the 'Good Morning' song and Yueping Zhang for the Chinese characters in Chapter 5. My past and present PhD students have always offered me inspiration as well as Margaret Meek and colleagues from both the cross-cultural intercollegiate group and members of the Multilingual Europe seminar series funded by the ESRC. Helen Fairlie, my editor at Sage, has given me support and encouragement throughout the writing of this book and I should like to thank her for that. Last, but by no means least, I should like to express my thanks to Karl Kimmig for his patience and helpful suggestions throughout this and with all my work.

Work leading to this book has been financially supported by Goldsmiths, University of

London, the ESRC, the Leverhulme Trust and the Paul Hamlyn Foundation.

I should also like to thank Editorial Panamericana, Inc. for the use of the cover and p. 4 of *Nuestra Cartilla Fonética*, Editorial Panamericana, Inc. (t. (787) 277 7988/f (787) 277 7240 (edpanamerican@yahoo.com), Thai Airlines for the use of *Elephant*, *English Quarterly* (Canadian Council of Teachers of English Language Arts) for use of excerpts from grandparents (Vol. 36, No. 4), Routledge for use of excerpts from *Many Pathways to Literacy: Young Children Learning with Siblings, Grandparents, Peers and Communities*, (2004, eds E. Gregory, S. Long and D. Volk, p. 118) and David Fulton for use of Elsey, a fuller version of which appears in *One Child, Many Worlds* (1997, ed. E. Gregory). I should also like to thank colleagues at the University of Vic, Spain, for use of excerpts from 'Ventafocs'.

Setting the Scene

He who knows no other language does not truly know his own.
(Goethe, in Vygotsky, 1962: 110)

KEY TERMS

Mother tongue	A term subject to much debate and sometimes referred to as home/heritage/community or first language. Definitions include: the language learnt first; the language known best; the language used most; the language with which one identifies; the language one dreams/thinks/counts in; and so on; none of which are acceptable to all. It is generally recognized that a mother tongue may change, even several times during a lifetime.
New language learner	A child who is at an early stage or who still lacks fluency in a second or additional language but whose ultimate aim is to become as fluent as possible, that is, able to communicate easily with others in the language and able positively to identify with both (or all if more than two are being learned) language groups and cultures.
Emergent biliterate	A child who is learning to read and write in more than one language simultaneously.
Metalanguage	A term in linguistics for language used to talk about language. Research studies show that young bilinguals have an advanced metalinguistic awareness as they are able to realize the arbitrariness of language, see word boundaries, and so on at an earlier stage than monolinguals.
Grammar	A description of a language; an abstract system of rules in terms of which a child's knowledge of a language can be explained.
Orthography	The principles underlying a spelling or writing system.

Annie is 7 years old and beginning her second year of primary school in Thailand. From time to time she escapes the crowded city of Bangkok to stay with her extended family in the countryside. Eventually, she hopes to live in Britain where she has relatives. She has already learned to read simple texts in Thai, her mother tongue, and loves to practise these with her mother at home. Like many young children in schools across different continents, Annie is also beginning to learn to read and write in English, a language chosen by many countries as a necessary asset for the education of all young children as they start school. Other children across the world will be learning in different languages, often the one that is politically dominant in the country in which they live. Some will be the children of refugees, others of economic migrants, others from indigenous families whose mother tongue is not the official language of the school and yet others from multilingual countries where children will be expected to become literate simultaneously in more than one language. Like many children across the world, Annie will need to learn that the new language will have a different script and very different rules from her own. Gradually, through becoming a reader in English, Annie will learn to make sense not only of new words but of other worlds, with very different customs, traditions and stories from her own. The aim of this book is to show how young children undertake the task of learning to read in a new language at school or at home and to argue that children like Annie have distinct strengths and weaknesses not explained in monolingual perspectives on early literacy. Later chapters will introduce Julializ from the USA, Pia and Nicole from France, Ah Si from Macau-Sar, China, Elsey from Australia, Sanah from Singapore and Dineo from South Africa as well as children from Britain. Although they will all be learning in very different cultural contexts, I shall draw out common patterns that hold these children apart from their monolingual peers. The book thus suggests principles and practices for all those interested in observing the learning of young new language learners and for those engaged in initiating them into new words and worlds.

In this chapter, I begin to outline the nature of the task through the example of Annie reading in both Thai and English. Annie is lucky, since her mother has enjoyed telling and reading stories to her since she was very small. She is now trying to find dual language Thai/English stories for her to read and finds *Elephant*, a traditional Thai fable.

Annie first reads the story with her mother in Thai. Afterwards, she reads the story again in English with a native English speaker. Looking closely at Annie's reading in both languages, we begin to perceive some of the differences between reading in a first and a new language, as well as the complexity of tackling a text in a language one cannot fluently speak. Since this book is written for English rather than Thai speakers, we can only dissect her achievements in Thai through the English language. However, the grammatical structure and rules of Thai are very different from English, as we shall see later in the chapter.

The animal story – Elephant

นิทานสัตว์

ช้าง The Elephant

ช้างโขลงหนึ่งพากันเดินหาแหล่งน้ำ ในที่สุดพวกมันก็พบสระน้ำแห่งหนึ่ง

A herd of elephants wandered to search for a pond. Finally, they found one. (p. 1)

ฝูงช้างต่างพากันเหยียบย่ำไปบนพื้นดินรอบๆสระซึ่งเป็นที่อยู่ของพวกกระ

ต่าย ทำให้กระต่ายถูกเหยียบตายเป็นจำนวนมาก

The elephants stepped on the soil around the pond which was the rabbits' shelter. This killed many rabbits. (p. 2)

เมื่อเห็นเข้าดังนั้น กระต่ายที่รอดชีวิตต่างก็ปรึกษากันว่าจะแก้ปัญหานี้อย่างไร

กระต่ายตัวหนึ่งเอ่ยขึ้นว่า 'ฉันมีความคิดจะไปบอกพวกช้าง

ว่าฉันเป็นกระต่ายที่มาจากพระจันทร์

และพระจันทร์ห้ามไม่ให้ผู้ใดดื่มน้ำจากสระนี้'

When many rabbits died, the rest of them discussed the problem. A rabbit said,
'I have an idea. I will tell the elephants that I am the rabbit of the moon, and the moon forbids anyone to drink water from this pond.' (p. 3)

เช้าวันต่อมา ฝูงช้างก็มาดื่มน้ำที่สระอีก

กระต่ายตัวที่ออกความคิดก็มารออยู่ก่อนแล้ว มันตะโกนว่า

The following morning, the herd of elephants came to drink water in the pond. The rabbit who had the idea arrived before the elephants. He shouted … (p. 4)

'เจ้าพวกช้างทั้งหลาย ฉันเป็นกระต่ายที่อยู่บนดวงจันทร์

นำคำสั่งจากพระจันทร์มาบอกพวกเจ้าว่า

ห้ามผู้ใดลงมาว่ายน้ำหรือดื่มน้ำจากสระนี้ ใครฝ่าฝืนจะโดนลงโทษ'

— Continues over —

'You elephants, I am the rabbit which is on the moon. I convey the moon's words to all of you. He forbids any animals to swim or drink water in this pond. Anyone who ignores his words will be killed.' (p. 5)

จ่าโขลงของช้างไม่ใช้ปัญญาไตร่ตรองจึงหลงเชื่อคำของกระต่าย

"ขอบพระคุณในความเมตตาของท่าน พวกเราทำผิดไปแล้ว

ได้โปรดอย่าให้พระจันทร์ลงโทษเราเลย" จ่าโขลงช้างอ้อนวอน

The elephant's leader which was very foolish believed the rabbit.
'Thank you very much for your kindness. We have made a mistake. We hope the moon will not punish us,' he pleaded with the rabbit. (p. 6)

'แล้วตอนนี้พระจันทร์ท่านอยู่ไหน ? โปรดพาเราไปพบท่าน

เพื่อจะได้ขออภัยที่ได้ล่วงเกิน'

'พระจันทร์กำลังว่ายน้ำอยู่ในสระ ฉันจะพาเจ้าไปพบท่านเดี๋ยวนี้แหละ'

กระต่ายตอบพลางนำทางช้างไป

'Where is the moon now? Please bring me to see him. I would like to apologise to him.'
'He is taking a bath in the pond. I will bring you to see him right now,' the rabbit replied and went ahead. (p. 7)

เมื่อมาถึงสระก็เป็นเวลาค่ำ มีเงาของพระจันทร์สะท้อนอยู่ในน้ำ

กระต่ายชี้ไปที่นั่นแล้วพูดว่า

'ทำความเคารพท่านแล้วก็รีบไปจากที่นี่เสียโดยเร็ว'

When they arrived at the pond, it was at dusk. The shadow of the moon reflected in the water. The rabbit pointed at it and said, 'Pay respect to him then hastily go away.' (p. 8)

จ่าโขลงช้างยกงวงขึ้นจรดศรีษะเป็นการแสดงความเคารพต่อพระจันทร์

หลังจากนั้นฝูงช้างก็ไม่กลับไปที่สระน้ำนั้นอีกเลย

The elephants' leader gradually lifted his trunk to touch his head to pay respect to the moon. Then the elephants went away and never came again. (p. 9)

⎯ Continues opposite ⎦

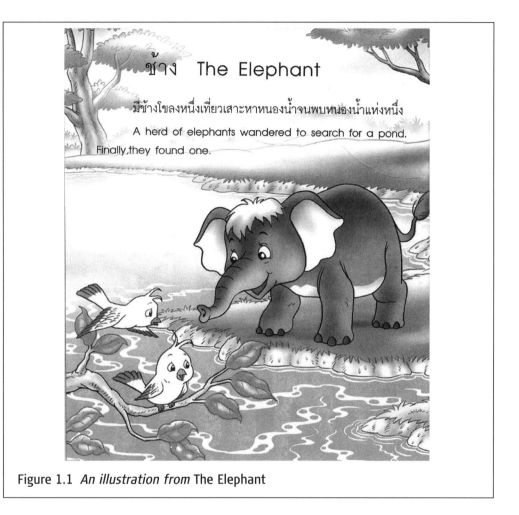

Figure 1.1 *An illustration from* The Elephant

Let us look first at what Annie can do in Thai after just a year of learning to read. Although both the story of *Elephant* and the book itself are new to Annie, she sets to reading confidently in Thai to her mother, holding the book herself and turning each page appropriately. As usual, her mother reads the first word on the page and Annie continues. Her reading appears fluent and effortless and she reads with obvious enjoyment. Her eyes search the illustrations for information and she comments on animals in the pictures as she goes along. But what is Annie actually able to do as she tackles the text? Through the dual-language version, we see that she successfully reads 19 different *nouns* (herd, elephants, rabbits, moon, pond, soil, shelter, problem, idea, water, morning, words, animals, leader, kindness, mistake, dusk, shadow, trunk), 30 different *verbs* (wandered, found, search, stepped, killed, died, discussed, said, have/had, tell, am, forbids, drink, came, arrived, shouted, convey, swim, ignores, pleaded, bring, apologise, replied, went, reflected, pointed, pay respect to, lifted, touch), nine different *prepositions* (on, around, of, from, in, before, ahead, at, away from) as well as a limited number of *pronouns*, *adverbs* and *adjectives*. Had she been reading in English, she would have read 22 verbs in *the past tense*, seven in the *simple present* and one each in the *present continuous*, the *future* and *future passive* as well as *future conditional*, and the *present perfect tenses*, *infinitives* and the *imperative* form. She uses prepositions of place, time and motion. Additionally, Annie obviously understands the content of the story and she is able to empathize with the characters. When questioned, after reading, on what she likes about the story, she replies confidently: 'the rabbits … because they are clever'.

In fact, Thai is very different from English and there are, consequently, a number of language-specific grammatical and orthographic rules that Annie has already learned. Although the intention here is not to describe in detail the Thai language and script, a few aspects are important to understand the task Annie faces of becoming bilingual and biliterate in her first and her new language. First, we see that she is already becoming a competent user of the Thai script, an Indic alphabet originally designed to represent the sounds of Sanskrit but with new symbols created during the thirteenth century to represent the sounds of Thai (Hudak, in Comrie, 1987). The script is by no means an easy one to learn. Thai is a tonal language with five different tones (low, high, falling, rising and mid-tone) with several symbols for the same sound. There are 44 *consonants* divided into three groups (high, mid and low) to indicate the tone in spelling, a complication when learning to read, as well as 18 *vowel* sounds. As in other tonal languages, for example Mandarin and Cantonese, use of the correct tone is crucial since reading a word or sentence using the wrong tone will entirely change its meaning. There are other aspects that make both spoken and written Thai very difficult – the Thai themselves regard their language as complex and stratified, even for highly educated people. Central to this is the proliferation of titles, ranks and royal kin terminology that has affected various aspects of the language. The choice of pronouns, for example, is highly complex. In contrast to a simple 'I' and 'you' in English, Annie will need to choose according to the sex, age and social position of herself and the addressee as well as her attitude or emotion towards the person at the time of speaking. She will later need to begin to learn elaborate, often ryhming, expressions. However, other aspects might make both spoken and written Thai easier to contend with than English. There are no *articles* ('a', 'an', 'the', for example) to distinguish between and no *inflections* for case, gender or number of nouns – these are indicated by either affixes (prefixes or suffixes), compounding ('parents' = 'father' and 'mother'), reduplicating ('dek' or 'child'; 'dekdek' or 'children') or repeating a word with the same word one tone higher in pitch than the normal tone, an effect usually used by women. Verbs also have no inflection for tense or number which are shown either by the context, an added time expression or a preverb, often showing that the action begun by the main verb has been completed. Finally, even a non-Thai reader may discern from the text above that, orthographically, there is no space between individual words; a space is used to denote the end of a sentence rather than a full stop. This very brief glance at the Thai language and script begins to highlight what Annie, like many young children, has achieved as she speaks and reads in her mother tongue by the end of her first year of school.

The task ahead: new languages, literacies and scripts

The child assimilates his/her native language unconsciously and unintentionally but acquires a foreign language with conscious realisation and intention … the child acquiring a foreign language is already in command of a system of meaning in the native language which s/he transfers to the sphere of another language. (Vygotsky, 1935, in John-Steiner, 1986: 350)

Reading in English, a language Annie is learning formally in school and beginning to learn informally with her mother, is a very different matter. A text she manages confidently in Thai is clearly too difficult in English and Annie looks expectantly to the native English speaker (a relative she trusts, yet sees and speaks to very rarely) for help. Instead of holding the book herself, she hands over to the adult to take control and to turn the pages. Eavesdropping on Annie and the adult reading together begins to provide a window onto the strengths and weaknesses of a young child as she embarks on the task of learning to read in a new language:

Annie: *I can't read English. But I can read 'b', 'd', 'c' and '1,2,3,4,5,6,7,8,9,10'* (said very fast and in a sing-song voice).

Adult: *But you know the story in Thai, don't you, and that will help you. I'll read it to you first.*
(She reads the whole story in English to Annie, pointing carefully to each word as she does so)

Adult: *Now let's find one page. You see if you can find me one word you can read in English.*
(Annie turns over the pages to page 5 and scans the page, pointing along the lines with her finger and then picks out and reads from the first line 'You elephant')

Adult: *'Elephant!' You can read 'elephant'.* (Turns to page 3) *Where's the word that says 'rabbit'? Can you find it?*
(Annie runs her finger along the line until she finds 'rabbit' and reads it)

Adult: *That's great!* (Turns to page 4) *How about a word that says 'elephant'?*
(Annie finds the word)

Adult: *Yes! There's another one that says 'elephant' there. Can you find it?*
(Annie finds the word)

Adult: *Yes! Two words for 'elephant' on that page. Let's have a look at this page* (turns back to page 3). *What can you read on that page? Can you find the word for 'rabbit' again?*

(Annie points to the word and reads it)

Adult: *Yes! How many words say 'rabbit' on that page?*

(Annie runs her finger intently along the lines of print and counts 'one, two, three')

Adult: *Yes! Three words that say 'rabbit'. Any more?*

Annie: *No.*

Adult: *What about 'elephant'? Is there any word that says 'elephant' on that page?* (page 4)

(Annie runs her finger along the print. 'Yes' She points to the word)

Adult: *What about that word?* (turning the page (page 5), *she points to 'moon')*

Annie: *Mmm ... 'Moon'*

Adult: *Yes. What about that one?* (points to 'pond')

Annie: *'Pond'*

Adult: *Yes! Very good.* (Turns two pages to page 7) *What about 'pond' again on that page? Can you find it?*

(Annie scans the line and finds the word, saying 'There')

Adult: *Yes. How about 'rabbit'?* (page 7)

(Annie points to the word and reads it)

Adult: (Turns two pages to page 9) *How about 'elephant'?*

(Annie points to 'elephant')

Adult: *You've read nearly all the words on that page. Aren't you clever?* (Turns back to page 8) *Where's the word that says 'pond' again?*

(Annie points to the word and reads it)

Adult: *How about 'rabbit'?*

(Annie points to 'rabbit' and reads it)

Adult: (Turns to page 9) *How about 'elephant'?*

(Annie points to the word)

Adult: *'Moon'?*

(Annie points to the word and reads it)

Adult: *So all those words you know how to read. You know 'rabbit' and you could write it too. You know 'elephant', you know 'moon', you know 'pond'. What else do you know? You know 'you'. What else do you know? You know 'the' ... You know how to read 'the' ... What else do you know?*

Annie: *I think I know 'he'.*

Adult: *Do you? Where's 'he'?*

(Annie scans the pages and finds 'he' on pages 4 and 5)

Adult: *So you know lots of the words! You can nearly read that book in Thai and in English.*

(Annie smiles shyly and shakes her head)

Adult: *Yes you can. Look!* (points to all the words recognized by Annie and reads them). *What about this one? This long stick?* (points to 'I')

(Annie reads 'I')

Adult: *There you are. You can read that one too!*

Upon a further shared reading of the text, Annie also reads 'head', 'go', 'in' and 'on'. She counts the rabbits and elephants, says 'rabbits die' (pointing to the illustration of the dead rabbits) and 'kill' (pointing to the elephant).

What is Annie actually able to do as she attempts to read? She starts off by stating clearly 'I can't read English', and, indeed, her achievements in English cannot be compared with those in Thai. However, what follows and is depicted above clearly differentiates her from a monolingual English beginner reader. Her lack of knowledge of the grammar of spoken English means she is unable to predict phrases and sentences from the context. For example, she cannot 'read' from an illustration and say 'elephants came to drink water in the pond' (page 4). However, she can memorize at first sight nouns important to the story (elephants, rabbits, pond, water, moon) as well as call upon other words she possibly already knows from different contexts (die, kill, he, I). Chapters 4 and 5 explain further why this might be the case and how teachers might call upon children's skill in using such words. Crucially, however, Annie is able to call upon her knowledge of literacy in her mother tongue to help her tackle reading in a new language. First, she knows that print carries meaning, that stories can be reproduced in written narrative and that reading can be enjoyable. Then, she realizes that both scripts and words themselves are arbitrary. In other words, 'rabbit' can be an entirely different word written in a different script in different languages, yet still mean the same thing. Written conventions are also arbitrary. Words in Thai are not separated by a space, as in English, and a space in Thai has the equivalent meaning of a full-stop in English. Her emergent biliteracy also gives her a heightened metalinguistic awareness and concepts as well as terms such as 'word', 'page', 'line' and so on are not new to her. Third, her early biliteracy has familiarized her with directionality (both Thai and English read from left to right and top to bottom), as well as in what way to turn pages and to look to the illustrations for help in understanding the text. Finally, through her knowledge of both the spoken and written story she is beginning to appreciate that certain cultural understandings are universal, for example the importance of a spiritual power (in this case the moon) in controlling things. She is also beginning to understand the struggle and conflict between different creatures (in this case the rabbits and the elephants) in sorting out their disagreements over the occupation of land and water in order to live peacefully together in the same territory. Through these understandings and skills, Annie moves way beyond the learning of new words to begin to make sense of new worlds central to her later life.

What might be the role of the adult in facilitating children like Annie's learning?

We see that the adult:
- provides a role model of a fluent reader and speaker of English by reading the story slowly and clearly to the child, pronouncing each word clearly, pointing as she reads
- emphasizes important key words, usually nouns 'rabbit, elephant, moon, pond' and so on and verbs 'die, kill' and so on
- wherever possible, links the word with the appropriate illustration, using mime, for example, for 'die' and 'kill' where necessary
- uses repetition by drawing the child's attention to key words in different contexts throughout the story
- provides a relaxed situation by showing the child that s/he is not expected to read the whole text, thus relieving her of any pressure to 'perform' in a difficult task
- understands that, as a new language learner, Annie can understand far more than she can say
- focuses on what the child *can* actually achieve rather than what she cannot do.

Through emphasizing and repeating the words that Annie *can* read in all sorts of contexts, the adult gives her confidence to see herself as a future bilingual and biliterate adult, able to function in both Thai and English worlds.

Different countries, different contexts

As they set about making sense of a new world, children like Annie will have very different experiences according to where they happen to live and go to school. In the twenty-first century, many schools across the world are receiving children who will be learning literacy in a language they cannot fluently speak. Some will be already able to read and write another language at home, at a community language class or at school in the same or in a different country. Others will speak another language, yet will be unable to read or write it. Yet others will be introduced to a new language and literacy at the same time as becoming literate in their mother tongue. We need to remember that a large majority of countries in the world are multilingual. Between 4,000 and 5,000 languages are spoken in fewer than 200 different states; in Nigeria over 500 languages are spoken natively, while India claims over 1,600 mother tongues. In some countries, literacies in several languages and scripts will stand side by side in different types of schools; Street (1984) explains how this takes place in Iran, and Wagner et al. (1986) describe parallel but totally different schools in Morocco where learning takes place in either French or modern or classical Arabic. In many multilingual countries there will be one lingua franca or common language for formal education which only the more affluent will use for business or commerce in later life. In some former colonial countries all children may be faced with the task of making sense of literacy in an unknown language. In Zambia, for example, initial literacy teaching takes place in English, a language which many children have no means of practising outside the classroom. However unpromising the conditions, then, we know that children can and do learn to read for the first time in languages which they cannot yet speak and that this need not be regarded as something strange.

Circumstances in some parts of the world will be more favourable than those outlined above. Countries which have two or more official languages hold out more promise to strangers because they need to ensure early bilingual competence for all children through carefully planned immersion programmes. In Singapore, where there are four official languages, it is taken for granted that children will be able to learn to speak, read and write simultaneously in English and their home or heritage language (Mandarin, Malay or Tamil). Within Europe, some countries, such as Luxembourg and Switzerland also expect children to become biliterate within a few years. Some linguistic regions such as Wales or Catalonia also hold out similar expectations for children. Although school language programmes are directed at developing bilingualism in two languages only (English/Welsh or Spanish/Catalan), children with minority languages (largely Arabic speakers in Catalonia and speakers of South Asian languages in Wales) will benefit from the focus placed on language through immersion programmes. Second-language teaching will also be high on the agenda of initial and in-service teacher education courses and an integral part of National Curriculum requirements.

Even within officially monolingual countries, provision made for non-native speakers varies greatly. According to the US census of 2000, nearly one in five people, or over 47 million residents over the age of 5, speaks a language other than English at home, an increase of over 15 million since the 1990 census. An impressive figure, this number also excludes 'unofficial' or illegal residents in the country. Until 1998, children's schooling had been largely influenced by the US Supreme Court's crucial decision in the *Lau* v. *Nichols* case (1974) which stated that 'there is no equality of treatment merely by providing students with the same facilities, textbooks, teachers and curriculum; for students who do not understand English are effectively foreclosed from any meaningful education'. A variety of different programmes were then created which combined immersion into the new language with mother-tongue maintenance. Some of these programmes also included monolingual children should this be the choice of their parents. However, in 1998, elections in California led the way to an English-only policy. In spite of being home to the largest number of non-native English-speaking residents in the US (39 per cent), Proposition 227 'English for the Children' initiative won 61 per cent of votes, a victory that virtually dismantled California's 30-year-old system of bilingual education. Arizona quickly followed under Proposition 203. Finally, the Bilingual Education Act (BEA) of 1968 was replaced in 2002 by Title III of No Child Left Behind, in which the sole emphasis was on the rapid acquisition of English. This preoccupation with providing only transitional support for learning English through mother-tongue teaching contrasts with bilingual education in both Australia and Canada which emphasize bilingualism as a personal and national resource rather than as an anti-poverty measure (Edwards, 2004).

During the twenty-first century provision of new language and literacy tuition has become a matter of urgency for Europe. Since 2007 and the expansion of the Economic Union to 27 member states, there has been considerable movement of families away from their country of origin to other European cities. Britain has added Eastern European languages to its already considerable diversity of languages in many cities. Germany has become host to many non-native speakers who may be guest-workers (largely from Europe and Turkey), ethnic Germans (largely from Russia) or political asylum seekers. Most wish to remain permanently in the country. Provision for the language and literacy education for newcomers is very different according to the country they enter and the policy at the time. In Britain, provision will be largely determined by the local education authority as well as the individual school attended. Children in areas with a high number of non-native speakers are likely (although not assured) of access to either an additional language teacher or language instructor in their class. At the beginning of the twenty-first century, however, mother-tongue teaching is not provided to young children and parents will need to make private provision if they wish this to take place. Families in the southern German region of Baden-Württemberg may expect their children to enter a full-time immersion class for up to one year where structured tuition following the normal curriculum will provide enough German to join the ordinary class as soon as possible. Children are spared from tests in German until considered fluent. Children belonging to one of the larger minorities should benefit from the provision of mother-tongue teaching by their consulate and it will be the duty of the school to ensure collaboration between the mother-tongue and class teacher for joint curriculum planning and assessment of each child. Turkish speakers (the largest minority group) in neighbouring Bavaria, enable children to participate in pilot projects promoting bilingual education (in Turkish and German) for all. In either Austria or Switzerland, sections of the national or local curricula will be devoted to ways of combining second language with subject-content teaching backed up by specialist initial and in-service education for their specialist teachers. Recognition of the mother tongue, however, disappears abruptly in France. Unless attending a private bilingual school such as that of Pia in Alsace, the emphasis is on teaching children to become French citizens with an excellent knowledge of the language and culture as quickly as possible. Equality here is interpreted as providing the same curriculum, which should be uniformly of a high quality, for everyone.

Later in this book, we meet children learning in a variety of different contexts across the world.

What's in a word? Terms and terminology

Words used to describe children like Annie reflect current official educational policy in different countries. Were she to move to France, the term is simple and has not changed during recent years. Annie will be described as 'non-francophone' (non-French speaker). In Austria and Germany there is a subtle change to 'Schüler mit nichtdeutscher Muttersprache' or 'non-mother-tongue German speaker'. In Britain, we find that the 'immigrants' or 'non-English speakers' of the Plowden Report in 1967 become 'non-native speakers' or 'English second language learners' (ESL) in the Bullock Report of 1975, 'bilingual children' of the late 1970s and in the Cox Report of 1988, and 'children with English as an additional language' during the 1990s and into the twenty-first century.

Deciding upon a satisfactory term to describe the children in this book was not easy. Use of the term 'bilingual' in educational circles in Britain during the 1980s and 1990s to describe children like Annie signalled acceptance of a wider definition of the word to mean those at any stage of second language learning. Yet to refer to her as 'bilingual' contradicts both common understanding and dictionary definition which describes a bilingual as 'able to speak two languages, especially with fluency' (*Collins English Dictionary*, 1992). Clearly, children like Annie are not fluent (or anywhere near it) in their new language. If they were, there would be little point in writing a book about them. Indeed, there is a danger that use of the term 'bilingual' might deflect attention from the fact that the children need help as they go about learning in a new language. For this very reason, the term has been rejected in the US (where 'English Language Learners' (ELL) has replaced 'Limited English Proficiency' (LEP), 'non-native speakers', 'English second language speakers', 'minority language speakers' or sometimes 'non mother-tongue English speakers') and Australia (where the terms 'English second language' alongside 'children with languages other than English' (LOTE) are preferred). Yet 'bilingualism', or at least a reasonable fluency, will eventually be the aim of children like Annie and terms like 'second' or 'additional language learner' do not adequately reflect this. Nor are they 'foreign language learners' whose aim to communicate might be very limited in the new tongue. Really, the children are just beginning on the road to bilingualism. But 'beginner bilingual' implies that they need to be taught, step by step. This is obviously not the case. Luckily, children are also learning informally, from their classmates, the television and life generally. For this reason, I refer to both Annie and all the children in this book as 'new language learners'.

So how might we define 'new language learners'? I do not wish to imply that the learning of a new language 'just happens'. This may well occur over many years, but most children cannot afford such a luxury. Some may well have to achieve after a very short time the same level of literacy as their monolingual peers. Rather, I want to emphasize a joint process of formal and informal learning *where the teacher and her teaching does matter.* New language learners are children who may be at an early stage of learning or simply lack fluency in the language they need to read and write. All the children in this book have recently started school and are learning to read in a new language. In some cases, this may be the official language of the school and a language they do not speak regularly at home. In others, it might be the heritage language, regarded as a mother tongue but which children might not be able to speak fluently. In other cases, it might be a new language yet taught alongside either the official language or mother-tongue literacy at school. The children in this book have come from very different linguistic and cultural backgrounds. However, they share in common an ultimate aim of becoming *bilingual or plurilingual or competent* which I understand as: 'being able to function in two (or more) languages, either in monolingual or bilingual communities, in accordance with the sociocultural demands made on an individual's communicative and cognitive competence by these communities …' (Skutnabb-Kangas, 1984: 90).

Young new language learners are largely absent from research into reading. Studies on the reading process, methods of teaching and materials tend to assume either oral fluency in the language in which tuition takes place or considerable literacy skills in the first language if the learner is an adult or older child. The example of Annie, opening this chapter, shows us clearly that learning to read in a new language is very different from learning in a language one can already speak.

Therefore, do young new language learners approach the task differently? If so, what special strengths and weaknesses might the children have? How do educators provide 'culturally responsive' teaching which considers the expectations and interpretations of both children and their families? If these children do use special strategies, what implications might be drawn for teaching approaches at home and at school? How might we learn from what takes place in homes and families, including interaction between siblings and grandparents with young children as they play and learn together?

A plan of the book

This book aims to provide a framework for observing and teaching young children learning to read in a new language. Examples from years of classroom observations, taped reading interactions, interviews with mainstream and community teachers, and work with families are seated within the findings from research on sociocultural theory, second-language learning and learning to read. The book assumes no specialist knowledge on the part of the reader. It is written for teachers, researchers, student teachers, bilingual instructors, parents and everyone interested in young children learning to read in a new language at home or in school. There is no claim to provide simple solutions. Rather, the book illustrates the complexity of the dual task of learning a new skill in a new language and a new language through a new skill.

The argument put forward is that young learners have particular strengths as they step into reading in a new language at home or in school, strengths which are not accounted for in 'mainstream' studies on reading. Throughout the book, case studies and taped interactions are used to urge readers to observe, in detail, ways in which new language learners approach the reading task. The book aims to encourage readers to examine carefully their own strategies as they work with the children and makes practical suggestions for linking the teaching of English with beginning reading, listening to children read, assessing their English and working with families and community schools. Above all, the book aims to highlight the importance of an awareness of different strengths (and weaknesses) if we are to provide equal access to literacy to the new language learners in our classrooms.

The book attempts to link theory and practice throughout. Nevertheless, the focus is different in each section. Part 1 situates the child within the wider context of the family and the community. Learning to read is viewed on three levels: the sociocultural (the outer culture in which the family lives), the interpersonal (the child's relationship with other learners and 'teachers') and the intrapersonal (processes within the mind). It examines the scope of existing theories of beginning reading and studies on the reading process in explaining the task ahead for these new language learners. Chapter 2 focuses on the way young new language learners in different countries across the world learn to situate themselves in the social context of reading. It investigates the literacy practices in young children's lives and presents a cross-cultural perspective of the role of the caregiver in structuring learning and initiating children into reading in the home. Chapter 3 moves to the interpersonal level and examines the role of different mediators in children's learning. It unpicks different patterns of interaction between young children and their siblings, grandparents and peers. Chapters 4 and 5 investigate reading as a mental and linguistic activity. They draw upon both existing research and classroom examples to examine the strengths and weaknesses children have as they use different clues to make sense of the reading task in school.

Part 2 moves to practice and focuses on ways in which educators might use their knowledge of current research to inform teaching, both in classroom reading lessons and by children's families and community teachers. Using the findings from Part 1, Chapters 6 and 7 outline two different but complementary approaches for beginning reading in the classroom. Chapter 8 presents ideas for using the approaches in the classroom. Finally, I give a voice to young adults whom readers met in Part 1 of the book as they look back on learning to read in a new language. How do they remember learning to speak and read English? How has it affected their adult lives today? What hints might they have for educators?

Throughout the book, readers are asked to question their own beliefs on what reading is and how it is learned. Cocooned within the membership of one culture and education system, it is easy to believe established theories and ideas to be 'natural' and unchangeable. Yet we do not have to travel far to realize that beliefs on how children learn to read are very different as borders are crossed. Countries throughout the world have considerable numbers of young new language learners in their schools and all have different approaches to introducing them to reading. Ultimately, educators will aim at a 'joint culture creation' (Bruner, 1986) within class-rooms, yet to be authentic, this will need to be culturally responsive to all the children in the class. During the last years of the twentieth century, teachers and researchers were uncertain whether migration would continue to be an issue for very long. However, the first decade of the twenty-first century has shown worldwide migration taking place on a scale which will affect us all. It is a phenomenon we cannot afford to ignore as we make the promise of 'equal opportunity' to young children learning a second, third or even fifth language in school.

Questions for reflection

- What are some important differences between learning to read in a new language and in the mother tongue?
- How might you read with a new language learner?
- What other terms are you familiar with to refer to 'new language learners' and what does each conjure up?

Further reading

Comrie, B. (ed.) (1987) *The World's Major Languages.* London: Routledge.

Crystal, D. (1987) *The Cambridge Encyclopedia of Language.* Cambridge: Guild.

Edwards, V. (2004) *Multilingualism in the English-speaking World.* Oxford: Blackwell.

Kenner, C. (2004b) *Becoming Biliterate. Young Children Learning Different Writing Systems.* Stoke-on-Trent: Trentham.

Skutnabb-Kangas, T. (1981) *Bilingualism or Not? The Education of Minorities.* Clevedon: Multilingual Matters.

Part 1
Learning to read differently

Introduction: cultures, codes and contexts

Any function in the child's development appears twice, or on two planes. First it appears on the social plane, and then on the psychological plane. First it appears between people as an interpsychological category, and then within the child as an intrapsychological category. This is equally true with regard to voluntary attention, logical memory, the formation of concepts, and the development of volition. (Vygotsky, 1981: 163)

KEY TERMS

Intrapersonal/intra-pyschological learning	Terms used to refer to individual cognition, mental capacity and the mind. Many studies on initial literacy acquisition take this as the starting point for children's learning and exclude interpersonal and sociocultural/intercultural learning.
Interpersonal/inter-psychological learning	Terms used to refer to the learning between individuals within or between social or cultural contexts. Interpersonal learning takes place in both informal contexts (within families, between friends and in communities) and in more formal arenas (between teacher and child and teacher and family). It provides the foundation for intercultural learning as children learn to learn in a new language in school.
Sociocultural learning	A term used to refer to learning that 'puts culture in the middle' (Cole, 1996: 116), focusing on the inextricable link between mind and culture. Within a sociocultural framework, children learn as apprentices within a community. Literacy is viewed consequently in terms of 'literacies' or 'literacy practices', each with a set of conventions children need to learn to become members of the group. Children learn these practices alongside a more experienced member of the culture. For children learning to read in a new language, sociocultural learning will also involve intercultural learning, whereby the child learns not just a language and literacy, but a new world to which they belong.
Syncretism	A term used to explain how young children blend existing languages, literacies and practices to create new forms. Syncretic literacy studies detail different ways in which this might take place in children's homes, schools and communities.

Vygotsky's interpretation of learning as essentially a *social* phenomenon is not common in studies on how young children learn to read in school. Rather, social phenomena have belonged within the disciplines of anthropology and sociology; initial literacy acquisition within the domain of psychology. Within this latter frame, learning to read in school is viewed as an activity of the mind; as 'psychological' rather than 'social', 'intra-personal' rather than 'interpersonal', 'cognitive' rather than 'cultural'. A psychological frame of understanding reading means that the task becomes both individual and universal: individually, children are each expected to perform the mental acts of memorizing sounds and words leading to the decoding of print; universally, children everywhere are expected to pass through the same stages at roughly the same time. Children who do not manage this risk being labelled 'less able' intellectually than their more fortunate peers. What might this separation of mind and culture actually mean for many young children learning to read in a new language in school as well as those teaching them? To illustrate, I begin with the story of one young child learning to read in the UK. I then introduce an alternative approach to understanding literacy learning in a new language, which interweaves three levels of learning: individual cognition, interpersonal learning between individuals, and the cultural learning of both teacher and learner. This approach is developed further in Part 1 of this book.

Tony's grandparents crossed from China to Hong Kong before they moved with his parents to Northampton, UK, ten years ago. His family now has a 'takeaway' above which they live. Tony enters school smiling at 4 years 10 months. During his first few weeks in school, he appears the picture of enthusiasm. Every morning, he leaves his father or grandfather eagerly and rushes to the 'name table' where he quickly finds his name. This task accomplished, he often chooses to draw. Tony draws methodically and his drawings are usually immaculate copies of the covers of books. The detail of both the illustration and print are exact to the dot over the 'i'; nothing is omitted. Meg and Mog covers appear to be his favourites. During class discussions in the first few weeks, Tony concentrates intensely, watching the other children and always putting his hand up when he hears the words 'Put your hand up' said by the teacher. One morning, Tony comes proudly carrying a plastic bag with Chinese script on it, which is shown to the class. During this early period he often amuses the teacher by his constant 'What's that?' questions, reminding her of a much younger English child.

However, after Tony's initial enthusiasm for school, his teacher feels that she has 'lost' him. Tony does not appear to enjoy speaking English, reading books or school in general. After a few months she sees his continual question 'What's that?' as part of his 'collection fetish' to 'possess words for their own sake'. Tony does not seem able to

——— Continues opposite ———

choose an activity and wanders aimlessly around the classroom. He does not mix with other children and is unable to play. Tony's teacher encourages the children to experiment with writing but he appears to want only to copy print exactly. Nor does he want to take work home to his parents. Tony's behaviour grows increasingly poor. On one occasion, she says: 'Tony seems to want to be told what to do all the time, to copy and imitate me'. Finally, she puts Tony's problems down either to his lack of ability or to his family's lack of encouragement or interest in his work.

As a researcher following Tony's reading progress, I take an attractive dual-language book for him to read with his father at home. These were my notes from the occasion:

I am surprised by the frosty reception I meet from his grandfather:

'Tony can't have his book yet. You must keep it and give it to him later.'
'But why?'
'Because he can't read the words. First he must learn to read the words, then he can have the book.'

Tony's grandfather pulls out an exercise-book from under the counter and shows it to the teacher. A number of pages have been filled with rows of immaculate ideographs. His grandfather says proudly that Tony has completed these at his Chinese Saturday school. With a sceptical look, he pulls out a screwed-up piece of paper. On one side was a shop advertisement from which it had been recycled. On the other was a drawing of a transformer. Tony's grandfather:

'This is from his English school. This is rubbish.'

Pointing to the corner where 'ToNy' is written, he says,

'Look. He can't even write his name yet!' (Gregory and Biarnès, 1994: 21)

His mother and grandmother speak little English, but nod agreement as his father and grandfather discuss Tony's progress. Tony's family remember learning to read as a difficult experience involving physical punishment if they failed to recite or repeat a word correctly. They look back to their own schooling in Hong Kong and China which presented them with a definite set of rules. These rules maintained a dichotomy between work and play, together with a belief in the authority of the teacher and the strict enforcement of obedience if need be. In practical terms, the rules meant that children sat in rows and learned by recitation. There was no choice of activity and they would receive homework from the very start as results would determine which kind of secondary school they could attend. There would be no talking to other children or

Continues over

to the teacher unless requested. The authority of the teacher also enforced duties on her part. It was seen to be the teacher's duty to 'teach' the children, telling them explicitly what they should or should not do.

It seems that Tony's father and grandfather repeat these rules in their expectations as Tony enters school. They are anxious that pressure should be put upon their child to learn to read and write and to be obedient, through force if necessary. The concept of 'wanting to learn' does not enter this frame. To support literacy learning in Chinese, Tony is to start his Chinese and English schools simultaneously. His parents foresee no difficulty in learning to read and write in both languages and his father appears keen to supervise the homework he assumes he will receive from both schools.

Further research tells me that literacy has traditionally been held in the greatest respect in the Chinese culture and China has been claimed as the first highly literate society in the world where a small group of 'litterati' or literates wielded immeasurable power in society. This tradition of respect is reflected today in the existence of a special 'educated' or 'beautiful' script alongside the everyday script. Mastery of the 'beautiful' script needs years of concentration and hard work. It is so special that children relate it to a folk tale 'The Chicken with Golden Eggs' ('The Golden Goose'). Attempting to rush the learning of this script will only spoil it. It is so complex that Chinese students will spend the first year of their Language and Literature degree learning to perfect it.

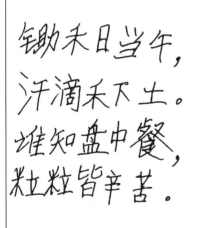

Figure I.1 *A famous poem learned at home by many young children whose family origins are from China. Tony was 6 when his grandfather taught him to write this:*

<u>*Working in the rice-fields*</u>
Having worked in the rice-fields all morning,
My sweat has fallen onto the fields
Now I have got to know all the rice on my plate
Every grain is the result of my hard work

Continues opposite

Although only the highly educated will aspire to mastering the 'beautiful' script, it serves as an example of what may finally be achieved through personal application and hard work. This need for application applies equally to the essential beginning stages of literacy. Tony's family and his Chinese school teacher explain how Tony has been given an exercise book where he must divide the page into columns and practise ideographs over and over again until they are perfect. This attention to detail is particularly important, for the misplacing or omission of a single stroke will completely alter the meaning of the symbol. At each lesson, Tony learns to read by reciting individual words after the teacher in chorus with the other children. Examining the appearance of the symbol is particularly important, for a number of ideographs are pictorial. Learning is based on first understanding the meaning of the word and learning how to pronounce it correctly in both Cantonese and Mandarin. This is followed by repetition, memorization and careful copying. After copying, the child will be taught how to use the word in different sentences. Tasks at school are carefully and clearly delineated and confined in scope.

The completed exercise book is important to Tony's family, for a number of these bear witness to a child's achievements and proficiency. Only when a child can prove this competence is he or she given a book to read. To have immediate access to books devalues both the book and the principle of hard work. Children must work their way towards knowledge step by step and the book is a reward for a child's conscientious achievements. A love of books, therefore, comes after reading is learned and not as a necessary prerequisite to it. For Tony's family, books have a talismanic value and the few family books which the family own are placed well out of the children's reach. In contrast to the high status and respect accorded to the Chinese script, English literacy is viewed as primarily functional in nature. However, they are very aware of the importance of English literacy for business, which for them means the running of the 'take-away' which they hope Tony might later extend. English literacy for Tony's family is seen as a means to opening doors upon which their financial security might depend.

Tony's story begins to highlight the danger of separating the mind from the interpersonal and cultural aspects when understanding the process of learning to read in a new language. At first, his teacher interprets Tony's lack of progress in terms of cognitive deficiency and, later, as a lack of interest by his family. Then, after seeing some of the work produced at his Chinese class, she realizes that the reading process is far more complex than she had been led to believe in her college courses. To understand Tony and his situation, we cannot just look at the way he performs in what 'counts' as reading in his classroom; we have to see him as a member of a cultural group, learning both at home and in his Chinese language class and bringing some of that learning to his English school. He will then need to learn with his peers and his teacher in a new cultural setting. In other words, we have to consider Tony primarily as a social being, interacting with his teacher on both a personal level and as a member of a cultural group. Of course, Tony will need to learn to develop the mental skills in order to read in his new language too. However, the crucial step is to recognize and acknowledge the intricate and intimate link between culture and cognition in the learning endeavour.

During the last two decades of the twentieth century, work in cross-cultural psychology began seriously to question traditional psychology that separated the mind and the individual from the wider context in which they functioned. Inspired by Vygotsky whose work had been translated from the Russian during the 1960s to 1980s, Gregory Bateson (1979), Michael Cole (1985; 1996), James Wertsch (1985), Barbara Rogoff (1990; 2003) and others were developing a separate branch of psychology, referred to and expanded by Cole as 'cultural psychology', a psychology that 'puts culture in the middle' (1996: 116), viewing mind as interiorized culture and culture as exteriorized mind. This is often referred to as taking a *sociocultural approach* to learning in that it integrates the fields of developmental, cognitive and cross-cultural psychology with those of cultural, social and cognitive anthropology, drawing also on work from linguistics, cultural history and philosophy. Indeed, a sociocultural approach transcends academic disciplines and focuses on the inextricable link between culture and cognition through engagement in social activities, tasks or events.

This approach is particularly relevant to young children learning to read in a new language, since they are becoming active members of the literacy practices of different cultural and linguistic groups. In this endeavour, they will need to interact successfully with others who represent difference, speaking different languages and inhabiting new worlds. Some children will be extroverts and will dive into new experiences and love to experiment. Others will be of a more introverted nature and will find experimentation with a new language more difficult. During close observation of 5-year-olds beginning to read in the US, Chittenden et al. (2001) found that children divided clearly into two groups: 'convergent' learners (more introverted, often neat and tidy children who found it difficult to take risks) and 'divergent' learners (extroverts, who were happy to take risks and experiment). This difference may be personal, but may also be cultural and the result of a different interpretation of what counts as learning in their family. Whatever may be the case, it is important for teachers to recognize and to learn about the different 'funds of knowledge' (Moll et al., 1992) within families as well as the different learning styles brought by children from home (Volk, with de Acosta, 2004).

Within this frame, a number of *syncretic literacy studies* conducted during the early years of the twenty-first century are focusing on ways in which young children are living in what

Charmian Kenner refers to as 'simultaneous worlds' (2004b: 55), acquiring membership of different cultural, language and literacy groups in different contexts or domains of their lives. These studies show how very young children are able to syncretize the languages, literacies, narrative styles and role relationships appropriate to each group and then go on to transform the languages and cultures they use to create new forms relevant to the purpose needed. Through playing out different roles and events in different languages, they learn to call upon a greater wealth of metacognitive and metalinguistic strategies. A similar syncretism is shown as children play with the different scripts of their communities, using a sort of 'mosaic language' (Mor-Sommerfeld, 2002).

In Part 1 of this book we meet a number of children who are at different stages of learning to live in simultaneous worlds: some, like Tony, Annie, Ah Si, Sanah and Hasanat are just beginning to move into the language and literacy of a new world; others, like Julializ, Pia, Curtis, Elsey and Dineo, although not yet fluent, are reasonably comfortable at making sense of different words and worlds. In Chapter 2, I introduce, with colleagues from the US, Australia, France, South Africa, Macau (China), Singapore and Britain, the contrasting social and cultural contexts in which children from different countries are beginning to make sense of literacy in a new language. Chapter 3 presents in more detail the interpersonal context. We see how young children learn both within and between cultures with families at home, in communities and in the more formal context of school. Chapter 4 focuses on the context of the mind and considers young new language learners in relation to the endless debates on beginning reading and how it is accomplished. Chapter 5 examines the different nature of 'making sense' for emergent bilingual minds. Thoughout all four chapters in Part 1 we see young children as active learners, making sense, through different mediators, of both words and worlds.

In Part 1, I focus on what educators of new language learners should *know about* rather than what they should *do* in homes and classrooms. Learning to read in a new language is understood to take place on three levels:

1 *The outer or sociocultural/intercultural level (Chapter 2)*
'Cultural patterns – social facts – provide the template for all human action, growth and understanding ... rather than rules, it is a set of associative chains which tell us what can be linked up with what – we come to know it through collective stories' (Rosaldo, 1989: 140).

In Chapter 2, I am joined by authors from the US, Australia, France, South Africa, Macau, Britain and Singapore who give examples illustrating the cultural patterns of literacies taking place in the homes and schools of children in different countries. A cross-cultural

Continues over

perspective is, therefore, taken that begins to introduce readers to the everyday collective stories that will become part of children's repertoires as they begin to learn literacy in a new language in school. The examples reveal home literacy practices that are dynamic, emergent and interactional in nature. The focus in this chapter is on the range and diversity of practices and languages rather than on the interaction between individuals as children learn.

2 The middle or interpersonal level (Chapter 3)

'[A] culture itself comprises an ambiguous text that is constantly in need of interpretation by those who participate in it ... Meaning, therefore, is in interpersonal negotiation' (Bruner, 1986: 122).

In Chapter 3, the focus shifts to the interaction between young children and the mediators of literacy in a new language, at home, in the wider community and at school. Interpersonal negotiation is thus shown to be crucial in learning. Siblings, grandparents and friends are seen to play as important a role as teachers in imparting school or traditional literacy practices in different languages to young children.

3 The inner or intra-personal level (Chapter 4)

'[L]earning takes place ... in the zone where culture and cognition create each other' (Cole, in Wertsch, 1985: 12).

Chapters 4 and 5 move from homes to classrooms, from informal to formal educational setting. They present an interactive model of the reading process whereby learning to read involves making sense of a number of different 'cues' or clues within an interpersonal context. Using examples of children from different language backgrounds learning to read in English, they unpick their particular strengths and weaknesses as they set about the task. These may be individual or cultural. For example, Tony's comfort with memorization and group rather than individual learning as well as his attention to fine detail in drawing and writing may have been entirely individual but may well have resulted from the approach taken in his Mandarin class. The chapters shows how important it will be for educators to recognize and build upon the different linguistic and cognitive strengths of children as they enter new words and worlds.

2 The social context: important practices

One of the most effective ways to learn about oneself is by taking seriously the culture of others. (Hall, 1959: 54)

KEY TERMS

Context	A term deriving from the Latin root 'contexere' (to interweave) and is interpreted here as 'the connected whole that gives coherence to its parts' (*Oxford English Dictionary*). The sociocultural context is the context inherently linked to the cultural, social, historical and institutional settings in which it occurs.
Cultural practices	A term referring to the regularly occurring patterned activities or ways of living in a community. Cultural practices are not static but have their own dynamic structure in terms of their purpose, who participates, when they take place, the materials involved, the interaction patterns between participants and so on.
Literacy practices, literacies	Terms referring to a variety of different 'literacy practices' or 'literacies' which exist in parallel both within and between different communites. These terms reflect a view of literacy that is inherently social and there-fore plural in nature in contrast with a view of literacy as a universal and neutral cognitive skill.

The setting is a narrow, inner-city 'lane' in East London with various shops which provide for the local Bangladeshi community. The warm, sunny day makes this busy area more friendly, even though a predominantly male population is seen frequenting the stores. Nasima and Eve have decided to buy a Qur'ān to add to their collection of materials for their project. Among the various food, clothes and music/book shops, they enter one which displays these holy books and other wares in its windows. On entering, a bearded man wearing a holy cap, nods and looks away. The two visually absorb the goods around them. The shop space is fully utilised, with shelves full of Arabic and Bengali books rising high above their heads. It looks like 'Aladdin's cave' with amulets, rosary beads and prayer mats decorating the walls and tables. The Qur'āns on show are beautifully embossed with gold Arabic lettering, in all shapes and sizes. Their eyes fall on one of the larger ones. 'Shall we take a look at that one?' asks Eve, as she points to a large green one. 'If you like,' replies Nasima. 'You are going to get it if we decide to buy it?' she continues awkwardly. 'What do you mean?' wondered Eve. 'You are going to hold it?' she says more specifically. 'I will if there's a problem, but why?' queries Eve. 'Well I can't hold it!' cries Nasima. 'Why, what's wrong with your hands?!' After which, Nasima explained that the washing of the body is essential before touching the Qur'ān, or one will be damned ... However, they were able to get the book wrapped before leaving the shop. (Gregory et al, 1993: 1)

The purpose of telling this story is to underline how easy it is wrongly to assume that we share common understandings and interpretations even with colleagues. In this case, the English teacher (myself) had assumed that buying a Qur'ān would be no different from purchasing a Bible. Similarly, Nasima (my colleague) of Bangladeshi origin had assumed that I would be aware of the reverence with which Muslims treat the Holy Book, hence the need to undertake 'wazu' (the washing ritual) before touching it. After all, I had been teaching and working with Muslim families for many years when the shopping incident described above occurred.

When travelling abroad, we tend to accept that expectations of how to go about doing things, words to use in sensitive situations, school learning and teaching and even what constitutes 'right' and 'wrong' are likely to be different. We know that, especially during the early stages of our visit, we need to make a special effort to observe the host culture and we know that mistakes will inevitably be made. Sometimes, we feel helpless and unable to understand what is required of us. At times like this, we may wish that the rules could be made more explicit by our hosts, particularly when a situation is formal and/or has important consequences (visiting a bank manager or even an invitation to a special meal). Yet it is easy to forget these experiences when we return to our own world as teachers in school. It is easy implicitly to assume that children's families share our own understanding of 'reading' and will find school methods and materials meaningful although they may well have learned to read in a world quite different from our own.

In his influential work, *Thought and Language* (written during the 1930s but translated only in 1962), the Soviet psychologist Lev Vygotsky examines the relationship between thought, language and learning and stresses that words need to be interpreted on two levels: their *meaning* (the dictionary definition) and their *sense* (the feeling called up by a word to an individual or a cultural group). He uses the example of the word 'flag' to show how the dictionary definition (or meaning) 'piece of cloth esp. bunting, often attached to a pole or staff decorated with a design and used as an emblem, signal or standard or as a means of signalling' (*Collins English Dictionary*, 1992) may be very different from the 'sense' of the word which may conjure up pride and honour or humiliation and shame according to the experiences of an individual within a cultural group. Words which have a high emotional content or those where experiences vary greatly are likely to evoke a very different 'sense' for individuals or cultural groups. 'Reading' is one such word. Its dictionary definition (or meaning) of 'comprehending the meaning of something (written or printed) by looking at and interpreting the written characters' (*Collins English Dictionary*, 1992) masks the vast span of 'sense' definitions it will conjure up both for different individuals and for cultural groups. The vital point about the 'sense' of words is that they are rooted in experience with others, perhaps caregivers, friends, colleagues at an institution or members of a cultural group.

In this chapter, we look at the 'sense' conjured up by 'reading' for families from different parts of the world. The chapter is, therefore, concerned with the outer *sociocultural context* in which learning to read takes place. Within this frame, reading is viewed primarily as a set of 'reading practices' rather than a particular cognitive skill. The notion of 'reading/literacy practices' has its origin in work conducted by two researchers from the US, Sylvia Scribner and Michael Cole (1981). Hitherto, literacy itself had been regarded as the great mental transforming invention underpinning cognitive development; in Vygotsky's words, 'written speech forces the child to act more intellectually' (Cole, 1996: 228). Scribner and Cole's questions were: is it literacy or might it be *formal schooling itself* that is responsible for superior performance in certain cognitive tests? And, if so, might local *cultural practices* rather be responsible for particular cognitive development and thus superior test performance? The Vai tribe in Liberia provided an ideal location for this work since, unusually, people participated in one or more of three very different types of literacy: Vai (a personal literacy used for traditional occupations such as record-keeping and letters, but not taught formally in school), Qur'ānic and general Arabic literacy (both informally taught) and English literacy (taught formally in school). After using a number of activities and tests as well as working closely with the carefully selected sample of participants, the researchers were able to show that, rather than literacy itself, *participation in a certain type of literacy* was responsible for particular test results. For example, those participating only in Qur'ānic and Arabic literacy (learned through incremental recall or memorization) performed better in incremental recall tests than those literate in either Vai or English literacy; those skilled in Vai literacy (learned through putting together syllables) outperformed the other groups in integrating syllables and the English literates (using logical reasoning and discussion of content in their learning) excelled in *syllogism tests* and free recall tasks. Generally, the researchers were able to deduce that formal schooling constituted a particular set of cultural, literacy and learning practices in the same way as Vai, Arabic and Qur'ānic literacy. In other words, people become *members* of specific cultural and *literacy practices*, often taking place in particular locations, for a particular time and involving certain materials, methods, participation structures and skills. This is not to say that we cannot transpose any one of these into a different practice in order to gain new memberships. This perception of literacy is, however, very different from the view that *literacy itself* transforms cognition.

Scribner and Cole's work provided a new frame for studying literacy and generated a number of studies comparing the different literacy practices both within and between cultural groups. Shortly after the Vai study, Brian Street (1984) produced a study of different literacy practices in Iran, leading him to argue that these are always *ideological* in nature, that is, rooted in a particular world view and a desire for that view of literacy to marginalize and dominate others rather than *autonomous*, that is, neutral, universal cognitive skills. He thus uses the term 'literacies' as opposed to 'literacy'. This term, alongside that of 'literacy practices' is now generally used by researchers taking a sociocultural approach to the study of reading taking place in the homes, communities and formal institutions of young bilingual children. Some of these studies focus on the mediators of literacy, alongside whom children learn as apprentices – siblings, grandparents, other relatives, friends and other members of the community as well as parents and teachers (Gregory et al., 2004); some highlight the *purpose* of the reading activity (Haight and Carter-Black, 2004; Robertson, 2004); others give a finely tuned analysis of the methods and materials used (Kenner, 2004b; Volk, with de Acosta, 2004) and yet others reveal the knowledge itself of families in order to participate in certain literacy practices (Gonzalez, Moll and Amanti, 2005).

The aim of this chapter is to highlight how important it is for teachers and others working with young children to find out about the reading experiences and practices as well as the expectations which new language learners and their families bring to school. Examples of families living in the US, South Africa, Singapore, China (Macau), France and Britain show us below just how varied these experiences may be. Finally, I ask: how can a knowledge of home and community reading practices help teachers and other adults as they introduce new language learners into reading in school?

Julializ and Bible reading in the United States

Dinah Volk

Julializ Torres is a 5-year-old Puerto Rican kindergartner who lives in a large Midwestern city in the US. Like a number of her peers, she is embedded in a network of family, friends and fictive kin, many of whom support her developing literacy. Julializ lives with her mother and her 9- and 12-year-old brothers, Francisco and Fernando. She is also raised with her two cousins, Zoila, 6, and Hilary, 3, '*como hermanitas*' (like sisters) by her mother, Sra. Torres, and her mother's brother and his wife. Another married couple, *hermanos de la iglesia* (church brethren), lived with the family for several months. And a church brother, a young man from the neighborhood, visits frequently, often helping the older boys with homework.

Sra. Torres receives government assistance and earns extra money caring for children in her home. She and her husband graduated from high school in Puerto Rico. Their family lived in the city for nine years after living elsewhere on the US mainland, in Puerto Rico, and in Europe when the father was in the army. Sra. Torres and her children belong to a Pentecostal church, attending services twice a week and studying the Bible almost daily at home. The children attend Sunday school where their mother teaches a class.

Julializ, like many people in her network of support, is bilingual in Spanish and English, with emergent skills in the latter language. She learned Spanish first and speaks that language primarily with her mother. She and her brothers and cousins often use English. They watch television in both languages, though many of the reading materials the children use – library books, school books, workbooks purchased in the grocery store – are in English. Her mother notes that it is difficult to find reading materials in Spanish for herself and for the children.

In school, Julializ attends a bilingual kindergarten where the children are learning to read in Spanish using a basal reader programme that includes small story books in Spanish. Concepts are taught through poems, songs and traditional Latin American children's rhymes. The teacher introduces English informally in songs, games and stories. At home, Sra. Torres uses the *Cartilla fonética* (see Figures 2.1 and 2.2), a primer from Puerto Rico which draws on the regular phonetic characteristics of Spanish, to teach Julializ to read in that language.

In both settings, Julializ and her family members – adults and children – regularly use both Spanish and English as resources when engaging in literacy tasks. For example, one day in school, while writing in her journal, Julializ used invented spelling to write about her favourite book, *WNI-TAPU* (*Winnie the Pooh*) (see Figures 2.3 and 2.4), beginning with the W from the English name but using Spanish sounds for the rest of the word. Another day at home, Zoila, a confident English reader, helped Julializ read a list of English words with scaffolding consisting of the Spanish vowel sounds as cues for the troublesome English ones. For example, Julializ was able to read the word *to* after Zoila cued the English O sound in *to* using the sound of U in Spanish. Zoila then cued the different English O in *not* using the Spanish A and Julializ was able to read that word too.

Figure 2.1 *A primer from Puerto Rico*

Figure 2.2 *A primer from Puerto Rico continued*

Literacy interactions at home take many forms. At times, family members provide direct instruction in valued knowledge and skills. Sra. Torres teaches Julializ to read in Spanish using the Puerto Rican primer and supervises her as she completes homework, usually in Spanish, as well as pages in her workbooks in English. Bible readings at home are sometimes transformed by Sra. Torres into reading lessons, syncretizing family, school, and religious literacies. Typically, prayers at the beginning of a reading invoke the assistance of God, his angels and all family members. Once that sacred/family context is established, Sra. Torres reminds Julializ of appropriate literacy behaviours (look at the page; follow my finger) and then the two go on to co-construct a number of strategies that give Julializ increasing responsibility for the reading task. First they read together with Julializ a beat behind her mother. Then they move to echo reading with Julializ repeating her mother's words. Finally, Julializ reads the familiar but complex biblical language on her own with her mother providing prompts.

Figure 2.3 *Winnie the Pooh*

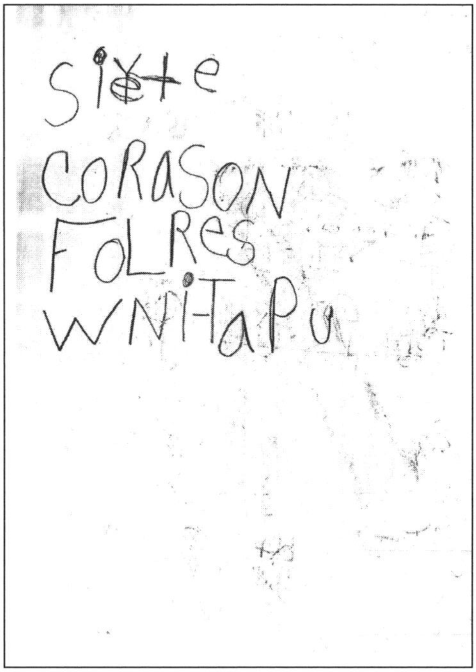

Figure 2.4 *Winnie the Pooh continued*

Sra. Torres encourages Francisco and Fernando to help Julializ with her reading and sometimes monitors their teaching. On one occasion, Francisco, a reluctant student who dislikes speaking Spanish, guides Julializ's reading in English by providing single words for her to repeat. Concerned about this method of merely providing text, Sra. Torres reminds him to ask Julializ about the meaning of the story and models her own comprehension question: '*Mami, ¿tú entiendes la historia?*' (Dear, do you understand the story?). Francisco then asks a similar question.

In contrast, Fernando, a competent, bilingual student, uses Spanish to cue Julializ to the meaning of English words, provides letter sounds to help her with word analysis, and directs her attention to the pictures as cues. When asked how he had learned to teach in this way, he cites his kindergarten teacher who has now become Julializ's teacher.

At other times, Julializ engages in literacy in less formal ways. She often chooses to work in her workbooks on her own and reads library books in bed before falling asleep. Her uncle reads to her and his daughters whenever they play together at his house. The girls play video games that involve print, with the two older girls helping Hilary, the youngest.

Julializ and her cousins often engage in dramatic play and, at times, play 'church'. Their play is syncretic as they blend and re-create literacy practices from home, school and religious contexts, as well as popular culture. Either Julializ or Zoila take the lead, depending on the competencies required. For example, on one occasion when they begin by gathering Bibles to use, Zoila announces that Julializ should lead the service since the Bibles are in Spanish and she can read in Spanish better than Zoila who attends an English-only first grade. After the planning is over, Julializ reminds Hilary about appropriate behaviours: close your eyes while praying; say 'amen' at the end. She then goes on to recite a prayer from memory and read a psalm that she had memorized. The girls sing songs, including a love song from the movie *Selena* – starring Jennifer Lopez – that they have been watching on video. Sra. Torres's protest makes them abandon that song and switch to another using similar language to express their love for Jesus. The service ends with Julializ imitating the pastor's distinctive preaching voice and testifying about her own love of God.

The family's understanding of 'what counts' as literacy is also syncretic, drawing on a range of approaches. Sra. Torres explains that she learned to read as a child in Puerto Rico using the *Cartilla fonética* with its phonetic approach and copying letters on the blackboard into her *libreta* (notebook). The approach she uses with her children – and the one nurtured in the older siblings for use with the younger ones – blends an emphasis on knowledge of letter sounds with a focus on understanding the meaning of a text, learned from the teachers in her children's schools.

In church and in religious interactions in the home, literacy also involves memorization and oral recitation of *la Palabra* (the Word; for Pentecostals, literally the Word of God). This approach is brought to life in the children's church play and is communicated by Sra. Torres when she tells a story about Julializ's first public reading in church. At 4 years of age, Julializ had begged her mother to allow her to read a psalm in front of the congregation just as older children and adults did. When Sra. Torres pointed out that Julializ could not read, Julializ practized a psalm until she could recite it in church from memory – holding the Bible open in front of her as she did so. Her mother helped her memorize it and stood facing her, coaching her performance during the recitation itself. Sra. Torres told this story often, explaining that it represented Julializ's promise as a member of the congregation and her promise as a reader.

It is important to note that, for this family, reading the Bible is never merely about reading. Its primary function is to inspire and to provide lessons about how one should live one's life, staying on '*el buen camino*' (the good path).

From Julializ's perspective, learning to read is a hard and important task and she looks ahead with concern, despite the teacher's assessment that she is the most advanced reader in the kindergarten. What is more, Julializ considers her ability to use Spanish and English useful but not remarkable, since so many people she knows are similarly bilingual. Thus, when she was asked to pick some books to read during an informal reading assessment in school she used a variety of strategies and both languages. The first book she chose was in Spanish and, using her knowledge of letter sounds, she worked at sounding out individual words. 'This is hard,' she commented in English as she continued to work. When given the opportunity to pick another book, she chose one in English without commenting on the change in language and began to tell the story using the pictures in addition to identifying individual words and repetitive phrases. She sighed, 'It's going to be hard in first grade.' When encouraged by the researcher that she was already reading a lot, she added, 'My mom is showing me.'

In sum, literacy in Spanish and English are woven throughout the daily lives of Julializ and her family and, literally, throughout their house. When Julializ gets home from school, she completes homework at the kitchen table while her mother cooks and her older brothers, cousins and the children her mother cares for move in and out, helping and distracting. Julializ and her cousins play – often integrating literacy into their play – in the living room, her room or the basement playroom while the young man from their church helps one brother with homework in the kitchen and their mother helps the other in the living room. Church services and Sunday school on Sunday are supplemented by almost daily Bible readings with the family and Wednesday Bible study in their home or in other homes led by church members. The teaching and learning of literacy in two languages is ongoing and pervasive.

Our second child is European, living in France with her English mother (of African Caribbean descent). Her father is German. Pia's day-to-day literacy practices differ in many ways from those of Julializ, as we see below.

Pia and letter-writing in France

Joan Bursch

Eight-year-old Pia attends a bilingual (French/German) school in Alsace on the French/German border. Her mother is English, of African Caribbean origin, her father German. Pia has been brought up trilingually (English, French and German). Although not taught to read or write in English, her mother read English stories to her and she simply took the books and started reading them herself. The family watches television in German only, listens to English music, has a computer with a French keyboard and software but uses it mainly to write in German. Pia speaks mainly French with her siblings, though there is little written material in French in the house. Her mother sees English as her most endangered language.

Me, Pia's mother (speaking English) with Pia (speaking French):

P: *Why doesn't anyone ever write to me?*

Me: *Well you know, Pia, lots of children your age don't think much about writing when they are not at school. I'm glad you like writing so much, but not everyone does.*

P: *I sent Jessica a letter, and she said she was going to send me a present, but she still hasn't.*

Me: *Maybe she doesn't like writing so much.*

P: *She said she would –*

Me: *Well, you send her a birthday card and maybe she'll write back.*

P: *Hm.*

Jessica is Pia's German penpal, arranged by the school. They write to each other in German when requested to by their teacher. Pia loves reading. And she loves writing. She does not need a teacher's prompt to engage in 'authentic' literacy. On 23 July 2004, she gives her mother a first draft of a letter to her penpal, written on the reverse, 'clean' side of paper her father has brought home from work for the children to use:

Hallo Jessica
Ich wünsche dir ♥-lichen Glüwuntsch zum Geburtag in August gehen wir in spanien wir Waren chon dort wo gest du hin? Ubernägste woche bleibe ich zu einer freundin und Whitney get in bretange mit mami. Wir sind haben (she crosses the latter word out herself) in ein urlaube für Kinder so zu sagen eine woche lang
Gruse (she crosses this out herself) tchüs
Pia
(Hello Jessica
Congratulations on your birthday in August we are going to spain we've been there before where are you going? The week after next I'm going to spend the night with a girlfriend and Whitney's going to Brittany with mum. We are for a week on a holiday for kids, so to speak.
Bye
Pia)

Pia wanted to come back for the corrected letter. Her mother insisted that she stayed there and participated in the corrections herself. Pia writes in red felt tip. Her mother corrects in pencil and explains in English. Her mother suggests improvements, sometimes soliciting

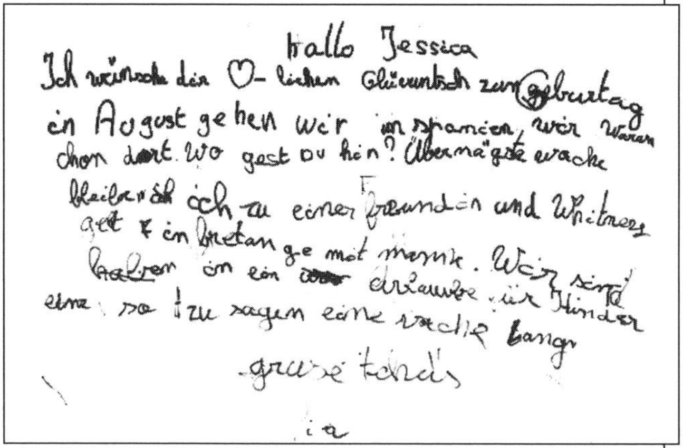

Figure 2.5 *Pia's letter*

Figure 2.6 *Bitte lösen*

Figure 2.7 *Pia's school literacy*

Figure 2.8 *Pia's school literacy continued*

them from Pia and writing them down on the draft once they have been agreed upon. The letter also exhibits certain spellings based on Pia's knowledge of French phonology (for example, 'ch' in *chon* instead of '*schon*'). On the reverse side of the sheet, next to a copy of a newspaper article relating to the car company Pia's father works for, her mother notes Jessica's address, which Pia later writes neatly on the envelope before posting the letter. This letter is not requested by the teacher, but stems from Pia's genuine interest and hope to receive mail in return.

Literacy is an activity which is based on the recipient's willingness to engage so as to understand the meanings intended. At school, the clearly instructive interactional style aimed at 'smooth' literacy behaviour may stand in direct contrast to the 'knottiness' of everyday literacy practice children experience at home. Two days after the letter to Jessica:

> Over a complete sheet of A4, on 27th July, 2004, Pia writes the following in German: *Bitte lösen.* She means '*Bitte lesen*', i.e 'please read'. Ten enormous letters in a mixture of basic print and capitals, sweep across the page, reflecting the emotive and earnest nature of the request. Squeezed in on the last remaining strip of free space, she continues in progressively bigger handwriting: 'bitte bitte bitte bitte bitte', i.e. 'please please please please please'. On the reverse side, she vents her indignation: '*Wiso hört mir nimand zu ich habe es chon mahl in den Kumer Kasten hinten kucken geschriebe und es wirkt nicht*'. 'Why doesn't anyone listen to me I have already written about it and put it in the complaint's box, look at the back of the box, but it's not working'. Her handwriting ranges from thick capital letters to joined up writing. An arrow directs you to passages which do not follow the conventional spacing of writing so that you get her meaning. The final words are squashed into the bottom left hand triangle of paper, and in the top right hand corner, Pia writes/draws, squiggles in addition to embellishing her name with curls and strokes the way mature writers absentmindedly do when writing and talking at the same time. The 'zu' in the text is noticeably bigger than the preceding letters, so that the text reads:

> 'why doesn't anyone L I S T E N to me'.

> Complete absence of punctuation. Complete presence of authenticity.

I only discover this paper as I hear it being pushed under my study door. I call my daughter. The study door opens immediately, for she was awaiting precisely this response. I speak to her in English. She responds in French using German to repeat her father's words:

> P: *I was talking to Papa. He was talking to someone else and I had to wait for ages even though I was talking first. When I finished complaining all he said was* (imitating): '*Huh, was ist denn los?*' (i.e. ('Huh? What's the matter?')

M: *Has Papa read this?*

P: *I don't know.* (looking at me) *You're writing in English?*

M: *Mhm*

       She is watching me all the time I stick this post it on her writing. She asks:

P: *What's the matter?*

M: *I stick this on cos I don't want to write on your work.*

P: *Are you taking this for your work?*

M: *Mhm.*

       She nods, then skips out of the room.

These excerpts provide a succinct insight into the literacy practices Pia experiences outside the classroom. It shows how the child resources skills acquired both at home and at school which are blended then deployed as an authentic expression of self.

A letter at school would never have been written in red (reserved largely for the teacher) or in felt (reserved for colouring). Interestingly, Pia's mother corrects in pencil, which Pia used when first learning to write in German at school. In this interaction, then, we can detect a subtle change in the classical balance of power associated with teaching and learning. For the final version, however, Pia not only switches to pen, but also pays much more attention to her handwriting. Clearly, different standards are consciously being applied, depending on the audience in question, for the 'in-house' text pushed under the study door is neither edited by Pia, as she does in the letter to her penfriend, nor is her spelling or presentation commented on by her mother.

The mother's correction techniques demonstrate that teaching strategies associated with the classroom are familiar to the child from home. By rejecting Pia's wish to just conveniently come and pick up a corrected version of the letter, Pia's mother invites her daughter to make a larger investment in the negotiation of meaning. Is the child used to receiving unexplained corrections on submitted work at school? Why does she assume this attitude appropriate at home?

She could have written 'herzlich'. She chose to draw a heart instead. Here, we see her sensitivity to logograms and thus to social uses of literacy that do not overlap with school. This blend of logogram and writing is sanctioned by her mother. Would it have been by her teacher?

The complaints box was introduced at Pia's bilingual French–German school by her German teacher in Year 1, autumn 2002, as a means of according the children the space to write about their true concerns. Two years on, Pia maintains this practice at home, and in German:

> Wenn ich sage 'Whitney darf nicht in den Kummerkasten schreiben' schreibt sie darin.
> *(When I say Whitney's not allowed to put anything in the complaints box, she does it anyway.)*
> 7 March 2004. Written in pen on a torn off corner of paper from Papa's workplace.

> Wenn ich hinfalle dann fält ein anderer auf mich und macht meine brillen kaput.
> *(When I fall down, another child falls on top of me and breaks my glasses.)*
> 6 May 2004, deposited in the complaints box at school and later returned to Pia, who then
> gave it to me. Written in various felt tips in a mixture of print and joined up writing.

The process appears to be internalized in the original language of instruction, German, even though at home her mother speaks to Pia in English and Pia speaks to her older sister, Whitney, predominantly in French.

These samples of domestic literacy attest to the child's sensitivity to contributions to her literate behaviour at every level as to her awareness that, depending on the context and audience, there is more than one way of 'getting it right'. We see how all the members of her family are implicated in her reading and writing, as are the wider social worlds of parental employment and her own institutionalized learning. The texts, thus, may be unpeeled like an onion and demonstrate how genuine reading and writing may be employed by young authors as a true expression of self to leave a mark upon their immediate environment.

We now move across continents to meet Dineo and her family, living in very different economic circumstances in South Africa. The excerpt below invites us into the literacy practices shared by the whole family.

Dineo and performing in South Africa

Pippa Stein and Lynne Slonimsky

> *You see, the generation of now are not like us, the generation of the 70s. I did not finish school because I was naughty. I don't want to blame my parents. But at least I was groomed. I want my children to be like me. I want to groom them not by thrashing, but by talking. (Interview with Mr Kapa, Dineo's father)*

Dineo Kapa is a 9-year-old girl who lives with her mother, father, brother and sister in a two roomed government-subsidized house in Thokosa township, on the outskirts of Johannesburg. Both parents are highly ambitious for their children, as Dineo's mother explains:

Dineo wishes to become a social worker when she grows. I pray to God that the closed doors can be opened so that I can take her to the level of her desire. That is my dream. I'm sure that this dream will become a reality one day because her father and I are positive.

This support is manifest in a strong commitment to their children's education. They spend several hours each afternoon assisting their children with their homework. This takes place regularly around the small table in a one-roomed 'shack' in the yard used as a kitchen. Often Dineo is assisted by her older brother. In the communal family bedroom where the children sleep on the floor, there is a small television and the children watch the 'soapies' each evening with their parents.

Every Thursday evening, Dineo accompanies her mother, brother and sister to a local church meeting held at the back of a small four-roomed house nearby. Mrs Kapa sings in the choir. The church is Pentecostal in orientation and the congregation worship in tongues, as well as in Sesotho and isiZulu. Mrs Kapa follows a combination of traditional African religious practices, mixed with forms of Christianity.

This exposure to 'both worlds' also functions at the level of the family language practices. The children are exposed to the languages and cultures of both parents – Sesotho and isiZulu – but the father's language, Sesotho, has more status as Dineo has been sent to a school where Sesotho is the main African language spoken and taught. In the parents' eyes, these languages and cultures are part of the local, African world. It is English, the language and culture of the world beyond, which the parents are desperate for their children to have access to, as part of their 'grooming' for the future. This 'world beyond' is the world of 'white schools' in town, literally and metaphorically places which give children access to exclusive, wealthy and powerful networks. Mrs Kapa talks bitterly about these differences.

I think the schools should have good teachers who can teach our children English. I am very proud that my children are doing well at school but my problem is, how can they compete with children from the white schools? There are many people who believe there cannot be equality in South Africa … If there is going to be any difference, it should be that the schools should have equal education for all the children.

Along with English, literacy is a highly-valued asset in this family, shaped by the parents' past experiences as literacy learners. Both of them describe their encounter with literacy as a kind of religious experience. As Mr Kapa recalled:

When I came to Std 3 [Grade 5], a light dawned on me. I was taught by a very great teacher, her name was Mrs Mofokeng. At the time I couldn't read or write, I could only count numbers, write my name and surname. By that time learning was difficult because I was always classi-

fied as a 'fool' … For the first time in my life with the help of Mrs Mofokeng I really understood what the mixture of vowels and consonants represented. She had patience for the 'fools'. I started to love my studies and I moved from the 'fools' to the 'clevers'.

This sense of literacy learning as a form of revelation is revealed again in Dineo's mother's story of her first encounter with literacy:

When I got to read isiZulu, I think I was in Grade 3, the feeling of knowing how to read was phenomenal, I can't describe it, it was like magic … Knowing how to read and write is very interesting because you remember the time you could not do it and suddenly your eyes are open.

The literacy event which we explore below took place one afternoon around the communal kitchen table. This kind of activity took place on a regular basis, although it was usually the mother, not the father, who played the major pedagogical role. The event, which is recorded on video, is multimodal in its complex, multi-layered combination of the use of spoken and written language, sound, image, gesture, body and space. It is constructed as a *whole family performance* involving the father, the daughter, the mother and the brother who all see themselves as co-participants in the development of Dineo's literacy. What is enacted is a form of ritual, almost religious in its reverence for the book, and for the spoken and written word. Like the weekly religious meeting where people as a group support one physically and emotionally through prayer, song and talk, Dineo's family group themselves closely around her like a blanket. The mother stands behind her daughter with her hand resting reassuringly on her shoulder, while the father and Dineo sit at the table, the father holding the text for Dineo, guiding her patiently and carefully through each text – one in Sesotho, the other in English.

The father's focus here is overtly pedagogical: he is training Dineo in the practice of how to read aloud, how to *perform the text* with skill and accuracy. This event is not constructed as a pleasurable bedtime story reading activity, but as a form of work, of labour. The first school book the father chooses is a Sesotho version of 'Jack and the Beanstalk', the second a geography textbook which Dineo reads in English.

The father is very concerned with how the written text *sounds*. He pays a great deal of attention to Dineo's inflection and intonation patterns in her reading aloud of the Sesotho text. He is acutely sensitive to her pitch and volume, asking her to project and enunciate the words carefully, to 'speak up'. He stops her repeatedly in the flow of her reading to model exactly, and somewhat pedantically, how the Sesotho language should sound, how she should be inflecting her Sesotho phrasing. She repeats his inflection patterns, as the following example shows:

Father: (showing the reader to the camera): *Ya, ha re ye he, tswela pele.* Yes, let's continue.

Dineo: *Nna le Mme ha re ne letho le re ka le jang? ka—-* [Me and my mother don't have anything to eat?]

Father: *Aa* [No]

Dineo: *ka ho* (She pronounces the words incorrectly) *reolo—*

Father: (correcting her pronunciation) *ho realo Thabang.*

Dineo: *Ho realo Thabang.* [Said Thabang.]

Father: *Thabang a kere ke ena a tjong jwalo ho ntho, ho monna ya mokgutswane.* [Thabang said that to the short man.]

On one level, the father's focus on inflection and intonation is developing Dineo's coding competence. Effective literacy draws on a range of practices including the skill of breaking the code of written texts by recognizing and using the alphabet, sounds in words, spelling, and structural conventions and patterns. However, Sesotho as a spoken language is a tonal language which depends on subtle variations of pitch and tone to inflect different meanings. Thus, on another level the father's focus on phonological features shows his appreciation of the relation between coding competence and semantic competence in reading aloud Sesotho texts. Pitch and tone *are* meaning. He is demonstrating and modelling that *the meaning of this story is in the performance*. Reading aloud is akin to oral storytelling: it requires shifts and intonations, an awareness of audience and an attention to poetics associated with oral performance.

The father's interest in performance is further shown when he indicates to her how the written text contains clues, like punctuation marks, which guide the reader in how the text is to be read. He is consciously developing her metalinguistic awareness. Here he introduces her to the concept of a 'full stop':

Father: *Ho.* (emphasis on pronunciation) *Ho realo monna eo, kgutlo. Ke eng kgutlo?* ['No. Said the man.' Full stop. What is a full stop?]

Dineo: *Ke full stop.* [It's a full stop.]

Father: *Full stop, wa bona he.* (pointing at the section to be read) *Ha re qhale he, ke mona he.* [Full stop. Let's start afresh.]

After the reading of the Sesotho story, the father turns his attention to teaching Dineo how to read English correctly. When Dineo is reading the geography book, he also draws her attention to the 'correct' pronunciation and inflection of sentences and phrases in English, modelling how she should be saying them. As they read this book, the father continues to emphasize inflection, pitch and tone but then stops at the end of a sentence to query the meaning of the word, 'rock'. Here he calls on Dineo's mother for help:

Father: (asking the wife) *Kana ke eng rock? Rock e jwang mm, ba bua ka eng mo?*

(asking the wife) *What is a rock? How is a rock? What are they referring to here?*

Mother: *Ke ntho eo o tholang geography?* [It's something that you get in geography?]

Father: *mm …*

Dineo: (points to the picture of the rock)

This is a significant moment in which, for the first time, Dineo takes the initiative, asserting her visual literacy skills as she helps her parents to understand 'rock' by pointing to the visual text on the page. It is a clear example of the insertion of the discourse of school in the home, where the child uses her knowledge to support her parents' understandings. Even though the father does not initially know what 'a rock' means, he still reads the sentence aloud with perfect inflections, caesuras and emphases in a manner that communicates that 'a rock' refers to some kind of object. Through this partitioning, he is demonstrating that text consists of units of meaning which are integrated into a textual whole.

Dineo's father is constituting and projecting Dineo as a certain kind of reader, communicating the message that while texts are meaningful, this meaning is closed. The task of the reader is to extract 'the' meaning in the text, from the text. Taken together, these practices signify that there is a 'right' way to read the text – which he authorizes – and that learning is achieved by adhering to the 'right' way. Certain language practices count, and not others.

Through all these textual practices Dineo learns how to read, what counts as reading and what it means to be a reader, all of which transform her consciousness, experience and identity. Dineo's father is 'grooming' her for the future by consciously developing and modelling certain kinds of navigational capacities which he believes will enable her to 'open the closed doors' to her aspirations. Skill in literacy and language is essential. He emphasizes the value of bilingual literacy: she needs to know how to read an indigenous African language as part of maintaining her local ethnic identity, and she needs to know English as part of a global identity, her identity beyond the township. In insisting on *his* language as the language which has value in the home (and not the mother's language, isiZulu), he is asserting certain forms of linguistic patriarchy in this household. Through his interest in reading as performance he is developing Dineo's navigational capacities in relation to specific local oral cultural practices, which are an integral part of church, schools, and homes.

It seems to us that Dineo's parents are quite comfortable exposing and projecting her into an environment in which diversity is the norm. Johannesburg is a cosmopolitan city, replete with a multiplicity of registers which are African, European and American. Dineo and her family are part of this city, and like everyone else, negotiating what it means to be both part of the West and the African. Her parents actively encourage her to participate in multiple worlds: it is naturalized practice in the households that the children are exposed to Christian and African traditional lifestyles. Through these hybrid practices, the children are introduced to forms of worldliness, beliefs that the future generation needs to be part of multiple 'elsewheres'. Dineo is not a passive recipient of these ideas: how she will react, resist and transform these ideas and practices remains to be seen. However, how she takes hold of and transforms these forms of linguistic and cosmopolitan capital for a productive future depends to a large extent on the material conditions of Dineo's life: on the day of this reading event, her mother and father were preparing to send all three children to the rural family home in KwaZulu-Natal because there was no money for food.

We travel across continents again to meet Ah Si, our fourth child, who lives in Macao, until 1999 a colony of Portugal, but now part of China. At 3, she is our youngest child, but nevertheless, already fully engaged in becoming literate in a new language.

Ah Si and nursery rhymes in Macao-SAR, China

Keang Vong

As a 3-year-old child, Ah Si has a long way to go before she becomes fluent in her mother tongue, Cantonese. Meanwhile, a second-language environment has been created for her by her mother, Anna, so as to support Ah Si's literacy learning in English. Like many children in Macao-SAR, Ah Si lives with quite a few close family members, namely, her mother, father, baby brother and grandmother (from her father's side). She is also very close to her cousin who is a primary school student and spends a lot of time at Ah Si's home. Nonetheless, Ah Si is a slow-to-warm-up and observant child. Since Ah Si has just left nursery and started kindergarten education, she has not got many friends at school. The whole family usually spends time together on weekends and holidays. Naturally, the main language used in Ah Si's daily life is Cantonese.

Only one English subject is offered at Ah Si's kindergarten. At the time of the interview, school had just begun three weeks ago and alphabets such as big and small letters have been introduced. Moreover, words like 'apple' and rhymes about apples, 'Red Red Apple, Yum Yum Yum' have been covered at school. But Anna does not feel that there is a strong need for the kindergarten to put more emphasis on English. Instead, Anna prefers a well-balanced curriculum for Ah Si. As Anna does not expect the kindergarten to provide a rich English environment for Ah Si, she does it herself.

Ah Si's English language environment is created primarily by Anna who highly values having a second or even third language, in particular, the mastery of English. During the interview, Anna stressed the importance in the following manner:

> *It's important in both everyday life and at work ... Work has become part of my daily life. At work, I have to communicate with a lot of foreigners, for example, Portuguese and Indians. People from many countries work at this company [an attorney's office]. If you have a second language, besides Chinese, it's a big help ... Someone good in English can benefit from a lot of information.*

In order to provide Ah Si with as much English as possible, Anna chose to start at an early stage. During her pregnancy, Anna listened to classical music and baby songs.

> *I heard that babies' ears are open 24 hours a day. So I listened to music and songs. It does not matter how much she [her baby] hears.*

These early efforts might have stemmed from her own schooling experience which was described by Anna as a hard one.

> *I finished my foundation education at Perpetual Help School. I transferred from a Chinese school to this English school while I was still a primary school student. The adjustment was so hard at the beginning. It was a lot of work to catch up with the English level [at this school] ...*

Besides listening to music, Anna makes use of books, real objects and oral English to enrich Ah Si's environment. Basically, the strategies Anna has employed to help Ah Si acquire English have been learned from her mother who used to spend plenty of time helping Anna with her English. The strategies include:

1   Using Chinese sounds that the child is familiar with in order to help memorize English pronunciation;
2   Repeating the pronunciation wherever possible, for instance, on the way to school, or while taking a walk;
3   Introducing the English words to the child for objects and people seen in the streets;
4   Checking periodically whether the word learned earlier remains in the child's memory.

According to Anna, these strategies worked very well for herself when she was young and for Ah Si now. In fact, Anna has further developed her mother's strategies. Anna believes that learning should involve the five senses. When writing a word, one has to look at the shape of the word and say it aloud. Using real objects will also facilitate a child's memory. Anna is a supporter of activity-based teaching strategies. Routines such as bathtime, playtime, and bedtime are taken as opportunities for learning.

When washing Ah Si's hands, I say in English 'Mommy is washing your hands'.

Anna also likes reading and playing word games with Ah Si. As observed when speaking to Anna, she has bought different English materials such as story books, nursery rhymes, flash cards, books on vocabulary and baby songs to facilitate Ah Si's English acquisition. When going through a book, Anna makes use of questions in order to check whether Ah Si has remembered the English words they had come across before. During this process, different teaching techniques can be identified. For example, questions are asked in English and then translated into Chinese.

Mother: (Flips the pages with Ah Si then stops at pages 8 and 9) *Ah Si, who is the lazy pig?*

Ah Si: (Points to the lazy pig on page 8)

Mother: *WHAT IS THE LAZY PIG DOING?*

What is the lazy pig doing? (the question was repeated in Cantonese)

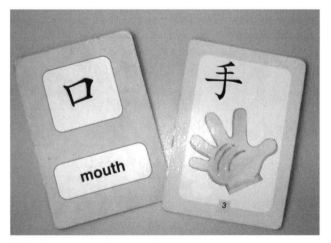

Figure 2.9 *Ah Si's dual-language flash cards*

Anna also models the usage of some English phrases for Ah Si.

Mother: *You have to greet others, say GOOD AFTERNOON to auntie Peggy* (Ah Si remains silent).

From time to time, Anna scaffolds Ah Si's learning by providing hints or prompts so as to trigger recall of the words and guide Ah Si to find the corresponding words by 'mousing' Ah Si's index finger on the page.

Mother: (Pointing to the banana on the page)
WHAT IS THIS?
What is this? (question repeated in Cantonese)
Ah Si: (Thinks for a moment)
Mother: *BA ...*
Ah Si: *BANANA.*
Mother: *That's right. IT'S BANANA.*

It's also interesting to witness that Anna will not ignore mistakes that Ah Si makes as each is followed by a correction.

Ah Si: (Takes the flash cards out of the box)
Mother: *ARE YOU READY?*
Are you ready? (question repeated in Cantonese)
Ah Si: *READY*
Mother: (Picks the first flash card from the pile and shows Ah Si the one side that depicts a hand and the Chinese character for 'hand' (手) on it)
What's this?
Ah Si: 手.
Mother: *What about in English?*
Ah Si: *EYE.*
Mother: *EYE? No. It's a HAND. Say HAND.*
Ah Si: *HAND.*
Mother: *AGAIN, HAND.*
Ah Si: *HAND.*

It is obvious that Ah Si loves English nursery rhymes as she can recite many of them with delight.

Mother: *Okay, I know. You like Twinkle, Twinkle, Little Star, don't you?*
Ah Si: (Stops at the page and nods)
Mother: *Let's read together for auntie Peggy.*
Ah Si: (Reads aloud with mother who is holding her index finger to point at each word)
Mother: (When Ah Si has finished, mother cheers) *Hurray. One more time?*
Ah Si: (Ah Si seems to have enjoyed the process and agrees to read aloud the rhyme one more time by nodding her head)
Mother
and Ah Si:(Read aloud again)

Figure 2.10 *Twinkle, Twinkle, Little Star*

Anna endeavours to apply as much English as possible to create an English environment for Ah Si and to make sure that Ah Si can learn from the mistakes made.

Anna is quite sure that her mother's teaching approach that she now owns work really well for Ah Si. In fact, during the interview, Ah Si was able to recognize many English words, recite nursery rhymes and understand some English phrases.

(When Ah Si was enjoying her ice cream, her mother showed me a book, published in Hong Kong, on ways parents should teach their children. I saw Ah Si shoving a spoonful of ice cream into her mouth, and she kept the spoon in her mouth. I wriggled the spoon and she smiled. Her mother said ...).

Mother: *Are you BRUSHING YOUR TEETH?*
Ah Si: Shakes her head while smiling (without saying a word).

According to Anna, Ah Si always surprises her by using English words and phrases that they have covered together playfully, that is, Anna would not have thought that Ah Si had actually learned the words/phrases.

All of a sudden, words such as Thank You, You're Welcome, pop up. You did not expect that she was able to apply them [to situations] … You can almost tell that she uses them purposefully, to show you that she remembers them and remembers exactly how to use them. Like in the morning, she will say mischievously, GOOOOD MORN…ING

Ah Si's comprehension of English commands also surprises Anna.

Sometimes I unconsciously say to Ah Si [without expecting her to understand], 'Give me the remote control please.' She responds by passing it on to me.

Even though Ah Si has already acquired a lot more English than her kindergarten offers, her English literacy is a result of her grandmother's and mother's teaching strategies. Anna proclaims that she has never read books or come across theories on teaching Chinese children English as a second language. In fact, her own learning experiences have provided her with a mental framework on how learning in English literacy occurs.

Our fifth child mirrors Ah Si in that his mother, who is Taiwanese, is determined that living in Britain should not prevent bilingualism and biliteracy. Below we see the literacy practices of Curtis and his mother which, interestingly, are similar to those of Ah Si and her mother seen above.

Curtis and fishing games in Britain

Yu-chiao Chung

'Lao Shi, this is my favourite book – A Story of Crayons.' Curtis told me that when I went to visit his family on a Sunday evening. (Lao Shi means teacher in Mandarin.)
'Oh, really? Do you like to read Chinese books?' I asked.
'Yes, I like to read Chinese books very much.'
He then pulled out another book from a big pile and told me me excitedly 'No, no, no! I think this is my favourite one – The Missing Moon. I like the story and the pictures in this book.'
He showed me the book with a big smile on his face, which was like the smiling moon on the cover of the book.

Curtis is one of my pupils of a Chinese complementary school in London. My class is the highest in the school; the average age of the pupils in this group is 11. At 7 years old, Curtis is the youngest, yet he has the best reading and speaking ability. He is always very motivated and confident in class.

Although Curtis is only 7 years old, he has a lot of experience of living in different countries.

He was born in Den Haag, Netherlands. When he was three, the family moved to Switzerland because of his father's work. They moved to London when he was four. He is from a mixed middle-class family; his mother is from Taiwan and his father is British. He is the only child in the family and has been brought up in English and Mandarin Chinese. Curtis's mother, Chin-hui, values the importance of maintaining their heritage language as well as the culture, so since he was born, she has always spoken to him in Mandarin. She has been his primary teacher of Mandarin.

> *Other parents play classical music for their children but I started to play Chinese nursery rhymes and Chinese poetry for Curtis as soon as he was born. I hope he can be immersed in a Chinese-speaking environment and get used to the language. This is very important because he doesn't have many opportunities to speak and to hear Mandarin.'*

Mandarin is a tonal language; each word consists of an initial consonant, a final vowel and a tone. Words constructed of the same consonant–vowel pair but different tones have different meanings. This tonal feature makes Mandarin very different from English as well as many other languages. This is often said to be the most difficult aspect for non-native speakers. In addition, the recognition of Chinese characters and reading are other challenges. The ideographic Chinese characters do not have a direct phonetic connection with their pronunciation. Other systems have been adopted to help learners to pronounce each word. For example, the character '山', which means mountain, is pronounced 'shan'. The origin of this character is from the shape of a mountain. There is no connection between the pronunciation and the character. Teachers, in this case, Curtis's mother, need to put a lot of effort into teaching children to learn Chinese characters before going further to read sentences and stories.

> *I have read some books about children's learning; I have also found it true in my own experience: when young children start to learn a word, the word is like a picture for them instead of meaningful text, especially for Chinese ideographic characters. I started to teach Curtis Chinese characters when he was 3 years old. I apply the ideographic feature to teach Curtis … In order to keep him interested and motivated, I often play different games with him and use various strategies. He has found learning Chinese characters interesting and these games leave him with a vivid impression of Chinese characters …*

Curtis and Chin-hui were playing a 'fishing game' together when I went to see them. This game is to help Curtis to remember characters. Chin-hui puts paper fish on the floor, each of them having a Chinese character written on it. Curtis was holding a fishing rod and trying to fish.

Chin-hui: *Curtis* 哪一個字是金?

(Curtis, which one is GOLD?)

Curtis' eyes darted between the 'fish' until they rested on the fish with the correct character on it.

Curtis: 我找到了！這一個是金！我要把他釣起來！

(I have found it! This one is GOLD. I will catch it!)

Chin-hui: 好棒阿！這是金。什麼詞裡面有金呢？

(Great! That's correct. Can you give me a phrase with a GOLD in it?')

Curtis: 金魚的金！
(Goldfish!)

Figure 2.11 *Curtis's fishing game*

Curtis could remember most of the characters written on the fish. However, there were still some he was confused about and he made some mistakes. Chin-hui gave him some hints by pointing out the roots of those characters. This helped Curtis recall very quickly.

When asked about reading Chinese books, Chin-hui and Curtis showed me the small library of Mandarin books on various topics they have at their home. When Curtis was younger, Chin-hui read Chinese books to him. As soon as he started to recognize some characters, Chin-hui started to read the books with him. Now, most of the time, she encourages Curtis to read for her and she only helps when Curtis doesn't recognize the characters.

> *When choosing books for him, I normally choose those by native writers instead of translated books, as these won't have any English in them. In this way, Curtis won't be able to rely on the English translation nor even just focus on English. Moreover, these books include Chinese culture, customs and traditional values. I believe cultural awareness is a crucial element when learning a language, especially when learning a heritage language.*

Figure 2.12 *Curtis and his mum working together*

> *I try to get different types of books for him. As he gets older, he does not just want to read children's stories. Therefore, I also choose books about science, animals as well as nature, etc. He enjoys reading these books very much.*

This evening, Chin-hui and Curtis read one of his favorite books together – a story of crayons. Curtis is very familiar with the story; he can recognize more than 90 per cent of the characters in the book. This is a story about crayons escaping from their box to draw a picture together on a blank poster. Different coloured crayons draw different things; the yellow crayon draws the sun and an island, and so on. Chin-hui put up a poster; she had cut out some pieces of coloured paper matching objects from the story, such as a yellow island, a green tree and a little boy, and so on. Curtis read the story with Chin-hui's help and then as the story progressed he was supposed to stick those parts to the poster.

Curtis: ....黃蠟筆說: 我是太陽的顏色, 所以我要畫大太陽。

(Yellow crayon said: I am the colour of the sun; so I am going to draw a big sun.)

Curtis read aloud and then picked up the yellow sun, walked to the poster and stuck it on.

Curtis: 接下來呢? 這個是什麼字? "?"到我了?

(And then? What's this word? My something?)

Chin-hui: 輪..., 輪到我了

(It is 'turn'. It is my turn.)

Curtis looked at the word closely and carefully again.

Curtis:　　喔！對！輪到我了！咖啡色的蠟筆說，我要畫站在島上的男孩。

Oh! Right! It is my 'turn'. The brown crayon said 'I am going to draw a boy standing on the island.'

Curtis continued to read:

咖啡色蠟筆還畫了兩根樹幹呢！

(The brown crayon drew two trunks as well.)

Chin-hui:　念得真好，現在要貼什麼呢？

(You read very well. What are you going to put on the poster now?)

Curtis:　　我要貼小男孩還有樹幹

(I am going to put on the little boy and the trunks.)

Curtis:　　等一下我要貼樹葉

(I am going to put on the leaves for the trunks later.)

……

Curtis:　　為什麼男孩看起來很傷心呢？

(Why does the boy look very sad?)

Curtis frowned to mimic a sad face when he read this line. Chin-hui said she always used gestures and facial or vocal expression to help to illustrate the stories.

By the end of the story, Curtis had completed his picture. He seemed to enjoy the entire process very much, devoting himself to the reading and the activity.

Chin-hui recalled teaching Mandarin to Curtis. She expressed that this has been a lonely and tough task in a non-Mandarin speaking country.

> *I am the only person with whom he can regularly speak Mandarin. Sometimes it is frustrating that he lacks the environment. He is getting busier with the school work; we have less and less time to read together. Now, we read and study Mandarin before he goes to bed … Even though my husband doesn't speak Mandarin, I really appreciate his support and understanding. It was hard for him. Imagine! He cannot understand the conversations between his wife and his son most of the time. It must have been very frustrating for him. Without his support, I could never have done this.*

However, this tough task has been rewarding. Curtis has not refused to learn Mandarin nor shown any frustration. On the contrary, compared with the other languages he started learning in school – French and Japanese – Curtis is very confident and comfortable using Mandarin in front of people. He is always very interested in reading Mandarin books and in watching children's television programmes in Mandarin.

Our sixth child marks a return to Asia; this time to Singapore. As a child of Malay background, Sanah will be expected to learn to read in both English and Malay now she has started school.

Sanah and story-reading in Singapore

Mukhlis Abu Bakar

1. Sanah:	*Mama jadi cik Noriha. [Mum, you be Miss Noriha.]*
2. Mother:	*Not now.*
3. Sanah:	*Ok Cik [Ms] Noriha.* ((pause)) *Are you ready, Cik Noriha? Are you ready?*
4. Mother:	*Now, I'm ready.*
5. Sanah:	*Can I to read? Come to read, come to read.*
6. Mother:	*Ok.* ((Both Sanah and her mother proceed to read the text.))
7. Sanah:	*Cat* ((pause))
8/9. Mother & Sanah:	*is looking*
10/11. Mother & Sanah:	*for a* (Sanah: *the*) *mouse.*

The above excerpt took place at home when Sanah was 4 years and 6 months old. It shows Sanah and her mother about to read 'Mouse in the House'. The excerpt features several of Sanah's traits as a budding bilingual literacy learner and the kind of literacy activities that she engages in at home.

Described by her parents as a talkative Malay girl, Sanah loves to play act either alone or with her only sibling, an older brother by a year. When she does play with him, she normally takes on the dominant character – the teacher as opposed to the pupil, or the police and hardly ever the thief. Her persistence is reflected in the above excerpt. Even though the mother is initially quite reluctant to participate in a role-play (turn #2), Sanah takes the microphone as a cue to play and pushes on (#3). She wants her mother to pretend to be the Research Assistant – Noriha – whom she has grown to like. When the mother gives in, it excites her (#5).

While Sanah is not yet able to read and does not take to books readily compared to her brother, she nevertheless enjoys being read to. Occasionally, she will 'read' aloud by herself but it is almost always from memory. In the event that memory fails her, she will improvise with much gusto whatever bits of textual information that she has retained. Her mother mediates her reading. Their reading activities usually involve Sanah and her mother reading the same text orally with the mother reading just ahead of her in overlapping turns. In this excerpt, between turns #8 and #11, Sanah and her mother are reading together, with Sanah a beat behind her mother.

	Transcript of reading or talk	Printed text or translation of talk
1/2. Mother & Sanah:	'Then baby wave her hand ...'	'The baby waves her hand ...'
3/4. Mother & Sanah:	'and we wonder, ...'	'and we wonder, ...'
5/6. Mother & Sanah:	'we will cry.'	'will we cry?'
7. Sanah:	*Kenapa baby dia dah nak nangis?*	Why does the baby want to cry?
8. Mother:	No, brother and sister worry. They ...	No, the brother and sister are worried. They ...
9/10. Mother & Sanah:	said ...	said ...
11. Mother:	((Reading off from the text.)) 'Then we wonder will we cry?'	((Reading off from the text.)) 'Then we wonder will we cry?'
12. Sanah:	((Looking at the pictures beside the text.)) *Siapa nak nangis?*	((Looking at the pictures beside the text.)) Who wants to cry?
13. Mother:	Brother and sister *lah.*	The brother and sister.
14. Sanah:	*Kenapa* brother *nya* sister ... ?	Why the brother and sister ... ?
15. Mother:	Because baby and mother cannot go in the class, you see.	
16. Sanah:	Yes. ((Pointing towards the teacher character in the book.)) *Kenapa dia nak ibu dia? Dia tak suka gi sek ...*	Yes. ((Pointing towards the teacher character in the book.)) Why does he want his mother? He doesn't like to go to sch ...
17. Mother:	((Realizing that Sanah has mistaken the teacher for the mother.)) It's not mother. This is a teacher. ((Pointing to the teacher.)) See.	
18. Sanah:	*Kenapa dia tak suka pergi ... Kenapa ibu dia tanya, ibu dia tanya tak boleh pergi seko ... ah tak boleh pergi tu apa tu* ((noise)) *sekolah.*	Why doesn't he like to go ... Why does his mother tell him he can't go to sch ... ah ... cannot go to ... what's that ((noise)) school.
19. Mother:	No, *ibu dia tak cakap macam tu. Ibu dia suruh dia pergi sekolah.*	No, the mother didn't say that. His mother told him to go to school.
20. Sanah:	*Tapi dia tak nak eh?*	But he doesn't want?
21. Mother:	*Bukan, dia good girl* and *good* boy. *(Mama) dia cakap, mama dengan adik tunggu dekat luar.* OK?	No, she's a good girl and he's a good boy. The mother said that she and the baby will wait outside, okay?
22. Sanah:	*Dia cakap dengan siapa?*	She spoke to who?
23. Mother:	*Dia cakap dengan ah, inilah* ah brother and sister. OK, *kita baca lagi.*	She spoke with ah, this ((pause)) ((pause)) brother and sister. Okay, we continue reading.

Malay is the dominant language in the home largely because Sanah's mother is more accustomed to Malay, having grown up in Malaysia and been educated in Malay. She picked up English after moving to Singapore with her Singaporean husband. Sanah and her brother are exposed to English at their kindergarten as well as through the television. They occasionally use English with one another. With their father, they speak more English than Malay, but with their mother, it is almost always Malay.

In the excerpt above, Sanah speaks with her mother in English in keeping with the language of the text and the language that she normally uses with Noriha. However, in situations where there is a real need to communicate, she normally uses Malay, as if respecting the language proficiency of her mother. This we see in another reading activity. In the excerpt above, Sanah and her mother are reading a book entitled *Off to School*. It is about a boy and his sister going to school for the first time, their mother and baby sibling sending them off and waving goodbye. The book has pictures on every page with a sentence or two at the bottom.

Sanah is 'echoing' (reading a moment behind) her mother's reading which is marked '…'. Underlining stresses the difference between the printed text (right-hand column) and what is actually read, for example, 'we will cry' is read instead of 'will we cry?' (5/6).

Notice how Sanah uses Malay to understand an English text. She is learning to read with the support of a mother whose linguistic preference and reading ability she knows. Sanah, who is herself more fluent in Malay, uses this knowledge to best effect by asking for clarification of the English texts in Malay. But, as if conforming to school practice, her mother continues to mark the language of the reading session by sticking to English. Thus for a stretch of eight turns (#7 to #8; #12 to #23), two languages work hand in hand – Malay carrying the questions, and English providing the answers. But the mother eventually gives in to Sanah's persistent questioning in Malay and switches to Malay until the end of the excerpt (#19 to #23). What Sanah has done (with participation from her mother) is to effectively 'syncretize' Malay and English texts, using what she knows about both languages to facilitate the development of her own literacy in English.

This excerpt also shows Sanah to be a 'reader' even as she struggles to recognize words. Her mother has misread the complex clause 'we wonder, will we cry?' as 'we wonder, we will cry' (transposing 'will' and 'we'). Sanah might not have detected the misreading (as she is only echoing what her mother reads, mistakes and all), but she detects the incoherence which the misreading creates. The restructured clause 'wonder, we will cry' appears to foreground the meaning of the embedded clause 'we will cry', and this foregrounded meaning (someone will cry) puzzles Sanah as there is no prior clue in the text that someone will cry. Attributing the crying to the baby does not make sense when it is all about the brother and sister who are going to school. So she asks '*Kenapa baby dia dah nak nangis?*'

[Why did the baby want to cry?] (#7). To clarify, her mother reads the relevant part of the text again, this time correctly (#11). But she still does not realize the mistake she makes earlier and the confusion it causes Sanah who, on her part, is still fixated on the meaning that there is someone who will cry: If it isn't the baby, who can it be? Thus the question '*Siapa nak nangis?*' [Who wants to cry?] (#12).

Since the mother is not aware of her daughter's struggle with the meaning, she cannot attend to her question appropriately. She assumes that Sanah is on track and takes her question at turn #12 to mean 'Who said they wondered if they will cry?' This also means that to the mother, Sanah is in effect asking a question whose answer has already been put to her. Thus, the mother does not hide her exasperation when she next replies. With a voice that sounds annoyed, she quips 'Brother and sister *lah*' (#13), the particle '*lah*' carrying much of the emphasis. But Sanah is still pursuing a different track and persists in knowing why the siblings want to cry (#14). To this the mother provides an explanation – 'Because baby and mother cannot go in the class' (#15) – that seems to cohere with both interpretive modes 'will we cry' and 'we will cry'. It resonates in Sanah's memory of her own first day in school and how she struggled stepping into class without her parents. She responds with an emphatic 'yes' indicating that she identifies with the imaginary characters whose actions and feelings she understands. For the next few turns, both mother and child continue to pursue the story on different tracks. Still on her 'we will cry' mode, Sanah tries different lines of inquiry, dropping one question and adopting another to get on top of the story.

Observations of this and other reading sessions show Sanah demonstrating reading-like behaviour. She attends to texts like a reader – comprehending, evaluating and questioning the texts others read with her. Sanah's development is facilitated by her mother who provides her with the space to 'venture', occasionally inviting Sanah to connect her thoughts with the text (for example, asking for an opinion or agreement) or relate the text to her own immediate experience. At the same time, when it seems that Sanah is only interested in the pictures and not the text, which normally happens in many of the reading sessions, the mother will rein her in by invoking her to 'look at the words' and telling her to 'see the word if you want to read' much like what teachers do if pupils do not pay attention. All these different literacy practices combine to illustrate how Sanah and her mother together co-construct a home literacy that is both similar to yet different from the literacy valued in school. They co-construct a lesson that not only uses elements of school talk and actions, but also draws on the culture of homes by using Malay and a local dialect of English in the reading and learning of English texts. Hence we see Sanah at home as a confident talkative child, already able to question, argue and predict in Malay and an emergent biliterate in Malay and English. Yet school will make new demands on her English where it will be difficult for her mother to provide help. She will need to switch from her current form of English (a mixture between Singlish and Malay) as well as improve her decoding skills before being recognized by her school as an English reader. We hope that Sanah's resources, so clear at home, will be recognized by a sensitive and knowledgeable teacher in school.

Our journey continues on to Australia to meet Elsey, a Torres Strait Island child.

Elsey and popular culture in Australia

Allan Luke and Joan Kale

Six-year-old Elsey has lived in the tropical North Queensland city of Townsville (with a population of 100,000) since birth. She and her family are part of the large Torres Strait Islander community which has been since World War II, an increasing presence in Australian mainland centres. In some urban schools, Torres Strait Islanders and Aborigines comprise 10–15 per cent of the primary class student body. Like many members of her community, Elsey is bilingual: she speaks English and Torres Strait Creole (TSC) a language which has borrowed and mixed features of phonology, vocabulary, syntax, semantics and pragmatics from traditional languages, English and another hybrid language used across the South Pacific for trade and cross-cultural communication. Torres Strait Creole is the preferred language for everyday communication among many Islanders living on the mainland. While many parents and grandparents might speak traditional languages still used in the islands (for example, Kala Lagaw, Kala Kawaw Ya, Meriam Mir), Elsey and most of her generation speak English and TSC. They are bilingual: switching from English to TSC depending on the particular site and situation for language use. This means that a group of Islanders may use English for a service exchange in a shopping centre, then proceed to use TSC amongst themselves for social exchange, and perhaps a traditional, vernacular language to address elders. This code switching occurs automatically and instantaneously.

Elsey has lived in several different locations over her six years, a reflection of the ongoing problem of finding affordable urban and suburban rented accommodation, and the Islander preference for three-generational family units as a strategy for providing social, emotional and financial support.

For the past year Elsey has lived with her paternal grandmother. From an Islander perspective, this household is unique in one respect: except for rare occasions, neither Elsey's brothers and sisters nor her parents are with her. Grandmother and child share a small, well-maintained maisonette in a fully integrated urban community. Without other live-in school-age children to accompany Elsey to school, Grandmother decided to place Elsey in a nearby Kindy. In the morning she heads off to the bus, carrying a lunch prepared by Grandmother in her backpack. She calls this backpack her 'letterbox', a reference to the activity sheets, notes and forms she brings home from Kindy. By observing the activities of other Islander children, her Grandmother and family friends, and by participipating in Kindy, Elsey is developing a sense of what literacy entails, its artefacts and objects, where it can be used, for what purposes and so forth.

Elsey's Grandmother is marginally literate, having grown up in the Torres Strait when schooling to third grade only was available. She occasionally scans a TSC dictionary and grammar test but she is reluctant to write in either of her languages and her reading is a laborious and uncertain process. Where possible she engages the assistance of clerks and trust-worthy relatives and friends to fill out the forms that she, as a pensioner, must contend with. She occasionally receives letters from her daughter on Thursday Island.

Yet Elsey engages with print, often enthusiastically, as part of her daily routines. One of her duties is to clear the mailbox each day, a responsibility she jealously guards. She has learned to recognize the addressee's name on envelopes and she can sometimes identify the logos and acronyms of familiar agencies. As she collected a letter one day, she glanced at the envelope and exclaimed, 'Oh shit, Telecom!', a signal of the significance such bills have in the house-hold. Both she and Grandmother scan and sort the mail daily, with Grandmother directing greeting cards to Elsey: 'Baby, this one is for you!' Elsey eagerly 'reads' cards and letters from brothers, cousins and aunties on Thursday Island, describing what is in them and making up possible stories and tales from the texts she technically might not be able to read.

Elsey, an emergent literate, uses writing and reading for a range of instrumental, recreational, and social interactional purposes (Heath, 1983). She writes her 'name' proudly for Grandmother and herself on scraps of papers, letters and cards; she can also write some close friends' names. For play, she sometimes asks for names and words to be written for her to copy. she sings church songs from books and lyric sheets, often prepared by her Grandmother: 'Mam, you write for me, "Jesus loves me".' These forms of writing are inte-grated with leisure-time drawing, making diagrams and simulations of writing: invented spellings and making letters which she has developed in imitation of those writers she has observed. What emerges is the kind of composite writing that Dyson (1993) calls 'symbol weaving'. In one early writing/picture, she explained to Joan about her family:

E.   *Yeah,*

          dhea, nau ai ken raitem [subvocalizing while writing] (there, now I can write it).

          Raiting atha pamili neim (writing other family name).

          *mai atha pamili is … am … ooh … now … oh … I know … am … ah, mai atha pamili
          neim is … Mamali* (my other family name is Mamali).

J.   *Mamali?*

E.   (louder) *Bamali.*

J.   *Bamali?*

E.   *Bob*

J.   *Oh? Bob Marley.*

Elsey accompanied this drawing of different letters with a picture of a man with a
Rastafarian haircut which she referred to as 'a sticky'. This was her representation of Bob
Marley, whose music and folklore figure prominently among many Islander youth. The
sources she draws upon are varied, including posters she has seen in friends' homes, pictures
in flyers and newspapers, television, radio and music texts. Elsey is using her early writing
as a way of 'naming' herself, her world, and her life – and that life is a blended, hybrid one
that combines images and texts of popular culture and Torres Strait Islander culture, with
those texts that she and Grandmother must negotiate daily.

Elsey's reading centres on functional print in her environment and she conceives of reading
as serving specific purposes:

J.   *Are you gonna read the paper or what?*

E.   *Mm?*

J.   *Gonna read the paper?*

E.   *Read the paper for what?*

She can recognize names and addresses, and the logos which appear on signs (for example,
McDonald's, Target). At home, literacy events centre talk around advertising flyers, news-
papers, forms and the texts that she and her grandmother jointly use. Here Elsey and
Grandmother are scanning an advertising flyer for a local store:

GM.   Shower curtain, plastic curtain, *yumi gede diswan* (we'll get this one).

E.   *Jest onli tri dola?*

GM.   *O, bokli your favrit* (oh, broccoli's your favourite).

E.   *En karit mai favrit* (and carrot is my favourite).

GM.   *Celery, not brokli.*

E.   *Which one?*

GM.   *That wan celery.*

E.   *You think brokli.*

GM.   *Mmm … this backet gud fo Astro* [a dog] *fo slip* (this'd be a good basket for Astro to sleep in).

E.   *Which basket?*

In this and other home literacy events, Elsey is an active participant responding to Grandmother's prompts, at times switching the focus and topic, and linking the text to her own likes and dislikes, experiences and intentions. She clearly initiates talk and discussion around text and is not the passive recipient of adult-initiated questions or prompts. She and Grandmother switch readily between TSC and English.

Elsey also has a knowledge of story forms and events (for example, how to signal beginnings and endings, what counts as a valid story, what can be done by tellers, by listeners, who has the right to speak), it diverges in many ways from the middle-class bedtime story events undertaken in many mainstream homes, eagerly supported by many educators, and emulated in many classrooms. Elsey already can hear and identify cultural differences between stories. At the end of the *Moon Story*, she asks of her Grandmother:

E.   *Black one?*

GM.   *No.*

E.   *Is this a white one?*

GM.   *Maybe … it's just a story.*

Elsey here is categorizing the cultural bases and sources of stories, already distinguishing those with women and girls who have faces 'jis' like me' as different from those that are 'white'. Not only does the form and content of the Torres Strait stories stand apart from that of conventional children's literature (whether Golden Books or award winners), but story-telling is an oral performance with very different roles, expectations and rules.

Another key environment for Elsey's language socialization is interaction with the spoken and visual texts of radio and television. Elsey and her Grandmother like to listen to a local commercial radio station which broadcasts popular and rock music, and features a high-profile local announcer who mixes local news, sports, birthday calls and competitive phone-in quizzes with advertisements from local businesses. Elsey knows the lyrics and melodies of dozens of rock songs, often dancing and singing in chorus with the songs when they come on the radio. The following conversation illustrates how she interacts with the announcer, music and radio:

E.   *Let's do the time!* [switches on radio to check the time].

        Thank you, Mam.

        'Thank you Mister 'ooker!' [quotes L.J. Hooker real estate advertisement].

E.   *Anyway, I need to … listen to one of my favourite song.*

GM.   [unintelligible, radio announces local 'Sky Show'].

E.   *Mama!*

        I go go Sky Show!

        the Sky show is coming

        ai go tel yu dhe (I'll tell you about it).

GM.   *Wha?*

E.   *I bin gad Sky Show dhe we kyu go kam daun iya* (the Sky show was there where you go down the hill).

GM.   *True?*

E.   *Yeah, iya spik/ andI/ and dem/wiskain dem polisman go do* (they're talking about/and 'e/ and they/the police are going to do something I think).

        Hey I friend all my life for you [singing along with song by Linda Ronstadt and Aaron Neville].

Here Elsey is talking with Grandmother around the radio text, in effect translating the broadcaster's comments into TSC for Grandmother, shifting codes fluidly and continuously. As she often does, she breaks back into song, accurately reproducing the phrasing and dialect of the popular songs she likes so much. This kind of diglossic behaviour requires fluency and excellent listening skills, in Elsey's case, frequently developed around the texts of popular culture.

From all the above, we see that Elsey has developed a seminal knowledge about literacy. She participates in various literacy events at home and at Kindy, from playing 'homework' and copying words, to 'reading' signs, newspapers, advertisements. She can write strings of letters and has a sense that this is a way of coding words, sounds and meanings. She often combines these 'words' witih her drawings. Further, she has developed a facility at 'yarning' in both TSC and English, participating with Grandmother in the oral performance of Islander stories and recounting events in which she has had a role. Diverse intercultural texts and resources are at play in her life: but not the conventional texts of children's literature that feature prominently in many middle-class Anglo childhoods, often defined as the precursors of literacy.

Our final child moves us back to Britain where we meet Hasanat, a 5-year-old living in Tower Hamlets, London. Although his schooling will take place only in English, Hasanat's mother is endeavouring to ensure that his literacy will extend to classical Arabic to read the Qur'ān and to Bengali. We see him beginning to read in Arabic, as a new language, below.

Hasanat and Qur'ānic reading in Britain

Mahera Ruby

Hasanat is a 6-year-old living in the heart of the East End of London. He is the youngest of three boys in the family. Not only does he live in a household of three generations, but he has a large extended family living in extraordinarily close proximity. He is one of 31 first cousins, of whom 25 live within 3 miles. What is more, is the fact that there are four boys (of whom he is one) all in the same year group attending the same school and doing the same extra-curricular activities together. He is of the third generation of British Bangladeshi families that have settled in the East End of London. His grandfather was the first to migrate, followed by his family of seven children in the early 1980s. His youngest and eighth child was the only one to be born in Britain. The importance of maintaining the mother tongue within the home was of utmost importance. It was the sheer determination of Hasanat's grandmother that all his aunts and uncles are literate in Bengali. She was also the drive behind the children learning to read the Qur'ān and write in Arabic at home. As with many children from the third generation, they are in a situation where they are fluent speakers of Bengali until they start attending school at three when English becomes the dominant language. Hasanat's parents are both biliterate, yet at the age of 6 he has very little command of Bengali. Like many other children of his generation he is being raised in an environment where both parents are using English due to convenience, at the same time carrying the guilt that a part of their children's identity is being compromised and in some cases being lost. In order to make up for this children attend supplementary classes where they are learning to read and write in both Bangla and Arabic. In Hasanat's case his parents have focused on the learning of Arabic due to the importance of the language in the practice of Islam and Bangla is used mostly with grandparents.

The day-to-day literacy events in which Hasanat participates are numerous and involve three languages, English, Bangla and Arabic. He attends evening Qur'ān classes three days a week and one on a Sunday morning. At home he reads both by himself, with his brothers, maternal aunties, uncles, other aunties (friends), cousins, grandparents and parents. He loves to read books as well as being read to in both Bangla and English, particularly before going to bed. The family home does not have a television and the boys from a very young age have been used to 'finding' things to do. As a result Hasanat spends a lot of time drawing and writing, which he particularly likes to do on the whiteboard that is on the wall in their room.

Hasanat started to attend a playgroup from the age of 3. At this playgroup there was a particular emphasis on teaching the children to memorize parts of the Qur'ān alongside the mainstream curriculum. There was a drill of recall first thing in the morning of what the children had memorized the previous day. Before the end of the day the children would be memorizing new verses. The teacher would read melodiously and the children would repeat until their pronunciation was perfect. This was done in a big group on the carpet. The children would then be chosen at random to recall while the others listened. The family would reinforce this in the evenings at home. I would put on a Qur'ān CD with the particular part he was memorising on repeat, which would be playing in the background while he played with his toys. His father, when leading the prayers at home with the boys, would recite the verses aloud.

Arabic reading continued at the basic level until the age of 5 at home It was very informal and when his older brothers sat in the evenings to do their homework there was a demand for him also to do some 'work'. He would get his own 'Qa'eeda', an Arabic primer and would demand that I 'learn' him his 'pora', reading. With him sitting on my lap we would go through the pages; he liked me to spell the words, read them out aloud and he would repeat. The pages he was confident in reading Hasanat would confidently move my hands off the pages and reverse the process with him leading. He often wanted me to read my Qur'ān with him on my lap and loved to point out the letters he recognized.

Hasanat has been learning to read in English using phonics since he started at a local state school. He seemed naturally to transfer those initial skills when he first began to learn the Arabic alphabet. I noticed he was using the sounding out system when I initiated teaching him the Arabic alphabet from the age of four. As soon as he identified my recognition of his method he was very happy in comparing similar sounds across the two sets of alphabets and noticing the fine difference between some very similar sounds.

Hasanat started to attend the supplementary after school Arabic classes from the age of five. In his weekday Arabic classes the system of learning is a mixture of memorization and recall. The class consists of 24 children between the ages of 5 and 7. There are two young female teachers who have been employed because of their skills in Qur'ānic Arabic recitation as well as being able to teach such young children effectively. The usual homework set would be for parents to revise the previous memorizations. He and his three cousins love attending on Fridays as the 'golden time' allows them to write Arabic. I have sat in on the classes a few times and watching such young children follow the high expectations of discipline is extraordinary. The children for most part of the evening sit on the floor. The cultural ethos is very evident in the way the children respect their teachers and the different learning culture from the one in their mainstream schools. Incentives such as little stickers, badges and sweets are used to encourage the children to learn. There are also the verbal ones 'you are growing up now, you need to learn', 'you need to teach others through your good example', 'you will be rewarded for all your hard work by Allah', 'Let's see which cousin can learn the fastest', and so on. A snippet from one of the classes is presented below.

T: *hin hin*

H: *behijaratim*

T: *no you missed it no look you're reading one thing and your finger is somewhere else which means you are not using the letters*

        Hasanat reads the sentence correctly

T: *good good*

H: *lowhann* (did not make the right vowel sound at the end of the word)

T: *huh*

H: *lowhann* (repeated the same mistake)

T: *no why are you saying hunn, you should know this, this is not the time for me to remind you about kasrataeen (ِ) or fathataeen (ً) or dhammataeen (ٌ) hinn, hann, hunn this is basic, when there two kasra at the bottom of the letter then it's a inn sound, when there is two fath-ha at the top then its ann, and two dhamma's its unn*

        Hasanat listens attentively and repeats the sentence with the correct pronunciation

H: *lowhinn*

T: *what is the ha (ح)joined to? You can't read the ha (ح) on its own*

H: *mim mim (م)*

T: *that is it joined to*

H: *lowhimm (لوح)*

T: *good if that was on its own that's how it would look but because it has another letter next to it which has got a shadda (ّ)shadda means the meem needs the help from the ha, so you have to join them both, low*

H: *lowhimm mahfuzin*

In the above piece the teacher sits between Hasanat and one of his cousins at a little table. He is reading from a page made up of words that are found in the Qur'ān. The intention is for the children to learn the words through spelling as well as recognizing the various rules of recitation. Listening to them reading I myself was amazed at how they picked up on the complex rules, but more impressed at the way they were engaged in listening and then applying. Hasanat's cousin sitting on the other side did not take his eyes off them and was soaking it all in, moments later the teacher did not have to repeat to him separately since he had learnt from observation.

In the last few months Hasanat has developed enthusiasm for copying. He loves copying text and pictures from books, but his passion is copying from his siblings' writings or drawings. He will spend countless minutes copying solved maths problems and written text from their school exercise books including the teacher's markings and comments. He is an observant and keen learner. He is also very conscious that he has access to three languages, and his regular query is 'when am I going to learn Bangla?' 'I need to learn Bangla so I can under-stand what nanu (maternal grandmother) and dadu (paternal grandmother) say.' Such utter-ances bring home to us as parents that we are concentrating so much on the Arabic and English due to their social and spiritual importance in the current context we are living in, but the nagging question remains: Where does that leave his Bangla which is also a very important part of his identity?

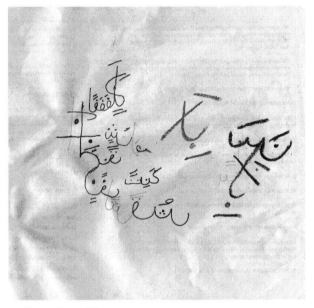

Figure 2.13 *Hasanat's early writing*

Questions for reflection

- If we focus on reading in terms of different *reading practices*, each with its own *purpose, materials* and *interaction between participants* (participation structures), what reading practices are each of these new language learners already familiar with as they enter school?
- How might each child's approach to learning to read in school be influenced by home and community reading experiences as well as the expectations of the home culture?
- What questions will the teacher need to ask to begin to negotiate a joint interpretation of the reading task with the child in school?

Making sense of reading

At an in-service course on reading in the multilingual classroom, a group of teachers were asked quickly to jot down an answer to the question 'What is reading?' When the responses were shared out among the group for discussion, it was found that almost every definition contained the word 'meaning'. When questioned about what they meant exactly by writing 'gaining meaning', most teachers said 'having pleasure', 'enjoyment' or 'fun'. Interestingly, teachers found it impossible to separate what reading *is* from what reading *does* for the reader and what is *needed* to begin to learn to read. Within our Vygotskian framework, their own 'sense' of reading involved the notion of pleasure from the very start of learning to read. If we return to the Qur'ān story opening this chapter, it is easy to see how it is but one step away to assume that 'gaining meaning from reading' must necessarily equate with 'fun' or 'pleasure' for everyone and from the very start of learning to read.

If we examine the *purpose* of reading in the lives of our families above, we find that *immediate fun* does not figure highly. Only Pia's family wants her to read simply for fun in the Western sense. She has a variety of reading and writing materials in French, German and English, and having a new story read by her parents is a treat. Of course, it is important to remember that the fun accompanies tuition as well as 'modelling' by her parents. But reading also serves other economic purposes in the life of her family. Her father often sits at his computer, he sends and receives faxes, they have work-related mail, and so on. Pia's mother studies for her PhD, writes poetry and other prose in English as well as marking students' scripts in French. Pia has been bathed in print since she was born. Although from very different circumstances, Elsey also shares Pia's love of letter writing and popular culture.

All the other families view reading more explicitly as a future investment. For most, pleasure and satisfaction are seen as the result of hard work which do not necessarily belong to the beginning stage of learning to read. Indeed, for all families, learning to read and write is a very serious matter. Even Pia sees her letter as an important means of communication that needs to be correct. Other families have little time for leisure. For Dineo's family in South Africa, literacy acquisition in English is crucial for economic survival and any hope in the labour market. To a lesser extent, both Julializ and Sanah's family are in a similar position, since English literacy is essential for any economic success and as a way out of poverty. Although comfortably off, Ah Si's mother also realizes the value of bilingualism and biliteracy for her daughter's future job prospects and wants to give her a head start. For Curtis and Hasanat who are both learning to read in a new language other than English, the purpose is just as serious; it means acquiring access to a religious or cultural heritage of which literacy is a vital part. Learning to read the Bible, Qur'ān or other prayers is an important purpose for literacy in the lives of Julializ and Dineo (whose families both belong to the Pentecostal Church) and Hasanat as a Muslim.

The purpose of a particular literacy practice also has a key impact on both the materials used and the interaction patterns between child and adult or more experienced reader. Children involved in religious literacies participate as apprentices in adult practices, using either the Bible or Qur'ān or other prayer book or a preparatory reader for these. They learn through repetition, echoing and finally performing in a way that they see as appropriate for God or Allah to hear. These materials and participation structures contrast with both the 'readers' brought from school by Julializ and Sanah and the taped songs or games played in Ah Si and Curtis's homes. During these 'school type' activities, mothers or siblings question and test their children on words or content in a way similar to teachers in school. Although initiating their children into different languages (English and Mandarin), both Ah Si and Curtis's mothers use similar materials and approaches as they read with their children in a new language. Both go to considerable effort to provide taped songs, flash cards, games and books and both correct, question and check their children rigorously. All the caregivers in this chapter give their children a very explicit introduction to home practices. Even Pia's mother corrects and discusses her writing with her as well as modelling writing through her day-to-day practices which are then taken on board by the child.

The families we have met in this chapter show us that terms such as 'gaining meaning' or 'taking pleasure' from reading will mean different things for different people. For some, it may be individual or an immediate feeling of satisfaction. For others, pleasure and meaning in reading may be intimately linked with becoming a member of a cultural or religious group. In other words, we cannot assume that teachers, children and their families enter school with the same 'sense' of reading. Recognizing the wealth of knowledge and reading practices brought by children from home at the same time as introducing them explicitly to the cultural rules of the school will be important first steps towards enabling children to 'situate' themselves in the social context of reading in the classroom.

Suggestions for teaching and learning

- Find out about the outside school literacies of the class. Show how they are valued by inviting children to bring materials they use at home and families to come and explain different practices, share different languages with the class.
- Build on children's home skills and networks by using dual-language books, games and other materials.
- Use a variety of approaches to literacy that draw upon children's home cultures and the popular media.
- Encourage children to use all their linguistic resources to make sense of texts.

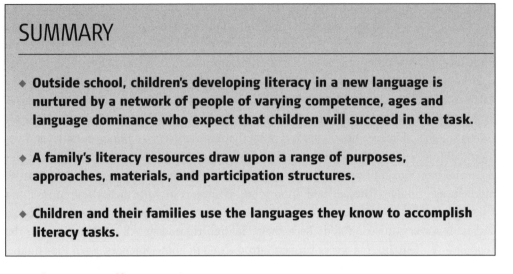

SUMMARY

- ◆ **Outside school, children's developing literacy in a new language is nurtured by a network of people of varying competence, ages and language dominance who expect that children will succeed in the task.**

- ◆ **A family's literacy resources draw upon a range of purposes, approaches, materials, and participation structures.**

- ◆ **Children and their families use the languages they know to accomplish literacy tasks.**

Further reading

Cole, M. (1996) *Cultural Psychology: A Once and Future Discipline.* Cambridge, MA: The Belknap Press of Harvard University Press.

Drury, R. (2007) *Young Bilingual Learners at Home and School. Researching Multilingual Voices.* Stoke-on-Trent: Trentham.

Heath, S.B. (1983) *Ways with Words: Language, Life and Work in Communities and Classrooms.* Cambridge: Cambridge University Press.

Rogoff, B. (2003) *The Cultural Nature of Human Development.* Oxford: Oxford University Press.

Tobin, J.J., Wu, D.Y.H. and Davidson, D.H. (1989) *Pre-School in Three Cultures.* New Haven, CT: Yale University Press.

3 Family and community contexts: important others

Conversational intelligence is a hallmark of the human mind.
(Trevarthan, 1998: 90)

KEY TERMS

Funds of knowledge	A term referring to the cultural artefacts and resources as well as bodies of knowledge that exist in households and communities.
Zone of proximal development (ZPD)	A term referring to the space between a child's actual development level as determined by independent problem-solving and the level of potential development as shown through problem-solving under adult guidance or in collaboration with more capable peers.
Scaffolding, guided participation, synergy	Terms referring to the interaction between a young child and adult/sibling/grandparent/more capable peer and so on who structure the child's learning while simultaneously learning during the process.
Prolepsis	A term referring to the way in which caregivers bring their idealized memory of a cultural past and the assumption of cultural continuity in the future to actual interactions with the child in the present.
Intersubjectivity	A term used in studies on Western child socialization to refer to shared conceptual understandings and an awareness of others.
Ethnotheories	A term referring to the cultural belief systems of families and communities such as concepts of education and childhood, as well as theories of learning, intelligence and instruction.

We come to every situation with stories; patterns and sequences of childhood experiences which are built into us. Our learning happens within the experience of what important others did.
(Bateson, 1979: 13)

In Chapter 2, we saw examples of a wide range of literacy practices in which children from seven countries participate as they learn to read in a new language. What also became clear were the skills, knowledge and resources held within the family and how different these might be. Interest in these resources led Luis Moll and a team of researchers in the US to work with teachers to tap into the 'funds of knowledge' (González et al., 2005; Moll et al., 1992) held in the homes of Mexican American children and their families. Norma González, a member of the team, explains the choice of the term 'funds of knowledge' instead of 'cultural or literacy practices' in that it emphasizes both the interpersonal relationships in families as well as the fluidity of practices in multilingual homes (González et al., 2005). This chapter focuses on the 'funds of knowledge' held by different family and community members (parents, siblings, grandparents, peers and school teachers) as well as their role in helping young children as they begin learning to make sense of reading.

According to Lev Vygotsky (1978), individual cognitive development occurs when children participate in joint problem-solving with others more skilled than themselves who bring intellectual tasks within their reach. This enables children to cross what Vygotsky refers to as the *zone of proximal development* (or ZPD). In this zone, Michael Cole (1985) stresses, culture and cognition create each other. In other words, through help, children can participate in cultural and intellectual activities they are unable to manage alone. The nature of this help given by a more experienced person has commonly been referred to as *scaffolding*, a term originally used by David Wood et al. (1976) who set up specific tasks and observed caregivers at work with infants as they completed them. They noticed that, as children learned the task, the adults skilfully removed their support, like the dismantling of a scaffold. Although the metaphor refers to very finely tuned support, it has since been used widely (and sometimes inappropriately) to refer to many adult–child interactions at home or school. Crucially, however, the emphasis in 'scaffolding' is on the role of the *adult* in assisting the child, often in instructional contexts. However, it may not always be appropriate when describing the caregiver–child relationship, especially in non-Western contexts. In her work on cross-cultural learning, Barbara Rogoff (1990; 2003) proposes instead the concept of *guided participation* to emphasize the active role of the child in participating in the societal activities of the caregivers. Guided participation emphasizes the way in which, rather than simply *internalizing* activities as Vygotsky suggests, children actively *appropriate* these practices and make them their own. Other cross-cultural studies focusing on the interaction between siblings, peers and grandparents with young children use the concept of *synergy* to emphasize ways in which both partners (younger and older or less and more experienced) learn equally from each other through the process of teaching and learning (Gregory et al., 2004). This chapter illustrates ways in which scaffolding, guided participation and synergy take place at different stages and in different contexts of young children's lives with particular reference to early reading in a new language.

Many ways of learning

It is generally accepted that knowledge itself originates within an interactional process and that children's learning takes place within shared conceptual understandings, structured behaviours and social expectations. The child only achieves a fully articulated knowledge of his world in a cognitive sense as he becomes involved in social transactions with human beings. (Newson and Newson, 1975: 438)

Research studies across the world point to the origins of knowledge in the interaction between infants and their caregivers. In the Western world, this often comprises a dyadic exchange between infant and mother. A number of studies show us ways in which pre-speech infants and their mothers participate in 'social dialogues' or 'conversations' with their infants almost from birth. Colwyn Trevarthan (1998) shows clearly through videos how babies as young as 4 months engage in reciprocal exchanges with their mothers through smiling, dance and rhythm. In her study of pre-speech 'conversations', Catherine Snow (1977) emphasizes the importance of noting that any utterance of the infant is accepted as a word and an initiator of a vocal exchange during this early stage. Through being prepared to follow up any opening made by the child, a 'real' conversation is set up. In this way, conversation gives the infant a shared frame of reference. The adult realizes that the child will interpret her correctly, as her speech is derived from the interaction itself. This reciprocity between caregiver(s) and their children is such that we refer to the child as possessing a linguistic system in terms of being able to express and understand a range of meanings before s/he knows any words at all. These early 'conversations' are often initiated by the child. Bruner (1979) uses the example of the game 'Peek-a-Boo' to illustrate this: the game depends upon the child looking the partner directly in the eye for signals at crucial pauses in the play. During these early interactions, the child is said to learn what developmental psychologists call 'intersubjectivity', which is another way of referring to an 'awareness of others' or an 'interpersonal concept'. All of this has been studied at length in one-to-one interaction in Western contexts where it is largely assumed that it is the child's mother who is of crucial importance.

However, we now have a number of studies on life in non-Western societies that begin to reveal very different patterns of socialization. From Sweden, Christina Olgaç presents a portrait of first-generation Somali families sending their children to Swedish kindergarten and reminiscing on their own socialization:

> Imagine a mother who have come to Sweden. Her childhood was like this. She had four, five siblings, neighbours, relatives and her mother. This little girl grew up. When she was one year her mother said to her: – Go outside. Come on, you can crawl outside. And she crawls out of the house. Outside the house there are all the relatives sitting. Everyone is there. The girl crawls, walks her first steps outside, not inside, outdoors. She becomes one year, two years. All the time she is outside. The weather is hot. She plays with other children, children and neighbours. Everyone who comes take care of her. The children of the neighbours, the neighbours take care of the children. Relatives, everyone. (Somali mother-tongue teacher in Sweden, in Olgaç, 2001)

This description of early learning is very different from that presented by authors research-ing Western communities. Care-giving is offered by a whole range of relatives and others in the community; life is lived outside rather than in a confined space. Other researchers from non-Western societies provide similar evidence. Nsamenang and Lamb (1998), working in Cameroon, describe the West African socialization process as 'project-in-progress' whereby stages are marked using social rather than biological signposts, the focus being rather on ways in which young children learn to take responsibility for themselves and others within shared community values than to take the highly individualistic role often expected in the West. Within this frame, infants learn with peers, older siblings and friends to observe and rehearse later roles expected of them. Heidi Keller et al. (2002) provide similar examples. Also working with caregivers and infants in northern Germany and Cameroon, they refer to the contrasting perspectives of 'independent' (Western) and 'interdependent' (African and other traditional) aims in socialization. These clearly result in very different understandings of what 'counts' as successful learning for young children.

From the very start of life, then, babies inhabit a 'cultural niche' where their development will be differentially patterned according to the care and cultural beliefs and practices of the community in which they live, sometimes referred to as the 'ethnotheories' of their care-givers (Super and Harkness, 1996). An international team of researchers from the US, Guatemala, India and Turkey, led by Barbara Rogoff (Rogoff et al., 1993), contrasted the ways in which caregivers assist their toddlers in learning different tasks. They noted vital similarities across all circumstances:

1 Caregivers collaborate with children in determining the nature of the activities and their responsibility, that is, they *create bridges* and *structure children's participation.*
2 They work together and, in the process, the children learn to manage new situations under the collaborative structuring of problem-solving attempts.

3   *Guided participation* includes both tacit communication and explicit instruction.
4   Children learn about the activities of their community with the support of a system of social partners including peers and a number of caregivers.

Within this overall common framework, the researchers found striking differences in explicitness, intensity of verbal and non-verbal communication and the interaction status of child and adult. Caregivers and toddlers from Salt Lake City, US, interacted much more through vocalizations than their Guatemalan Mayan counterparts where caregivers spoke much less, but interacted much more through non-verbal communication such as gaze and guiding children's hands. The status of adult and child also differed considerably in the Mayan and Salt Lake City groups. Salt Lake City caregivers participated in their toddlers' play as equals, negotiating meanings using simplified talk and co-operating with the infants to build propositions. However, the children remained largely excluded from the economic functioning of the household. Mayan caregivers, on the other hand, did not play with their infants nor engage with them in playful talk. But infants were integrated into adult activities and ensured a role in the action, even if only as observers. Their asymmetrical role vis-à-vis adults enabled them to 'eavesdrop' on activities outside the mother's circle and become powerful informants at home. What the Salt Lake City child learned through careful talk and play with an adult, the Mayan child learned through observation. Crucially, through their comparison of caregiver and infant pairs in similar situations, Rogoff and her colleagues show that what counts as teaching and learning will be very different in different countries and that, therefore, infants can be skilled in many different ways. Her team points clearly to the fact that the school system will largely represent Western values that 'provide practice in the use of specific tools and technologies for solving particular problems' (Rogoff, 1990: 191).

The above examples show that different cultural groups differ in both what they 'teach' their infants and what 'counts' as learning at all. Judy Dunn (1989) provides a neat metaphor for comparing child-rearing in different cultural groups. She claims that all children are given finely tuned tutoring but that the nature of the 'curriculum' is different according to the family's cultural background. We know that from birth, caregivers begin attributing infants with having definite intentions which will be framed within their own experiences and those of their cultural group. At its simplest, a child's cry might be interpreted as 'she's hungry, she wants ...' or 'she's sad because she can't see her teddy/the television/her daddy's gone', 'she's tired', and so on. In this way, the adult or older sibling gives a crucially important 'model' of the conventional interpretation of intentions within the culture. Caregivers introduce children to how others interpret their intentions in using particular words on particular occasions. Eventually, this may mean that children unconsciously adopt the caregivers' interpretation of the context and the activity. This kind of intergenerational link is referred to by Michael Cole (1996: 183) as 'prolepsis', or 'the cultural mechanism that "brings the end into the beginning"'. In Cole's example, the caregiver brings her idealized memory of her cultural past and her assumption of cultural continuity in the future to her actual interactions with the child in the present. This is a non-linear process whereby the child's experience is both energized and constrained by what adults remember of their own past and what they imagine the child's future to be. Clearly, the process of prolepsis is likely to be particularly complex when families, like those of the Somali community above, move countries and there will be a rift in obvious cultural continuity. New opportunities and challenges will present themselves in everyday life, including relationships between child, family and the school. Later in this chapter, we see ways in which different generations work with such challenges.

Figure 3.1 *A mother from Burma (Myanmar) teaching her baby to pray*

LEARNING TO TALK: A KEY TOOL IN INTERACTION

> *[T]he process of acquiring language and the process of acquiring socio-cultural knowledge are intimately linked. (Schieffelin and Ochs, 1998: 61)*

Scaffolding

In every culture, caregivers of whatever age support children's early language learning. This is widely referred to using the term 'scaffolding'. 'Scaffolding' is a useful metaphor to explain the language learning process as it reveals precisely the way in which assistance can be gradually removed as the child gains competence in a task. It is an important term which we shall return to later (Chapters 6 and 7) in relation to the teacher's task in school. The type of 'scaffolding' given will be different across cultures according to how 'learning' and 'interaction' are perceived. The Western approach is to *extend* a child's utterance, to *question* and to *model* appropriate speech. At different stages in children's language development, this will look as follows.

Stage 1: the holophrastic stage

Here the child first understands that meaning can be expressed in a word, for example, 'doggie' = particular dog > all dogs > dog.

The following incident took place recently on a crowded No. 73 bus in Oxford Street, central London. An infant of about 15 months sits with obviously adoring parents on the seat nearest the conductor. The child is holding a book open with a picture of a bus which he shows the harrassed conductor, mumbling something which could be 'bus'. The conductor at first ignores him, but when the parents say 'He's showing you his bus. He wants you to talk to him about it', the conductor eventually repeats 'Bus'. Other passengers who get on and stand close by are more forthcoming. 'Yes, it's a *big* bus,' says one. 'What a *lovely* bus,' says a second. 'You *have* got a nice bus,' says a third. The parents and their infant smile contentedly.

Stage 2: the 2-word stage (around 2 years)

Vocative (child):   *Oh, look!*
Question (adult):   *What's that?*
Label (child):   *Fishy.*
Confirms (adult):   *It's a fish. That's right!*

The adult's question is embedded in the child's attempts to complete a new task (naming the fish); the question implicitly models an appropriate structure of narrative (What's that?); after the child's response the parent directly models the appropriate form (It's a ——). In this way, the adult 'frames' the interaction, keeping the child's attention on the task, and finally provides an evaluative feedback. The form and content of the question as well as the nature of the feedback are just about the level the child can understand.

Stage 3: 'telegraphic speech' (usually between 2 and 3 years)

K (child):   *Mummy sock dirty.*
Mummy: *Yes. They're all dirty.*

K:	*Mummy sock.*
Mummy:	*There.*
K:	*Mummy sock.*
Mummy:	*That's not mummy's sock. That's your sock. There.*
K:	*Kathryn sock.*

Although the adult is said to 'scaffold' unconsciously, the pattern is unchanging and the repetitive tutoring quite explicit. Bruner (1986) refers to this assistance as a 'loan of consciousness' which the adult freely offers and the child has the confidence to 'borrow'.

Modelling

Another type of assistance given by adults is 'modelling' for the child. Luke (1993: 24) provides us with an example of an Australian middle-class mother talking with her 2-year-old child while standing in line in a restaurant:

> *We're in a long line, Jason, Aren't we? There are lots of people lined up here, waiting for a drink. Look (pointing) they're carrying a Christmas tree with lots of things on it. They're moving it. Do we have a tree like that?*

The child did not answer during the 20–30-second monologue by the mother. Linguistically, we see how the mother is providing the child with a number of quite complex structures: two different ways of constructing questions (Do we …? Aren't we …?); the present continuous tense (waiting, carrying, and so on); various prepositions (in, on, up, for). In addition, Luke maintains that the mother is 'situating' the child in the culture through talk, that is, she is naming salient objects (Christmas tree) and foregrounding reasons, norms and ethics for actions (for example, 'why' we line up, how to move things, what 'we' have). So we see that, with adult help, children learn to 'situate' themselves in different contexts long before learning to read in school.

These ways of 'tutoring' are probably familiar to many of us. Nevertheless, although finely tuned interaction will take place between infants and caregivers from all cultures, it will follow a different pattern from one cultural group to another. Bambi Schieffelin and Eleanor Ochs (1998) describe very different tutoring patterns taking place among the Kaluli in Papua New Guinea. Here dyadic exchanges are much less important than those involving at least three participants. Infants are also not treated as 'partners' in conversations until they have built up some vocabulary. At this point, they are seen as ready to learn to speak and will be directly taught by the caregiver's instruction to 'say it like this'. When mistakes are made, the infant will be corrected and asked to be more specific. The whole process is seen as 'hardening', culminating in the use of 'hard words'. Other studies show how child rearing in non-Western societies often falls mainly to older siblings who 'teach' infants through play (Keller et al., 2002).

Even in Western societies, child-rearing will vary considerably according to the beliefs and practices of different social and cultural groups. Longitudinal work by Shirley Brice Heath gives us detailed information on the language tutoring given by the caregivers of different cultural groups living in the US. In her classic book, *Ways with Words* (Heath, 1983), she traces the child-rearing practices of three groups (black working class, white working class and white middle class from the larger town whom she refers to as 'mainstream') living within close proximity to the Appalachian mountains. Heath's study shows how even groups speaking the same language socialize their infants into using words differently.

Heath traces the way in which the language learning process is quite different for her 'Trackton' infants (the name given to the black working-class group in her study) and those from Roadville (the white working-class group). Roadville infants receive very explicit tutoring of names. Here is two-year-old Sally being taught by her aunt:

> When Sally was just a little over two years old ... Aunt Sue was peeling tomatoes ... She was trying to get Sally to say tomato, but each time Aunt Sue asked 'What is that?' and pointed to the tomato, Sally would answer 'red'. Aunt Sue kept insisting 'Yes, it's red, but it's a tomato.' 'You like *tomatoes*, don't you?' Repeatedly, parents reject children's descriptions of things by their attributes before they have learned to respond with the *name* of the item. When adults misunderstand or mishear a child's statement, they ask for clarification most frequently by saying 'A what?' 'You want a what?' requesting a noun or a noun phrase rather than a repetition of the entire statement or another part of the sentence. Children are expected to learn through incrementally acquiring knowledge which includes names, attributes, phrases and stories. (Heath, 1983: 141)

The experiences of a Trackton infant are very different. Rather than participating in topic-centred question/answer routines or direct labelling activities, children between 12 and 24 months learn rather through repetition, repetition with variation and finally participation. Lem's progress, therefore, looks like this:

Lillie Mae: *'n she be go in' 'down dere 'bout every week, but I don't believe dey/: got no jobs =*
Lem: *= got no jobs:/* (Lem at 16 months)

This pattern of repetition is continued throughout the adults' conversation. By 20 months, Lem participates in the following way:

> Lem ... was playing on the porch while his mother and several other women were talking. He had been repeating and varying the ends of her utterances, when suddenly he stopped his play and went to his mother, pulling and tugging at her jeans: 'Wanna pop, wanna pop, bump, bump, bump.' His mother looked at him and said 'Stop it, Lem, you wanna, wanna, wanna, you ain't gettin' nut'n, Darett ain't home. Go ask Miz Lula. (Heath, 1983: 94)

In contrast with the Roadville children, Lem is not the centre of attention, nor is he being explicitly tutored into labelling objects or events. Instead, he enters into the conversation on equal terms; his mother attends to the message itself rather than the language used to express it – even if she does misinterpret it (she overhears the word 'pop' and focuses on the 'bumping' Lem received from Darett the night before). The examples of Lem, Jason, Sally and Kathryn will begin to help the reader understand strategies used by young new language learners later in this chapter and throughout the book.

Heath's work teaches us to observe all our children carefully as they first step into the classroom. Do they find it difficult to ask questions even if we think they know the words to use? If so, why might this be? Do we need to assist new language learners in 'situating' themselves in a whole new context, of which the language is only a part? Chapter 6 will illustrate one way of doing this with very young children.

LEARNING APPROPRIATE 'RECIPES': LANGUAGE SOCIALIZATION IN CROSS-CULTURAL CONTEXT

> Mamma and daddy just talked to me and made me talk to them. They'd ask me questions; it was then that I began to learn how to talk to other folks. They'd uh, ask me over and over again, to tell my aunts and uncles things, and I'd know they wanted me to say it right. They taught us children to be polite, too, to talk right when other folks were around. Mamma would always say: 'What do you say?' 'Did you forget your manners?' Jf I didn't say something when I was supposed to, they'd fuss at me for not *acting* right, not *doing right* by other folks. Saying 'I'm sorry,' 'excuse me' and 'thank you' were important, showed the kind of person you were. If you couldn't learn to say the right things, seems like they thought you couldn't do nothing right. (Heath, 1983: 142)

All children – given normal neurological and physiological functioning, and interaction with other humans – will learn to use oral language appropriately in their own speech community. Before starting school, they will already be able to use many acceptable verbal 'recipes' (more formally referred to as 'speech genres' by Bakhtin 1986) during different cultural routines of typical situations. Examples of such 'recipes' spring to mind from different countries in Europe. Think of meal-times which are preceded by the politeness recipe of *Bon Appetit* in France or *Mahlzeit* in Germany (translated literally 'Good appetite' and 'Mealtime' or more freely as 'I hope you enjoy your meal') for which we have, no equivalent in English. These recipes are often the most difficult aspects of language for foreigners to learn, perhaps because they call upon knowledge taught to us at a very young age by our elders which we then share implicitly with members of the same culture.

The sociolinguist Dell Hymes (1974) provides the useful term 'speech events' into which we can slot both recipes and other different types of oral language use needed for particular cultural practices. At first glance, these may seem spontaneous, like, for example, a telephone conversation, ordering in a restaurant, and so on. But we need only imagine our situation as a foreigner in a strange country appearing, perhaps, at a wedding or a funeral to realize that our interpretation of the situation (or our own cultural practices of 'weddings' and 'funerals') are no longer valid and we lack the appropriate words. In cases like this, we are, perhaps, most aware of language as an 'event'. Like any other 'event', language events are not random or arbitrary, but rule-governed and structured, following exact protocols and patterns and with definite boundaries.

Cross-cultural studies show us how caregivers undertake quite explicit and conscious tutoring of their infants to make sure that they participate using appropriate language in important cultural practices. Yet in each culture, what was referred to earlier as the 'curriculum' delivered to the child will be very different. 'Speech events' which are likely to be particularly important for the child to feel at home upon entering school are those linked with politeness and disciplining recipes and narrating or storytelling. But what might 'difference' look like?

Politeness and disciplining recipes

Tapes made of 'mainstream' Western caregivers in ordinary interaction with young children at home reveal distinct rules of politeness as well as a variety of language structures used in enforcing politeness or disciplining children. One important rule is that children should listen if the caregiver is reading from a book; another is not to interrupt if adults are talking; another is to say 'please', 'thank you' or 'sorry' at certain times. Requests or 'tellings-off' may be encoded by the adult as questions underlying the adult's statement – 'What do you say?', 'What do you think you're doing?', 'Do you mind?' – or indirect statements – 'I'm waiting', 'I'm speaking', and so on. We know that both politeness rules and the formulae used to enforce discipline are likely to be different in different cultural groups. The politeness recipes used by Heath's Roadville group might strike a familiar note to teachers in British classrooms:

> We grew up with a lot of shoulds in our house. 'You oughta do so and so', 'You should say 'thank you', 'I'm sorry'. 'You should write a thank you note.' Uh, I remember whenever I, uh, when I first learned that 'I'm sorry' could take care of most anything. We learned to do that at school too. Most anything you did, if you talked right afterwards you'd be O.K. (Heath, 1983: 142)

In a number of cultural groups such recipes will not be at hand. In many Asian cultures it is not customary constantly to say 'thank you' if the person you are speaking to is considered a friend. In the other extreme, a German-speaking child will be taught to reply 'please' or 'you're welcome' (*Bitte!*) immediately after hearing 'Thank you' (*Danke!*) from a conversation partner. 'Sorry' is not used as widely in many cultures as it is in the English-speaking world. We see that it will not automatically be easy for our new language learners to situate themselves in the 'classroom manners' of reading. Picture again Tony, whom we met in the introduction to Part 1 of the book, who has just started British school. Remember that Tony's family originates from Hong Kong. For the first few weeks at school he is so quiet. His teacher constantly tries to get him to play in the home corner with others, to talk, play, make a noise and move about. One day, at story-time, he starts clicking his fingers while she is reading. She stops and says quietly 'We're just waiting for Tony'. It takes Tony some time before he understands that his actions are inappropriate in this context. Should he have known? It seems that politeness is very much a cultural matter.

Narrating and story-telling

Narrating itself is a universal experience, beginning with the human urge to tell about an event, person or feeling. It may be 'the oldest and most basic human-language activity. Someone telling someone else that something happened … Basic narrative is preoccupied with holding on to occurrences by telling about them, thus creating sequences of events ordered in time' (Whitehead, 2004: 111). However, we know from studies in homes and classrooms that the idea of 'story' calls up different meanings for children from different cultural backgrounds. Difference concerns both the *purpose* for which a story is used and the *manner* in which it is told. Roadville (white working-class) children in Heath's study are brought up with the tradition that stories must be factual and must have a moral which highlights the weakness admitted in the tale; stories, then, are similar to testimonials given at their prayer-meetings. Trackton (black working-class) children grow up with quite different traditions. Their stories start with a kernel of truth, but aim then to rivet the interest of their audience even if this means massaging the facts. Mainstreamers (white middle-class) children see story differently again. They learn that 'telling a story' means relating a story from a book; even indirect story items (for example, pictures of Humpty Dumpty on wallpaper) may well be linked with both the rhyme and the book.

The manner of narrating may also differ according to the type of stories children are accustomed to. In her study of the different participation of white and black American 5-year-olds in 'Show-and-Tell' (news-time) classroom sessions, Sarah Michaels (1986) shows how the white children use a 'topic-centred' approach (tightly organized centred on a single topic and leading quickly to a punch-line) whereas the black children prefer a 'topic-associating' style (series of episodes which are implicitly linked in highlighting a person or theme). Michaels's point is that the teacher implicitly expects all the children to adopt her own 'topic-centred' approach, but never makes her expectations explicit to the black children. The result is that the black children do not understand what is expected of them and simply learn to resent the 'Show-and-Tell' lessons. Like Heath, Michaels shows how the quality of tuition given to young children will depend upon a teacher's knowledge of the resources and interaction patterns a child brings to school as well as the ability to make her own expectations explicit. In the second section of this chapter, we begin to investigate both the funds of knowledge children bring with them into school and ways in which this knowledge is transmitted in home and community contexts.

Questions for reflection

- How far can we take over the role of 'scaffolding' a new language learner in the classroom? Which aspects might be most effective and which will need to be adapted?
- How many of our new language learners already relate to us as responsible caregivers and what might be the implications of this?
- How much do we know of the languages in the lives of our pupils and how they might differ from that important in school?
- Which language resources will our new language learners need to learn in order to be able to 'situate' themselves in the context of classroom reading?
- How explicit do we make these to all children?

We return to these questions in Part 2 of the book.

Siblings as expert reading teachers

Eleven-year-old Farjana is 'playing school' with Farhana, her 8-year-old sister. The children live in East London and were born in Britain of parents who came across from Bangladesh. Like a number of schools in the neighbourhood, theirs receives almost all its pupils from Sylhet, a region in the north-east of Bangladesh. Both girls attend community language classes to learn Bengali literacy and Qur'ānic classes to learn to read the Qur'ān in classical Arabic. However, when playing school, they always use English. This excerpt comes near the middle of an hour-long tape made at home in which Farjana 'teaches' her sister numeracy, spelling, science and poetry as well as listens to her read. Although living in an area with a strong London accent, the girls' voices echo the standard English of their teachers. Apart from the occasional grammatical error, their voices are indistinguishable from those of middle-class mother-tongue English speakers:

Jana: *Very good. Now let's have poems. OK, let's have a look. We're reading it from a red poetry pink box. There are loads, there are 62 pages. Now let's see, what ones do we want? OK. Let's have wolf. No, let's have two short ones. OK.*
'Golden chips.
Brown potatoes white potato change them if you can
Turn them into golden chips' – What do you think comes next?

Hana: *'Catch them if you can!'*

Jana: *'Frying in the pan!'*
Now let's have another one.

'Roses are red. OK?
'Roses are red, spiders are black.'
What do you think comes next?

Hana: *'Don't look now but there's one on your back!'*

Jana: *Very good. I think you knew that one …'*

The importance of siblings in non-Western communities in infant caregiving and preparing young children for everyday tasks as well as school learning has been widely recognized (Nsamenang and Lamb, 1998; Rogoff, 1990). These studies show ways in which older siblings 'tutor' young children through initiating play, modelling or direct teaching. For their part, younger siblings participate in or observe the skills and performances of the older child. Only recently, however, has attention been given to the role siblings in Western societies such as Britain and the US might play in preparing young children for school language and literacy. However, as Farhana and her older sister show, sibling tuition in multilingual homes might be significant. Older children are skilled mediators of both reading and other literacy-related activities, thus taking on a unique role in initiating younger siblings into a new language.

Let us invite ourselves into the lives of siblings of different ages and in different countries, either 'playing school' or listening to children read at home.

PRE-SCHOOL: SAMIA AND JULIALIZ

Samia is 4 and has recently started nursery class near London. She was born in Britain of Pakistani parents and her mother tongue is Pahari, a dialect of Punjabi. She is at a very early stage of English learning and her teacher is concerned that she does not speak at all in class unless able to speak to the mother-tongue teacher. At home, however, there is a different story. Equipped with a radio-transmitter microphone, she allows us to listen in to her play with Sadaqat, her 2-year-old brother:

(The italicized text indicates English and the plain text indicates Pahari.)

Samia:	Sadaqat, stand up
	we're not having group time now
	group time
	you can play, Sadaqat
	shall we play something?
	you want to do painting?
	[noise from Sadaqat]
	OK get your water
	let's get a water
	let's get a water
	let's get a paper
	baby didn't cry
	hurry up [whispering]
	you want paper
	and put in the painting
	do that and what you are
	choose colour
	black
Sadaqat:	*back*

Samia: *no, there's a black*
                                                did you finish it?
                                                painting
                                                you make it

Sadaqat, do it with this finger
do it like this, do it like that

                                                wash
which *colour* are you going to choose? (Drury, 2004: 47)

In contrast with her teacher's view that she is not yet able to comprehend or speak English, Samia reveals considerable skill in understanding the rituals of the nursery day and the corresponding formulaic language in English attached to these. She is also beginning to provide a model for her younger brother in the new language he will have to learn. In this and other episodes, we see how Samia competently switches languages in order to hold her brother's attention at the same time as 'teaching' him the new language. She uses Pahari in order to invite him into the game, then switches into English as the 'play school' takes place, using classroom lexis such as 'painting, hurry up, choose, did you finish it? let's get …, wash, group time' and so on. She carefully blends the languages in order to facilitate his understanding: 'which *colour* are you going to choose?' At the same time, she is giving herself considerable practice in the new language. In this sense, we see how *scaffolding*, *guided participation* and *synergy* are appropriate in describing the process of learning taking place. Samia clearly scaffolds her younger brother's attempts at a very new language; he is obviously an active participant in the learning; Samia is simultaneously learning as much as she teaches. Samia and Sadaqat thus begin to show the unique role played by siblings in each other's learning while they play together.

Our second example revisits Julializ and her family from the US, whom we have already met in Chapter 2. In the examples below, 5-year-old Julializ, a Spanish speaker with emergent English skills, is practising her reading with Fernando, her 12-year-old brother who is a confident bilingual and biliterate and Zoila, her 6-year-old cousin who is also brought up in the family. With Fernando, she works on word analysis and comprehension:

1. Fernando: *Recuerda la W hace 'wh'.* [Remember the W says 'wh']
2. Julializ: *Wa.*
3. Fernando: *Mhmh. No. We.*
4. Julializ: *We.//Are.//*
5. Fernando: *//Went.//Went.*
6. Julializ: *Went.To.The.Zoo.*
7. Sra. Torres: *Mhum.*

8. Julializ: *It.Whhhas ... A.*
9. Fernando: *Grande.* [Big.]
10. Julializ: *Big. Park. Www//www//* ...
11. Julializ: *... With*
12. Fernando: *Mucha.* [A lot.]
13. Julializ: *A lot.*
14. Fernando: *Mhum.*
15. Julializ: *Animals.*
16. Fernando: *Mhum. Of.*
17. Julializ: *Of.*
18. Fernando: *Diferente. En inglés.* [Different. In English.]
19. Julializ: *Different animals.*
20. Fernando: *Mhum ...*
21. Julializ: *The lllions wwwear.*
22. Fernando: *Mhumh. Cubs.*
23. Julializ: *Qué?* [What?]
24. Fernando: ((points to picture)) *Qué son éstos? ...* [What are these?]
25. Julializ: *Cubs.* (Volk, with de Acosta, 2004: 34)

In the episode above, Dinah Volk (with de Acosta, 2004) shows how Fernando gives his younger sister a phonic cue to help her recognize 'w - ent', then focuses on comprehension by telling Julializ the Spanish for the word she needs. He also directs her attention to illustrations, using a strategy he remembered from his own teacher when he was young. Julializ gradually gains confidence and manages some text on her own, often translating the Spanish cues offered by her older brother.

Meanwhile, her cousin Zoila, aged six, tries a different approach to facilitate word analysis:

1. Zoila: *La O (ō) es U (ōō).* [The O is U.]
2. Julializ: *To. Go.*
3. Zoila: *P.A. (ā)// P//*
4. Julializ: *// P// lay.*
5. Zoila: *La O (ō) es A (ŏ).* [The O is. A]
6. Julializ: *Nnnn ot. Not.*
7. Zoila: *U (ŭ). I-U (ĭ – ŭ). Ruuuuuuun*
8. Julializ: *Run.*
9. Zoila: *Oo (oo). Ll ook.*
10. Julializ: *Look ...* (Volk, with de Acosta, 2004: 35)

With considerable skill, Zoila uses Spanish vowel sounds to help Julializ learn English vowels (for example the Spanish sound U for 't o̲' in turn 1 and the Spanish A for 'n o̲t' in turn 5. She then goes on to demonstrate further sounds in turns 7 and 9. Both examples show scaffolding, guided participation and synergy taking place, although Fernando is now firm in his knowledge of English literacy and thus has less need to practise than his young cousin. The last example begins to show the complexity of learning to read using phonics for emergent biliterate children, a topic to which we return in Chapter 4.

EARLY DAYS AT SCHOOL: A LIFELINE TO READING FOR 5- AND 6-YEAR-OLDS

The resourcefulness and stamina of older siblings 'teaching' young children to speak and read in a new language is often invisible outside the home and especially to the school. In a study taking place in East London during the 1990s (Gregory and Williams, 2000) we found that older siblings of all ages were devoting an enormous amount of time and energy to reading classroom texts with younger siblings who had just started school. This was an especially significant finding, since the children's parents were first-generation immigrants from Bangladesh who, in many cases, were unable to read English themselves. Not only were older siblings reading regularly with the novice readers at home, their tutoring also revealed a finely tuned 'scaffolding' in the graphic sense of the term. Young children were firmly supported, never expected to achieve more than they could manage, never allowed to fail, yet at the same time challenged to make progress. In this respect, the 'lessons' shared much in common with the children's Qur'ānic classes – except that there were no tests. The pattern of participation was quite unique, moving from a 'Listen and Repeat' sequence for the very beginner reader where the young child repeated each word in quick succession, sometimes over hundreds of turns:

	Child	Sibling
1.		*gave*
2.	*gave*	
3.		*her*
4.	*her*	
5.		*fishy*
6.	*fishy*	
7.		*gifts*
8.	*gifts*	

to *telegraphic speech* where the child attempted to repeat larger chunks of text but only managed some words (underlined denotes repeat):

	Child	Sibling
1.		*Peace at last*
2.	*Peace in last*	
3.		*The hour*
4.	*The hour*	
5.		*was late*
6.	*was late*	
7.		*Mr. Bear was tired*
8.	*was tired*	
9.		*So they all went to bed*
10.	*all went*	
11.		*to bed*
12.	*to bed*	

This was followed by an *'echoing'* (reading one beat behind) of the older child's words and *'chained'* reading where the young child read until a mistake was made. The mistake was swiftly corrected, the correction always repeated immediately by the young child and reading resumed (underline denotes repeat):

	Child	Sibling
1.		*Okhta (this one)*
2.		*It's*
3.	*It's a whobber. Meg …*	
4.		*Mog*
5.	*Mog catched a fish*	
6.		*caught*
7.	*caught a fish. They cook*	
8.		*cooked*
9.	*cooked a fish*	
10.		*and*
11.	*and Owl had a rest. Meg was looking*	
12.		*looked out*

The young child was always expected to repeat the corrected word before continuing – a strategy learned in both the Qur'ānic and Bengali classes – and proceded to more complex comprehension questions only once a secure grasp of reading had been accomplished. In this way, older siblings provided a lifeline to very young incipent readers, boosting their confidence in a way parents could never have done.

DEVELOPING LITERACY AFTER THE FIRST YEARS IN SCHOOL

Teachers in schools where most children speak a different language at home often fear that the classroom is the only site for practice of academic forms of the target language. This is understandable, since school literacy demands increasingly difficult lexis and grammar that are often beyond the grasp of parents who have recently migrated. However, the fear is often unfounded. Increasingly, evidence of siblings 'playing school' in bilingual households reveals ways in which older children 'teach' their younger brothers and sisters using the specialist language (as well as the accent and mannerisms) of their teacher. Farjana and Farhana who opened this section provide a typical example of a 'lesson' taking place. Eleven-year-old Wahida also provides 'teaching' sessions to her eight year old sister Sayeda which are remarkable in both the skill required and their similarity to the lessons given by her real teacher:

Wahida   *Sayeda*

1: Well done! Only two wrong.
Now we're going to do homophones.
Who knows what's a homophone is?
No one? OK. I'll tell you one and then
you're going to do some by yourselves.
Like watch – one watch is your time watch,
like what's the time, watch. And another watch
is I'm watching you, I can see you. OK?
So Sayeda, you wrote some in your book,
haven't you? Can you tell me some please.
Sayeda, can you only give me three please.

                                                                 2: Oh I have to give five.

3: No, Sayeda, we haven't got enough time.
We've only another five minutes to assembly.
And guess who's going to do assembly –
Miss Kudija.

                                                                 4: OK.

5: OK? So tell me one.

                                                                 6: Son is the opposite of daughter …

7: Yeah

                                                                 8: and sun is … um … its shines on the
                                                                 sky so bright.

9: Well done! That's one correct one.
   The next one?

10: The cell means you go … to jail … in prison … you're going to prison and another sell means the selling money … they are giving money.

11: The last one is ?

12: Hear. Hear is you're hearing something … people are telling you something and here is come here, come.

13: Well done! Now you can go to assembly. Sayeda line up in order. Otherwise you'll come back and do lines. So remember your order. OK? Well done, Sayeda, you're in your correct order and Miss Kudija is going to take you down because I have to do some more things.

Freedom offered by the frame 'this is play' allows Wahida to take the role of a rigorous 'teacher' yet for Sayeda to remain unthreatened and even to question what is required of her: 'Oh, I have to give 5'. Crucially, however, we see how both children learn from each other. Wahida, the older child, learns through practising what she already knows about homophones and through modelling the task to be taught (turn 1); Sayeda has recently learned the concept of a homophone in her classroom and needs the reinforcement and confidence given through further 'teaching' by her older sister. This is just one example of the *synergy* taking place where both children learn equally from each other.

All the excerpts above show the very special role played by siblings when young children are learning to read in a new language.

SIBLINGS: A SUMMARY

- ◆ Siblings are unique mediators of language and literacy in a new language.
- ◆ This occurs particularly during socio-dramatic play and especially during 'play school'.
- ◆ A *synergy* takes place whereby both older and younger children learn from each other.
- ◆ Older children learn through modelling, guiding, demonstrating, instructing, coaxing, looking after, comforting and socializing younger children as well as generally practising their existing skills.
- ◆ Younger children learn through watching, listening, repeating, echoing, requesting help, following directions, imitating, challenging and experimenting.

Grandparents as mediators of literacies

My grandmother Mu Wye was the first woman who influenced my way of thinking. Her influence was as strong as the teachings of the Church. She was illiterate, but her memory was immense … To sleep with the grandparents was an immense privilege, because it meant we had the joy of hearing folklore and fantastical stories. Except for a few school textbooks and my father's veterinary reports, there were no books at all in the house. Nor was there television. Radio was a source of merely alien legends, and so my grandmother's role as oracle and storyteller came into its own. As with the myths of the tribe, so with my grandmother's stories – Grandpa would lie quietly in the darkness, occasionally confirming her stories, extraordinary as they were, with grave remarks such as, 'That is what my mother used to tell me.' (Thwe, 2002: 58 and 59–60)

Children cannot always rely on having siblings with whom they can learn. Fortunately, grandparents will be present in many young children's lives and, like those of Pascal Khoo Thwe growing up as a member of the Padaung tribe, a minority group in Burma (Myanmar) during the 1970s, will mesmerize young children through their stories, skills and knowledge. Grandparents have long been neglected in terms of their role as language and literacy 'tutors' of young children. This is particularly the case where families have migrated and the grandparents' knowledge of the language and literacy of the host community might be limited. Yet we know that grandparents across the world play a significant part in child-rearing in the twenty-first century. In families that have recently migrated, grandparents may be highly mobile, frequently visiting grandchildren in different countries and carrying to each their knowledge of a heritage language and literacy. Razia is one such grandmother. Now in her fifties, she was born and still has her home in Chittagong, Bangladesh. Her three sons and two daughters, however, have moved to New York, Canada and London and she spends much of her time travelling to visit her grandchildren. Her aim is to keep alive the language and cultural heritage of her country of origin, 'I speak to them in Bengali and they speak to me in Bengali.' In London, she shops with her grandchildren (aged 4, 3 and 2), takes them to the park, tells them stories, sings songs and rhymes with them, uses the computer, watches television and videos with them as well as initiating them into religious activities (in Arabic) and family history stories.

On this occasion, she is reading with 6-year-old Sahil:

When asked what he would like to read with his grandmother, he (Sahil) is seen carrying a book and running enthusiastically into the room where Razia is sitting:

Sahil: I can't find the *golpo* (story) book but I can see the ABCD book.
Researcher: Is that Bangla ABCD?
Sahil: Actually it's just *Chora*, yeh yeh, it is the *Chora*.

... He realizes that the book that he has found is the Chora book, a collection of rhymes or poems illustrated with pictures, popular among Bengali children. The poem chosen on this occasion is about how a child will plan his day from the moment he wakes up and how he will take his teaching from the respected wisdom from the elders in the community. The type of text grandmother and grandson read can be seen as helping to define their relationship. In fact it is a text that Razia is able to recite as much as read and the presence of the printed version may at times act as an aide-mémoire rather than as a script to be followed precisely.

Razia leads by reading a few words from the text; her tone of voice becomes more serious and this is taken to signal a more formal mode of learning. Sahil repeats, he takes great care in how he sounds the words: where sound comes from, such as the throat, the nose, which part of the mouth he uses and even how he forms his cheeks will all have a bearing on how effective his pronunciation in Bengali is judged to be. Razia's presence is also very important in that she can demonstrate, correct and support Sahil continually as the session proceeds. The cycle of Razia reading with Sahil repeating continues; this is a traditional teaching pattern in Bangladesh especially with new or unfamiliar material. Although Sahil's Bengali is good enough to allow him to understand parts of the story, there are also unfamiliar words, and he perseveres with his grandmother's help:

Sahil: *Akhane ki bole?** [What does it mean here?]
Razia: *Korta?* [Which one?]

*All quoted Bengali speech has been transliterated and is in italics. (Jessel et al., 2004: 18)

Figure 3.2 *Sahil reading a chora with his grandmother Razia and his younger sisters*

On other occasions, Sahil takes the lead, such as with computer activities. In the excerpt below, as in those taking place in other families, young children provide dexterity and confidence when using the mouse as well as a familiarity with both the game to be played and the purpose of the computer in 'partnering' him in the game:

Sahil has set up the card game Solitaire on the computer.

Sahil: *Asho akhane.* [Come here.]
Razia: *Oita ami akhono khelte parbo na tomi khelo.* [I cannot play that yet, you play.]

Razia knows some group card games but not those that are usually played alone such as Solitaire. However, she is now becoming familiar with the game through Sahil showing her on the computer.

Razia: *Amake bolo tomi ki ki korso.* [Tell me what you have done.]
    Dekhi to tomi. [Let me have a look.]
    Erm bolo na Dadu ... bolo na. [Erm tell Granny ... tell me.]
Sahil: *Aita akhan rakhte ...* [This one put ...]

She appears to take an interest and watches Sahil who tries to explain what he is doing as he repositions the cards on the computer screen.

Sahil: *Aita khotai rakhi, akhane?* [Where shall I put this, here?]
Razia: Hmm
Sahil: *Na aikhane okhane airokom kore.* [No this there like this.]
Razia: *Dadu tho computer khelte pari na tomi dekhai dou.* [Granny does not know how to play computer, you show me.]
Sahil: *Akhane akhane* [Here here]
    Ami jani ... tomi koro. [I know ... you do it.]

Razia then reaches for the mouse and begins to move it while attempting to press the centre scroll wheel. As she does this Sahil places his hand on top of hers (see Figure 3.3) while indicating that she should click the left mouse button. Sahil then continues to guide Razia's hand. Sahil continues to take the lead and the transcript of the dialogue suggests that he feels confident in this role:

Figure 3.3: *Sahil guides Razia's hand on the computer mouse*

——— Continues opposite ———

Sahil: *Akhane koro, na akhan ... akhan koro.* [Put it here, no here ... now do it.]
Ata kothai rakhbe ... daraou [Where will you put it ... wait]
Ata ... eh akhane akhane parbe ne. [This ... eh you can't put it here.]
Okhane rakhte parbe r, aita r aita akhane rakhte parbe? [You can put it there and, this one and this one can you put it here?]

Razia: *Tomi dekhaidau.* [You show me.]

Sahil: *Eh kotai kotai kotai rakhbe.* [Eh where where where to put it.]

Razia: *Aita akhane.* [This one here.]

Sahil: *Akhane?* [Here?]

Razia: Hmm.

Sahil: *Korte parbe na.* [Can't do that.]

(Jessel et al., 2004: 21)

Figure 3.4: *Learning with the computer with grandmother and a younger sibling*

Razia and her family were just one of a number in East London who were recorded cooking, gardening, reading the Qur'ān and using the computer with young children. Crucially, bilingual literacy skills as well as cultural practices from the heritage country were being exchanged in many activities. The relationship between grandparents and young children during literacy activities was a very special one; it was characterized by a 'mutual vulnerability' (Kenner et al., 2004c) whereby each was aware of the other's weaknesses in contrast with the parent generation. This vulnerability was symbolized by the use of touch and physical guidance. Sahil's guiding of Razia's hand when using the computer was reversed when Razia helped him to practise his Bengali handwriting. The computer also revealed a synergy taking place comparable to that between siblings whereby both taught and learned equally from each other.

Irma Olmedo (2004) reveals a similar mutual vulnerability typifying learning in her work taking place in Chicago. She depicts an intergenerational project 'Project Generation' in a dual-language school whereby elderly Latinos (*abuelitas*) told stories from their earlier lives to pairs of young children in Spanish (a Spanish-speaking child was paired with a monolingual one) and the children later wrote the stories down into a dual-language book which was presented to the women at the end of the year. Through both teaching young children and gaining confidence in themselves as teachers, the women were placed in the position of both teachers and learners. Likewise, the children learned both the Spanish language and literacy and, through thought-provoking questions, they promoted learning in the grandmothers. A similar synergy was likewise taking place in the British households:

> *The women initially claimed that they could not teach anything to the children since they themselves had had so little formal schooling. However, they came to appreciate how much they knew about a whole range of issues … The group sharing of stories took on a performative quality as the women became actresses and audience for each other, trying to dramatize features of the experiences they wanted to share. Because of the performative skills that the abuelitas exhibited during the story-telling episodes, they were able to actively engage the children as an audience. The adjustments that the abuelitas made in their language use meant that the stories were made more comprehensible for the children who were developing their Spanish skills. (Olmedo, 2004: 87)*

Olmedo concludes that Project Generation enabled the school to infuse its curriculum with the authentic funds of knowledge in terms of language and literacy offered by its community. In so doing, it enhanced the language and literacy skills of all its young emergent biliterate students who were able to participate in the work.

GRANDPARENTS: A SUMMARY

- Grandparents are excellent mediators of language and literacy to young children since they often have more time and patience than parents.
- In bilingual or multilingual families, grandparents often provide unique access to the language, literacy and cultural heritage of the country of origin.
- Grandparents and young children both teach and learn from each other. Thus a synergy similar to that between siblings takes place. Their relationship is also a very special one, typified by a mutual vulnerability

---

Friends as new language and literacy teachers

The second-language learner below is a 5-year-old Taiwanese child during his first two months of English learning:

First language child: *I got a real gun.*
Second language child*: I got a real gun.*
L.1. child: *You gotta parachute?*
L.2. child: *Yeh. Gotta parachute.*
Adult: *What's a parachute?*
L.1. child: *It has a man go down.*
L.2. child: *Yeh? go down, down, down*

Even children without siblings and grandparents will have friends with whom they learn and practise their new language. The example above shows how a very early stage English learner has a meaningful interaction through play. In fact, the only new word uttered by the L.2. child is 'Yeh'. All the rest is repetition of his friend's words, yet it is entirely appropriate in the play situation.

Like siblings, friends and peers often have a special relationship with each other based upon trust, reciprocity and playfulness. This is especially important in bilingual contexts where children become more conscious of language learning. Susi Long, with Donna Bell and Jim Brown (2004) provides examples from a classroom in South Carolina, US, showing ways in which three 5-year-old emergent Spanish/English bilinguals (Juan, Martita and Marcial) were supported by their English-speaking peers. All three children were bussed to the school and declared at the beginning of the year that they were only able to read in Spanish. At the beginning of each day at school, they sat side-by-side with other children sharing a story-book together:

> *During free activity time early in the school year, Marcial walked to the school bookcase and selected an English picture book. He sat on the floor and began to read the pictures (a reading strategy that had been demonstrated by the classroom teacher) aloud in Spanish. A few feet away Kiesh, an English-only kindergartener, sat on the floor reading the book, 'Jack Be Nimble'. She used the pictures to read the story aloud in English. Kiesha finished the book, closed it and looked at Juan. He looked at her, she moved closer to him and she opened her book again, holding it so that he could see the pages. Then, Kiesha began rereading her book in English, this time reading directly to Juan. Martita moved closer so that she could also see the pages. Both Martita and Juan looked at the pictures in the book as Kiesha turned the pages and read the book aloud to them. Later, Martita and Juan sat with one another and picture-read using the same behaviours that had been demonstrated by Kiesha. (Long, with Bell and Brown, 2004: 98)*

In the excerpt above, we see Kiesha modelling reading in a way similar to the siblings earlier in this chapter. Through her reading, Marcial, Juan and Martita were beginning to learn the patterns of written English as well as when to turn the pages and read with a friend. More direct assistance was also provided during the early stages by peers who were bilingual. In the following excerpt, the teaching assistant is reading an English book to a group of children including Marcial. She asks him, in English, to describe an illustration:

Ms. Alvarez: *Tell me what you see here.*

Marcial: [Looks closely at the illustration]

Ms. Alvarez: *What do you see here?*

Marcial: [Looks confused]

Maya: *Qué ve usted aquí? What do you see?* [Maya translates Ms. Alvarez's question into Spanish and then says it again in English]

Ms. Alvarez: *Tell me about the picture.*

Maya: *He is looking.*

Ms. Alvarez: *Marcial, what do you see here?*

Marcial: *Hay un chico y un perro.* [There's a boy and a dog]

Maya: *He sees a boy and a dog.* (Long, with Bell and Brown, 2004: 99)

The researchers describe Maya's role as being a skilled mediator of language, culture and literacy in the new language. She first translates Ms Alvarez's question into Spanish and then repeats the English question for him. She then explains to the teacher that he needs time to respond: 'He is looking.' Finally, she translates his response for him, thus allowing him to complete the task successfully. Her skill, therefore, lies in her ability to provide a 'bridge' for Marcial to reach the new language in a friendly and non-threatening way – a considerable achievement for a 5-year-old child.

Maya shows how bilingual peers are able to provide the special help new language learners need during literacy activities in class. The following excerpt returns to a school in London, where 8-year-old Yuan (a fluent English speaker with some Cantonese) is helping 9-year-old Wington who has recently arrived in Britain and is fluent in both spoken Cantonese and written Mandarin but new to English. The content of the reading in English was obviously difficult, since this was a mainstream class, but the children teach and learn from each other. We see how this happens through translation below:

1. Wington: *Come on, du nido la*
   [Come on, read here]

2. Yuan: constraint and relax

3. Wington: *Mieye yici?* [What is the meaning]

4. Yuan: *xiushu tongmai fansong*
   [constraint and relax]

5. Wington: *Xu nido yaomo gon guo*
   luolai zuo mie yong?
   [Does the text tell us what these

6. Yuan: *yiding yao la, wo taitai*
   [it should, let me have a look]

bones are used for?]

7. Wington: *Hai ng hai nido?*
          [Are they here?]

9. Chen: Did she manage to follow you?

8. Yuan: *Hai* [Yes]

10.*Yuan:* Um … yes.

(Chen and Gregory, 2004: 124)

Through her friend's translation, Wington begins to make sense of the text. However, learning is not a one-way process. Although Wington is just beginning to read in English, she is the older child, and clearly directs Yuan to the text to find answers to her questions. Yuan has the complex task of translating specialized and difficult words as well as explaining their meaning – a task that taxes her own knowledge of Cantonese and makes her more aware of her bilinguality. Thus both children teach and learn from each other in a way similar to both the siblings and grandparents/grandchildren earlier in this chapter. The children use other strategies, such as repetition, where Wington carefully repeats at first single words and then, as her confidence grows, whole phrases after Yuan and shared problem-solving in two languages whereby Wington, as the older child, quickly understands the task, such as practising the use of different conjunctions (although, in case, whenever, and so on) and offers the Cantonese, while Yuan translates into English and in so doing understands both the task and the Cantonese word. In this way 'bilingual exchange teaching' (Chen and Gregory, 2004: 117) takes place between peers in school.

The final episode in this section highlights specifically the teaching skills of young emergent biliterate children who attend formal mother-tongue language classes outside school. Charmian Kenner (2004a: 105) asked 6-year-old children attending mother-tongue classes in Mandarin, Arabic and Spanish to 'teach' their monolingual peers. The results were impressive. Here is an excerpt from a more detailed analysis of Ming's 'lesson' with Amina:

Chinese writing consists of thousands of characters, each of which represents a different meaning.The characters are built up from a repertoire of basic stroke types and stroke patterns. At Chinese school, Ming learned to write each stroke with precision in a particular sequence, to produce a correctly rendered character which could not be confused with any similar-looking one. Considerable importance was also placed on the aesthetic value of the final product ... As Ming taught Amina, he put these principles into operation. He demonstrated the character for 'seven' and Amina tried to follow his model.

At times her version began to look like the English numeral '4'. Ming realized that Amina was likely to interpret Chinese writing from an English point of view; a few moments earlier she had written one of the curved Chinese strokes as if it was the

Continues over

English numeral '2' and he had commented 'No, not 2, do it in Chinese'. In this case, he told her 'That's a 4 – that's wrong'. At another point Amina's writing resembled the English letter 't' and again Ming noticed this: 'That's wrong – that's a T'. When showing her for the second time, he made an aesthetic evaluation of his own work, saying, 'That's too lumpy'. (Kenner, 2004a: 108)

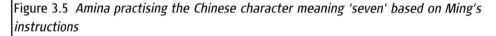

Figure 3.5 *Amina practising the Chinese character meaning 'seven' based on Ming's instructions*

Later in this excerpt Amina goes on to self-critique her own attempts at writing. She also began to understand the pedagogic strategies of the Chinese class, which involved practising the same character many times, rubbing out where necessary, until the character was harmoniously balanced and both student and teacher were satisfied with the work.

Suggestions for teaching and learning

Siblings:
- Find out about the play activities of siblings which involve literacy (possibly through children audio-taping themselves, keeping literacy diaries or simply telling the class during newstime.
- Build adequate time and collect appropriate materials for socio-dramatic play in the curriculum.
- Provide reading materials, suggestions for games and other activities, and so on that siblings might complete together.

Grandparents:
- Conduct a survey to find out about the activities taking place between grandparents and young children in the class.
- Invite grandparents into the class to share a skill, teach some of their heritage language or literacy, produce dual-language books and tapes which they read with the children, and so on.
- Invite grandparents to keep a scrap book with young children that can periodically be shared by the class.
- Make a chart of all the languages spoken and written in children's families including those of the grandparents.
- Invite grandparents into class to talk about their earlier lives in different countries and/or their favourite stories which the children can reproduce.

Friends:
- Allow children time for 'paired learning' where they complete both oral and written tasks together.
- Set up socio-dramatic play areas with provision for community (mother-tongue) language learning and encourage children to 'teach' each other.
- Encourage children to complete homework tasks with friends.
- Pair a newcomer to the country with a more fluent speaker who may compose a simple dictionary/phrase book for the child.

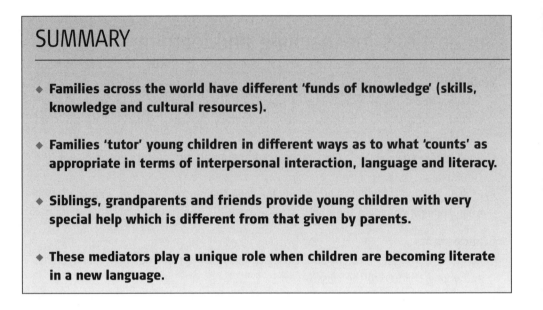

SUMMARY

◆ Families across the world have different 'funds of knowledge' (skills, knowledge and cultural resources).

◆ Families 'tutor' young children in different ways as to what 'counts' as appropriate in terms of interpersonal interaction, language and literacy.

◆ Siblings, grandparents and friends provide young children with very special help which is different from that given by parents.

◆ These mediators play a unique role when children are becoming literate in a new language.

Further reading

Brooker, E. (2002) *Starting School – Young Children Learning Cultures.* Buckingham: Open University Press.

González, N., Moll, L.C. and Amanti, C. (eds) (2005) *Funds of Knowledge: Theorising Practices in Households, Communities and Classrooms.* Mahwah, NJ: Lawrence Erlbaum Associates.

Gregory, E., Long, S. and Volk, D. (eds) (2004) *Many Pathways to Literacy: Young Children Learning with Siblings, Grandparents, Peers and Communities.* London: Routledge.

Kenner, C. (2004b) *Becoming Biliterate: Young Children Learning Different Writing Systems.* Stoke-on-Trent: Trentham.

Woodhead, M., Faulkner, D. and Littleton, K. (1998) *Cultural Worlds of Early Childhood.* London and New York: Routledge.

4 The context of the mind: important knowledge

A word without meaning is an empty sound; meaning, therefore, is a criterion of 'word', its indispensable component. (Vygotsky, 1962: 120)

KEY TERMS

Symbolization	The use of symbols to convey meaning. Young children learn that spoken words and, later, written marks are symbols for objects. Emergent bilinguals learn that objects may be symbolized by two or more words and possibly by different scripts, thus making them more aware of the arbitrary nature of language.
Bottom-up approaches	View reading as proceding from the smallest level of meaning (the phoneme) outwards to words, sentences and meaning. 'Bottom-up' approaches start with phonics as a method of reading instruction.
Top-down approaches	View reading as starting from the text as a whole and its meaning and working inwards to individual words and the phonemes they comprise.
Interactive approaches	View reading as the result of the interaction between knowledge centres (the phonic/orthographic/phonological; lexical; syntactic; semantic and bibliographic) each of which needs developing concurrently for meaning to ensue. For new language learners, the knowledge centres are viewed as an integral part of interpersonal interaction between the novice and more experienced reader.

'Can you remember how you learned to read, Nicole?'
(Nicole) 'I learned to read in English first. When I was five, I picked up a book and just read it out.'
'Can you tell me what you do when you read?'
'Well, you look at it, and when you finish reading one line, your eyes go down to the next.'
'What about when you read in French?'

'When you're reading French, your lips come out.' (demonstrates)
'Which language is easier?'
'French is easier to pronounce. In English, you have to break it into syllables, like this "ti-r-ed"
(claps to each syllable), but there are some syllables I can't read.'

Nicole's family moved from England to live in France when Nicole was just two. By 6, she was able to read well in both French (which she learned in school) and in English (which she learned with her family at home). Asking any young fluent reader about learning to read is a frustrating business, for it is so difficult to ask the right questions. We learn much more from observing children's strategies as they go about the task. As they read, we find that even when children learning two or more languages do not mix them at all in speech, they will often transfer reading strategies learned in one language to another. In Chapter 3 we saw how 6-year-old Zoila, living in the US, taught Julializ, her younger cousin, to read by showing her how to equate the English letter with the Spanish sound:

1. Zoila: *La O (ō) es U (ōō). [The O is U.]*
2. Julializ: *To. Go.*
3. Zoila: *P.A. (ā).// P//*
4. Julializ: *// P// lay.*
5. Zoila: *La O (ō) es. A (ŏ). [The O is. A]*
6. Julializ: *Nnnn ot. Not.*
7. Zoila: *U (ŭ). I-U (ĭ – ŭ). Ruuuuuuun*
8. Julializ: *Run.*
9. Zoila: *Oo (oo). Ll ook.*
10. Julializ: *Look … (Volk, with de Acosta, 2004: 35)*

We also saw how 5-year-old Hasanat in Britain was able to transfer his phonic awareness from his English class to learning to read the Qur'ān in Arabic. Similarly, when shown a difficult English word in isolation Nicole would always try the 'clapping out in syllables' approach learned in her French school. If she saw an English word in a sentence, she first read ahead, leaving it out to see if she could come back to it. If not, she tried the syllable approach again. Because she first learned the importance of syllables and sound blends in French, for example, 'ou' (m<u>ou</u>ton, d<u>ou</u>ble, l<u>ou</u>p, and so on), her first instinct was to pronounce 'double' as it is in French if she saw the word separately. However, she had no problem at all in seeing it as the English 'double' (as in 'double your money') if reading in English. Her eye went to the central vowel sounds in English words too; she, herself, pointed out the different sounds of 'ea' (as in 'h<u>ea</u>ven', 'r<u>ea</u>d', and 'l<u>ea</u>d' as in 'lead paint' or 'the dog's lead').

Like Nicole, most young children seem to be of one opinion that learning to read has to do with the brain or mind ('knowing', 'spelling') and language ('saying', pronouncing').

Teachers and researchers agree with them but argue about the extent and nature of the link between word recognition and understanding. Is there an inextricable link between the two or can they be separated? Would Nicole have been able to read the words 'heaven, lead and read' and use them appropriately if she had not understood them? This chapter and Chapter 5 focus on reading as a mental and linguistic process, with particular reference to learning to read in a new language. We examine the way new language learners learn to 'situate' themselves in what Cazden refers to as the inner context or 'the context of the mind' (Vygotsky's 'intrapsychological plane') as they set about making sense of reading.

This chapter, therefore, addresses the following questions:

Questions for reflection

- What is the nature of early symbolization?
- How far do different theories of reading consider new language learners?
- What is an alternative approach for new language learners?

Symbolization and new language learners

Four-year-old Tajul and 6-year-old Muijtaba help us understand the very first steps of reading. Tajul is a Sylheti speaker and Muijtaba speaks Urdu at home. Both have just entered school in England with no experience of formal literacy tuition and speaking just a few words of English. Tajul sits with his teacher with a book and Muijtaba works on his own with the computer. Eavesdropping on their work allows us insights into the very early literacy learning process:

Tajul's teacher is reading *Joseph's Other Red Sock* (Daly, 1983) and Tajul is joining in:

Tajul: There's dog. (points to illustration)

Teacher: Is it a dog? Or is it a tiger?

Tajul: Tiger.

Teacher: It's a tiger. There's Joseph with one sock on (points). He's lost a sock. (Reads) 'Did you look in your toy-box?' asked his mum. 'Yes,' said Joseph, 'but I could only find Harold ...'

Tajul Question mark! (points to it)

Teacher: (continues reading) '... and a rabbit there' There's another question mark, that's right. (Reads) 'Did you look in your cupboards?'

Tajul Question mark! (points to it)

Teacher: Yes, and here's another one, look! (points) (continues reading) '... asked mum'

Continues over

> Muijtaba sits by himself using a computer and a CD provided with a simple English/Urdu
> word encyclopedia (Mantra, 2005). He has been shown how to complete the task only
> once but competently opens each exercise. For example, he clicks onto the word 'The
> Body' which opens a photo of a boy with word bubbles for each body part with
> connecting lines to various parts of the body. After listening to the voice saying, for
> example, 'stomach' in both English and Urdu, he clicks the appropriate bubble which
> highlights the word in both Urdu and English. When asked what the word 'says'. he is
> then able to 'read' it as well as distinguish which word is Urdu and which one English.

Tajul and Muijtaba illustrate clearly the very first steps in becoming literate. Step 1, then, is the realization that an object can stand for or symbolize another object and, consequently, that a 'label' or word can be separated from the object it represents. Step 2 is understanding that the 'label' or word can be represented not just by another word or object but by a written mark on a page or a screen which, if one wishes, can be permanent. Muijtaba, at 6, is able to go one step further and distinguish which word is Urdu and which is English, despite having had no formal literacy tuition. Vygotsky (1978) views these steps as part of the unique development of humankind. He uses the example of a broom handle to illustrate how early symbolization takes place. For the young infant, a broom handle is simply the object it stands for. A giant step is taken on the day the child picks up the broom and makes it become a horse. In other words, the broom is no longer a broom; it symbolizes or represents something else. Written language, says Vygotsky, can be called 'second order symbolization' as the object is represented not just by another object or a 'label' but by a written symbol on the page.

In *Thought and Language* (1962: 110), Vygotsky claims that becoming bilingual enables a child 'to see his language as one particular system among many, to view its phenomena under more general categories … [which] leads to awareness of his linguistic operations'. How does this awareness come about? An example from the classroom may help to illustrate the process. When young monolingual children hear the teacher say 'Go and get your writing book, a pencil and a ruler and get on with your work' they may wonder whether they actually want to do as they have been asked or even try not to do it, but they focus on the message itself and are able to overlook individual words. For children unfamiliar with the language the task set is a different one. They need first to sort out the words 'writing book', 'pencil', 'ruler', 'work', and so on. Often the teacher helps them to do this by holding up the object in question and labelling it. In this way, children are forced to focus on the words themselves as necessary means of communication from the very first word learned in the new language world of the school. This process itself forces children to become more conscious of language as a grammatical system with words to name and describe objects and actions and so on.

Although neither boy can read in Bengali or Urdu, it is their incipient bilingualism that already enables Tajul and Muijtaba to realize that objects can be 'labelled' differently in speech according to which language you happen to be using. For example, Tajul realizes that something we know as 'an object to play with' can be labelled 'khelna' if you are speaking Sylheti but will be 'toy' when you switch into English. Muitjaba begins to realize that 'stomach' is a different label from the name in Urdu. They also realize that when you are speaking one language you try not to use another if your partner cannot understand – even if this means swallowing what you would really like to say. In other words, from the very start, learning another language means learning that labels cannot be 'stuck' to objects. It is but a short step for them to realize that the labels can be represented in different scripts too. Both boys pinpoint how complex these first steps into reading are as well the potential advantages of bilingualism even from the first day of entering another language. Similarly, in Chapter 2, we saw that, even at the age of 3, Ah Si realized that she was expected to respond in English when her mother used it to address her. By 4, Sanah was clearly aware that her book was written in a different language from the one she used to discuss it with her mother. By 7 Annie was very aware of the word boundaries of 'elephant' and so on, even though they were written in a very different script from the Thai she knew. We referred to this in Chapter 1 as an enhanced *metalinguistic awareness* (see page 1). Does this mean that it is potentially easier for new language learners to 'situate' themselves in the mental context of learning to read? By the end of the chapter, readers may be able to make up their own minds. But first we need to consider the nature of the task ahead for these children.

SOME USEFUL TERMS AND DEFINITIONS

Analytic phonics – the analysing of words into sounds to detect patterns which may then be compared with other words having similar patterns, for example, 'sh-ould, w-ould, c-ould', and so on. These words can often be divided into onset and rime: 'onset' (initial sound), for example, 'str-', and 'rime' (the ending), for example, '- eet'; rhyming with 'f-eet, bl-eat and eat' or 'c-ast, f-ast, p-ast'.

Blend (verb) – to draw individual sounds together to pronounce a word, for example, s-n-a-p, blended together, reads snap.

Cluster – two (or three) letters making two (or three) sounds, for example, the first three letters of 'straight' are a consonant cluster.

(Vowel) digraph – two letters making one sound, for example, sh, ch, th, ph. Vowel digraphs comprise two vowels which, together, make one sound, for example, ai, oo, ow.

Split digraph – two letters, split, making one sound, for example, a-e as in make or i-e in site.

Grapheme – a letter or a group of letters representing one sound, for example, sh, ch, igh, ough (as in 'though').

Grapheme–phoneme correspondence (GPC) – the relationship between sounds and the letters which represent those sounds; also known as 'letter–sound correspondences'.

Mnemonic – a device for memorizing and recalling something, such as a snake shaped like the letter 'S'.

Phoneme – the smallest single identifiable sound, for example, the letters 'sh' represent just one sound, but 'sp' represents two (/s/ and /p/).

Phonemic awareness – an awareness that every spoken word can be conceived as a sequence of phonemes.

Phonics – instructional practices that emphasize how spellings are related to sounds in systematic ways.

Phonological awareness – more inclusive than phonemic awareness; the ability to attend to the sounds of the language as distinct from its meaning, for example, rhymes, counting syllables, and so on.

Segment (verb) – to split up a word into its individual phonemes in order to spell it, for example, the word 'cat' has three phonemes: /c/, /a/, /t/.

Synthetic phonics – the conversion of letters into sounds and the blending of individual sounds into words.

VC, CVC, CCVC – the abbreviations for vowel–consonant, consonant–vowel–consonant, consonant–consonant–vowel–consonant, used to describe the order of letters in words, for example, am, Sam, slam. (Adapted from www.literacytrust.org.uk)

'Simple' versus 'complex' views of reading

How do research studies help us in understanding how new language learners are tackling learning to read and how teachers can best assist them? Briefly, there is no consensus of opinion. Nor has there been much interest in the special situation of such children. The relationship between reading, language and the mind, however, has long been a question of debate. In his revolutionary book, *The Psychology and Pedagogy of Reading*, published in New York in 1908, Edward Huey claims reading to be 'a highly complex task which involves very many of the most intimate workings of the mind' (1908: 6). Since then, there have been contradictory ideas on exactly how these 'workings of the mind' take place and how complex or simple they are.

The traditional debate (sometimes referred to as 'the great debate' by Chall in 1979 and explained fully by Adams, 1995) which took place throughout the twentieth century was between those supporting 'bottom-up' and those upholding 'top-down' processes as children learn to read. Such specialist jargon can be confusing, but it is important to understand these and other important terms for they reflect contrasting theories which have been influential in informing beginning reading tuition throughout the twentieth and into the twenty-first centuries. So what do they mean and how might they explain what children like Annie, Nicole, Julializ and our other children from Chapter 2 need to do as they learn to read?

At its simplest, the 'bottom-up' theory claims that learning to read proceeds from the particular to the general; from the smallest unit of meaning (individual sound or *phoneme*) to the largest – knowledge of the world (*semantic knowledge*) and knowledge of the structure of language (*syntactic knowledge*). Those supporting the 'bottom-up' process of reading maintain that learning requires a reconstruction of the sound forms of a word on the basis of its graphic representation, whereby understanding arises as a result of correct re-creation of the sound form of words. In other words, decoding sounds and pronouncing words is seen as a *means* to gaining understanding. Early reading tuition based entirely on the 'bottom-up' theory will stress the need to teach children first to match *phonemes* (sounds) to *graphemes* (symbols) which are gradually built up into words (*lexis*) and larger units of meaning. This is sometimes referred to simply as taking a 'phonic approach' to beginning reading.

The 'top-down' theory is a reversal of the 'bottom-up' view. It states simply that understanding proceeds from the general to the particular; from general experience of life and a knowledge of the language of the text to predicting and reading individual words and letters. Those supporting the 'top-down' process believe that the recognition of printed or written symbols serves only as stimulus for the recall of meanings built up through past experience and the reconstruction of new meanings through the manipulation of concepts already possessed by the reader. Early reading tuition influenced entirely by this view will stress the importance of teaching beginner readers to use existing semantic and syntactic knowledge in order to be able to select from alternatives and predict the written word. This is sometimes referred to simply as taking a 'top-down' approach.

In the twenty-first century, it has generally been acknowledged that both *decoding* (bottom-up) and *meaning-making* (top-down) are essential components in fluent reading. Researchers and teachers from both sides of the debate also agree that some systematic phonics training is beneficial for all children as they begin to learn to read. However, they substantially disagree on the following: how much phonics training should be given, at what age and what type? How much training in meaning-making should be given, at what age and what type? And, crucially, can and should decoding and meaning-making be split up and taught separately or are they intrinsically interdependent in the process of learning to read?

Theories and consequent policies on beginning reading instruction have been in constant flux from the last three decades of the twentieth century until the present day. During the

1970s, 'Look-and-Say' (whole word recognition) was the most common approach, followed in Britain in the 1980s by the 'apprenticeship approach' (guided book reading alongside a more experienced reader). By the end of the twentieth century, official policy in Britain was to use an eclectic approach (combination of whole texts with guided reading, phonics and sight word recognition) rather similar to the Whole Language approach in the US. However, during the early years of the twenty-first century, official policies in both the US and Britain have swung sharply in favour of the 'bottom-up' members in the reading debate, with some claiming that phonics training should be taught 'first, fast and only'. Beginning reading policies in Britain and the US during the first decade of the twenty-first century are informed by the 'simple view of reading', a model originally put forward by Gough and Tunmer (1986) and taken up in the US by the National Reading Panel in 2000.

The 'simple view' argues that decoding and language comprehension are separable. This model is accepted by the National Reading Panel but in a modified form which proposes that 'a balanced approach' should be taken, whereby only approximately half a programme should be devoted to decoding and word comprehension; the other half to integrating and applying skills in meaningful texts. In Britain, however, the 'simple view', as interpreted by the Rose Report (2006), goes one step further. It agrees that 'meaning or language comprehension' and 'word recognition or decoding' skills are, indeed, separable and should be taught separately, but also directs teachers of beginner readers to focus on decoding first; only after this skill has been developed should a shift be made to include comprehension. Further, children should be discouraged from using any form of context clues to aid recognition (for example, illustrations or grammatical or sense contexts) on the grounds that this strategy indicates a poorer reader.

So how should early decoding or word recognition be developed? The 'simple view' as understood in Britain proposes restricting reading instruction for approximately the first four to five months entirely to the use of a 'synthetic phonics programme'. Synthetic phonics starts with single letters and the sounds they represent (Lloyd, 2003). As soon as a few letters and sounds (including one or two vowels) have been taught, children are taught to look at simple words containing those letters, and to produce a sound for each letter (no *digraphs* are used at first), then to blend the sounds all-through-the-words into normal word pronunciation. Letters are shown in all positions in words from the start. Generally the first letters will be 's, a, t, i, p, n' and the first digraphs 'sh, th, ai, oa'. The aim is for children to blend an increasing number of words as their number of word to sound correspondences increases, for example, at, dog, hen, spot, hill, and for this learning to take place quickly so that children can work words out for themselves. In this way, it is claimed, the programme 'empowers children' (Miskin, 2005), since, if they decode effortlessly, all their energies can go into working out what the book is all about.

Crucially, supporters of the 'simple view' of reading claim that children during these early stages should be introduced only to reading books containing sounds and digraphs they have already learned (that is, only books belonging to the relevant published scheme) in order not to confuse them or demotivate them if shown words they cannot decode. During the second stage of the programme children are introduced to digraphs (two letters making one sound) and the children practise blending regular words using these, for example, b-oa-t, sl-ee-p, sh-ou-t, and so on. During a third stage, less regular words are taught, usually at the rate of two or three per week. If children pronounce a word inaccurately, they are asked to look for the irregular part, for example, 'do' (where the 'o' is an 'oo' sound). The key strategy is that of blending sounds, gradually moving from the smallest sound to building up to the word itself. The Rose Report grounds its argument for a single method of instruction and the omission of 'meaning' from these early stages on one central assumption: that children have already made considerable progress in language development by the time they have entered school, meaning that their oral language skills are considerably advanced and that they can both understand and express themselves (Rose, 2006: 79). Since, of course, the 'language' referred to is unquestionably English, this hypothesis will be crucial as we weigh up the advantages and disadvantages of this approach for young new language learners.

But people supporting this view are not the only discussants in the debate; a second, and equally strong, group exists for whom 'top-down' approaches are as important as 'bottom-up', for whom phonics teaching is only one strategy amongst others (and synthetic phonics only one type of phonics teaching amongst others) and for whom 'meaning' and 'decoding' are intrinsically linked. These researchers and practitioners are from a number of countries in the English speaking world. They share little in common apart from a deep-seated belief that there is *no* simple solution to learning to read, nor can there be any such thing as a 'universal method' (Adams, 1995: 23). After a comprehensive review and analysis of both basic and applied research on the topic, Marilyn Jager Adams at the Center for the Study of Reading, University of Illinois at Urbana-Champaign argues the case strongly in her book, *Beginning to Read* (1995), that decoding (or phonics) and meaning (or context) are inextricably linked and that both should be taught simultaneously in beginning reading programmes. Although Adams views phonemic awareness, in which she includes not only a knowledge of sound patterns but phonological awareness and a knowledge of spelling (orthographic) patterns as essential for a base upon which to build, she sees meaning as an inherent part of the reading process too. After reviewing all studies available, she argues that both should be taught side by side to young children from the beginning. She concludes:

Across this book, we have examined each of a number of domains of study ... each has pointed toward the conclusion that skillful reading depends crucially on the deep and thorough acquisition of spellings and spelling–sound relationships. On the other hand, none of these programs treats phonics in a vacuum. Nor, to be learnable, can phonic skills be treated in that way. Their proper acquisition depends on articulation with both lower- and higher-order knowledge about language and text. Nor do good programs succumb to the simplistic hypotheses that letter–sound relations are the most basic of reading skills. Rather, with respect to the knowledge that is critical to reading, that which can be developed through phonic instruction represents neither the top nor the bottom, but only a realm inbetween. Before children will learn to read, they must learn to recognize individual letters. They must become aware of the structure of language, from sentences and words to phonemes. And, most important, they must develop a basic understanding of the forms and functions of text and of its personal value to their own lives. (Adams, 1995: 422)

Thus, although recognized in the US as an advocate of the 'phonics first' camp, her writings do show support for a 'balanced' perspective.

From the other side of the Atlantic, and a decade later, a very similar message has been given by Greg Brooks and his team from Sheffield University, England. In *A Systematic Review of the Research Literature on the Use of Phonics in the Teaching of Reading and Spelling* (Torgerson et al., 2006) the team conclude the following: children definitely benefit from some systematic phonics instruction but there is no conclusive evidence to show how much is necessary or whether the synthetic phonics method is any better than any other type of phonics. By this, the team referred to two types of phonics teaching that had been widely used until overtaken by the synthetic phonics movement: *analytic phonics* where words are not seen in isolation but a common phoneme in a set of words is analysed by children (for example, how are 'put, pet, park, push, pen' alike?) and *onset and rime* teaching whereby children learn to segment a word into its 'onset' (initial sound) and rime (the remaining sound) (for example, n-ail, p-ail, r-ail; c-ast, p-ast, f-ast; c-all, f-all, h-all, all; c-at, f-at, h-at, p-at; Y-ork, f-ork, p-ork). Both Adams and Brooks and his team go on to stress the importance of meaning and context in order for successful reading to take place. How else, they say, could we know whether we should *lead the horse* or *repair lead pipes*? let alone whether *does eat oats* but *a wolf does not* or distinguish between *pig pens* and *fountain pens* or *an inaugural ball* and *a ping-pong ball*? So might reading *not* be such a simple matter as one side of the reading debate has proposed? We are gradually returning to Nicole and Julializ who opened this chapter.

SUMMARY

♦ The first step towards literacy is learning second-order symbolization (that an object can be replaced by a mark on the page). Emergent bilingual children have advantages in this since they know that an object can have different 'labels' in different languages.

♦ The 'simple view' of reading (or 'bottom-up' approach) proposes that decoding and meaning can be taught separately and that the focus should be on phonics first.

♦ This view is based on the assumption that children have a wide understanding of spoken language and can both understand and express themselves before learning to read.

♦ The 'phonics only' view is disputed by others who believe that decoding and meaning are both integral to reading and should be taught concurrently.

♦ New language learners have been largely omitted from the beginning reading debate.

Questions for reflection

- Is Nicole's skill in reading 'lead' (for a dog), 'lead' (as in lead paint) and 'heaven' as well as 'double' (as in French dooble) and 'double' (as in English) simple or complex? How does it compare with Julializ's skill in decoding?
- On what does Nicole's successful reading depend?
- How far can decoding and meaning be split in the teaching of reading?
- Why might the reading task be different for monolingual children and new language learners?

Where do new language learners fit in?

How can the above theories be applied to real children reading in classrooms? The excerpts below are from emergent bilingual children learning to read in the classroom, separated by

12 years of different ideas on reading instruction. They require careful reading before analysing the children's strengths and weaknesses which may reflect those of the methods used to teach them.

Five-year-old Husna and Naseema are in their second term at a multilingual school in East London during the 1990s. Following official policy at the time, their teacher is using a 'top-down' approach whereby she reads aloud to the children everyday using a Big Book (Holdaway, 1979). The children first 'read' the book with the teacher pointing to the words. They then gradually focus on individual sentences, phrases and words, counting where a word is repeated and discussing its similes and opposites and so on before they come to its phonemic make-up. At this point, they partially cover the word and find other words that have the same onset or rime or that share the same letter(s) or sound (s). The children always have some time each day to read freely with a friend or other adult using a book of their choice. Here, we eavesdrop on Husna and Naseema reading together:

The setting is an inner-city classroom of five- to six-year-olds. Husna and Naseema are reading *Each, Peach, Pear, Plum* by Janet and Allen Ahlberg, together. Despite the attractions of the illustrations, their eyes are drawn to the print and they read quickly and fluently. Husna points carefully to each word to help Naseema who is more hesitant. 'Each, Peach, Pear, Plum, I spy Tom Thumb. Tom Thumb in the cupboard, I spy Mother Hubbard. Mother Hubbard down the cellar, I spy Cinderella. Cinderella on the stairs, I spy the Three Bears ...' Husna breaks off with 'I can count to ten in Bengali: Ek, dui, teen, chaar, panch, chhoy, shaat, aat, noy, dosh.' 'Gosh?' asks the teacher. 'Mmm. But this is ten/dosh, not like gosh in "Oh, my gosh, my golly".' The teacher laughs, knowing she is referring to one of the 'Storychest Big Books' with which she is very familiar. The children continue with the text glancing only occasionally at the illustrations which complement this nursery rhyme world. As they reach the page featuring a magnificent plum pie, the teacher interrupts and asks 'Can you show me the plum pie in that picture?' The children stare blankly at the teacher and the page. Eventually, Husna points quickly to something nondescript in the background. The teacher shows them the pie and allows the children to get back to their reading. They finish the text and are impatient to change the book for another. (Gregory and Kelly, 1992: 144)

Briefly, what are these children's strengths and weaknesses and how might these be reflected in the methods their teachers are using? Let us look at their skills as beginner readers first. Like Tajul and Muijtaba earlier in this chapter and Annie in Chapter 1, they know that words or 'labels' are not tied to objects and that 'dosh' or 'gosh' (as they heard it) can mean different things in different languages. They have a strong one-to-one correspondence, pointing to each word as they read. They also have a strong linguistic awareness and an excitement in words themselves, shown by wanting to pick out individual words and compare them. They are able to use and enjoy rhymes – a short step from more formal onset and rime work. They show an awareness of the importance of syntax. They know that 'dosh' in Bengali is not just semantically different from the English, but is a different part of speech and must be used differently in sentences. They can use whole chunks of quite complex English 'in the cupboard, down the cellar, Oh my gosh, my golly …'. We could say that they are empowered by their fluency in reading the text – knowledge drawn from many readings where they have been able to read along with the whole class. However, they also have distinct weaknesses. First, they have only a very limited knowledge of phonics. Although aware of the similarities between 'gosh' and 'dosh' – transliterated from Bengali script – Husna would have been unable to sound it out. Nor did she really notice the difference between the sounds. Second, and most importantly, where does meaning fit in? Although fluent in 'reading' the text, neither girl was able to understand large parts of it, as we see from the 'plum pie' example.

Let us jump more than a decade and pass straight to 6-year-old Lina entering a similar London school. Lina's family has recently arrived in Britain from Lithuania, where Lina had already attended school. Lina entered her class unable to speak English and was at first very distraught. She has now been in her multilingual class for five months and has settled happily into learning. Following official policy, Lina is learning to read English with both her class and her language teacher using a synthetic phonics programme. Every day she practises one or two new sounds orally, writes them on her whiteboard and tries to make them into words:

Lina has already covered a number of sounds, including 's, a, t, i, p, n' etc. as well as a number of digraphs 'sh, th, ee, ai, oa'. She learns these very fast and with few problems. At six, she has no problem with one-to-one correspondence and directionality. Lina appears to have learned her sounds in Lithuania, since she confidently applies very non-English rules. For a while she prefers 'likee' (as in sticky) to' like', 'braf' (as in half) for 'brave' and 'know' (pronouncing the k). She gradually comes to terms with these as she learns their meaning. The children are allowed to choose from a variety of reading scheme books on a certain level, since their teacher is anxious that they should develop their English as well enjoying a chosen text. Lina therefore chooses a book at her appropriate level. As usual, her eyes go straight to individual letters, ignoring any surrounding text or illustration – even if a word is repeated in the picture (thus making it obvious):

( ) indicates word unknown and provided; **bold** print indicates word misread and correct word appears in brackets following it; **-ed** indicates pronunciation emphasized, as in 'rugged'

Bif's (aeroplane).
Bif made an (aeroplane).
Mum **help-ed** (helped) her.
The aeroplane **look-ed** (looked) good.
Bif **went-ed** (wanted) to fly **in** (it).
Share (she) went to the park.
The aeroplane **fly** (flew) up.
It went **o'er** (over) the trees.
It went **o'er** (over) the houses.
Bif **look-ed** (looked).
Everyone **help-ed** (helped)(her).
Bif **look-ed** (looked) and look-ed (looked).
Share (she) couldn't find **in** (it).
She **went** (wanted) to cry.
She went upstairs.
The aeroplane was on the bed.

How does Lina's reading differ from that of the two girls? Like Husna and Naseema, Lina has a number of skills which we may assume link with her teachers' methods of instruction. She is very aware of one-to-one correspondence and has a strong linguistic awareness. Her mother tongue is much more similar to English than the other girls' and consequently she sometimes thinks she can transfer meanings and sounds. Her reading of 'braf' for 'brave' believing it means 'good' on another occasion is one such example of this. Her awareness of phonics from Lithuania gives her confidence; at the same time, she has to learn that almost every letter sounds somewhat different. Nevertheless, she has made a very good start on this. She manages 'made, her, fly and everyone' as difficult words, learns 'she' and knows 'the' and 'couldn't' as sight words. She almost manages 'over'. Her pronunciation of '-ed' on the end of all the words she comes across shows how she is applying the rule she has just learned! Yet she too has a number of weaknesses. Because her attention is fixed solely on letters, she fails to recognize 'areoplane' (it dominates in the picture) even when it is repeated on the next page. Since she does not look either side of the word to be tackled, she often reads nonsense – and, crucially, does not know whether she is reading nonsense or not. She lacks any fluency or ability to 'chunk' words into expressions or phrases. When asked to talk about her story, she finds it very difficult. And so, Lina's reading epitomizes both her own strengths and weaknesses and those of synthetic phonics as the sole initial method for teaching emergent bilingual children – especially those who are familiar with a very different phonic system and who hear little English spoken outside school. Instead of being freed up to concentrate on meaning, all her energies are focused on sounding out each word. In some cases this works (for example, br-i-cks) from another book, but even then, she often has no idea what the word means. She is most successful in reading her 'sight words', for example, 'couldn't' which do not stop her flow in reading. In contrast with Husna and Naseema, she cannot 'chunk' language into phrases and expressions; her English syntax is very poor. She is, indeed, empowered by being able to tackle phonically new words she cannot understand, but, like the girls, she lacks understanding.

And so, in spite of all their strengths, the three girls are still worlds apart from Nicole whose *understanding* of English and French enables her to read the words accurately.

Questions for reflection

- How might Husna and Naseema's reading have been different if they had followed a synthetic phonics programme?
- How might Lina's reading have been different had she followed a 'top-down' approach?
- Would either approach have solved their inability to understand the text?

Neither 'bottom-up' nor 'top-down' views alone will suffice in explaining the reading task for Husna, Naseema and Lina because both theories assume that children share a knowledge of the language they are learning to read as well as the culture in which it is situated. However, we see from Lina that pronouncing words will not necessarily lead to understanding them; nor will Husna and Naseema be able to call up words linked to a past memory if there is no such memory or it exists in a different language from that in the text. In other words, while Nicole has no problem in reading 'We swim in the sea (pronounced -ee or as in 'lead' for a dog)', Lina reads 'We swim in the sea (pronounced -'e' as in 'lead' for lead pipe) and has no idea why it is wrong. While for Nicole 'plum pies' are her grandparents' treat, Husna and Naseema cannot even see whether the yellow top in the illustration is pastry or blancmange – or, indeed, even something to eat!

Putting meaning in the middle

The examples of Husna, Naseema and Lina begin to show that a different framework whereby *meaning* is central will be needed to explain the reading process for new language learners. A framework known as the *'interactive' model* (Rummelhart, 1977) gives us a starting-point here. This approach stresses that information from four sources (*grapho-phonic*, *lexical*, *syntactic* and *semantic*) must be synthesized in the process of reading.

Each of the four sources of information can be seen as a *knowledge centre* providing different sets of clues or 'cues' which children draw upon as they learn to read:

- **The grapho-phonic knowledge centre** comprises *orthographic* and *phonological* knowledge which sends out clues concerning the patterns of letters in words and the sounds they make, for example, 'splash' which is acceptable in English rather than 'sjcit' which is not.
- **The lexical knowledge centre** sends out clues concerning the word and the company it keeps, for example, 'knife and fork' rather than 'knife and powder puff'.
- **The syntactic knowledge centre** sends out clues concerning the structure of the language, for example, 'Catching rats is as easy for ratcatchers as catching toves is for — —'.
- **The semantic knowledge centre** sends out clues concerning the meaning behind the words (within the culture or within the text), for example, John tried hard to persuade his father that, far from being the — report in the class, his was, in fact, the —. (Readers know from their experience of life in our particular culture that 'worst' and 'best' could never be the opposite way round!)

Of course, information from different knowledge centres constantly interacts. Interaction might look like this:

LEXICAL/ORTHOGRAPHIC

- More letters can be remembered in a given unit if they spell a word rather than a non-word, for example, alligator rather than rllaagtio.
- More letters can be remembered in a nonsense string which conforms to the rules of English spelling than one which does not, for example, vernalit rather than nrveiatl.

SYNTACTIC/SEMANTIC/LEXICAL/ORTHOGRAPHIC

- Semantic knowledge influences word perception. It is easier to read a word if presented with one which is related, for example, bread/butter; doctor/nurse rather than doctor/butter.

- Our perception of syntax depends upon the context in which a word is embedded, for example, 'They are eating apples' where our comprehension depends upon whether the question was 'What kind of apples are they?' or 'What are the children eating?'
- Our interpretation depends upon the context in which the text is embedded, for example, 'The shooting of the hunters was terrible' where our understanding depends upon whether the prior text indicates that 'Their markmanship was terrible ...' or 'Their cruelty was awful ...'

All these knowledge sources provide simultaneous input into our 'pattern synthesizer'. This can be viewed as a general message centre which accepts them, holds the information and redirects it as needed. The message centre, then, keeps a running list of hypotheses or hunches about the nature of the input; each hypothesis is evaluated by the knowledge source and confirmed or disconfirmed. The procedure is continued until a decision is reached and the hypothesis is deemed to be correct.

For new language learners, however, an adaptation of this framework is needed, whereby *meaning* and *personal interaction* are central. One way of representing this framework is through the mnemonic of a child's hand, where each of the five fingers represents a different clue. The hand of a child also indicates that it needs to be held by a more experienced person (an integral part of the interactive approach as understood here) until it is ready to hold the hand of others as competence grows.

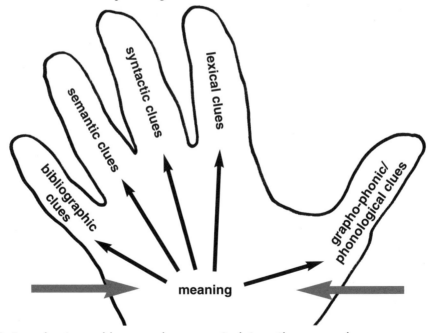

Figure 4.1 *Learning to read in a new language: An interactive approach*

Obviously, all fingers will be needed for certain difficult jobs. Nevertheless, fingers can compensate for others that are lacking and thus manage to cope, in a limited way, with most tasks. In the next section, we shall consider the special strengths and weaknesses of new language learners as they draw upon all the clues they can from each 'knowledge centre' to 'situate' themselves in the mental context of reading.

Questions for reflection

- How far does the use of 'knowledge centres' demand a fluency in the language in which reading is taking place?
- Which 'knowledge centres' are new language learners most and least likely to call upon as they begin reading?
- How can certain clues overcompensate for others which are lacking during the early stages of learning to read?

Suggestions for teaching and learning

- Tape yourself sharing a book with a new language learner. What knowledge does the child bring to the book and how does s/he participate in talking about the illustrations and the text?
- Tape young children as they read their scheme book and then a simple 'Book without Words' (wordless picture book). How does the child's use of the new language differ in both?
- Find a simple dual-language tape (or CD) and story-book in the child's mother tongue. Tape the child talking about the story both before and after listening to the tape and note the differences. Can the child distinguish words on the page in the different languages and/or scripts?

SUMMARY

◆ New language learners come to reading with distinct *metalinguistic* (knowledge about language itself) and *metacognitive* (awareness of their knowledge and the ability to use it strategically) advantages.

◆ Debates on learning to read have hitherto revolved around 'bottom-up' (starting with phonics or the smallest unit of meaning) or 'top-down' (starting with knowledge of the world and whole language structures) processes.

◆ New language learners have largely been omitted from this debate.

◆ An interactive view of reading is proposed whereby meaning and interpersonal interaction are central.

Further reading

Adams, M.J. (1995) *Beginning to Read: Thinking and Learning about Print.* Cambridge, MA: MIT Press.

Clay, M. (1991) *Becoming Literate: The Construction of Inner Control.* Portsmouth, NH: Heinemann.

Goodman, K. (1996) *On Reading: A Common-sense Look at the Nature of Language and the Science of Reading.* Portsmouth, NH: Heinemann.

John-Steiner, V. (1986) 'The road to competence in an alien land: a Vygotskian perspective on bilingualism', in J.V. Wertsch (ed.), *Culture, Communication and Cognition: Vygotskian Perspectives.* Cambridge: Cambridge University Press.

5 Using the same clues differently

Teacher: (reads with Tajul from *The Hungry Giant*, a Big Book for the class with small accompanying books for groups and individuals) '*... and got the giant some bread.*'

Tajul: (points to the bread, a French stick loaf) *This not bread. These are finger.*

Teacher: *It's supposed to be bread, actually. Some bread looks like that. It's not supposed to be fingers. It's supposed to be bread.*

Tajul: *It's not bread.*

Teacher: *Well, if you go into Tesco's supermarket, you can find some long thin bread like that. What does your bread look like? Does your bread look different from that?*

Tajul: *My bread is square.*

Teacher: *Oh, your bread is square, is it? Well, some bread is long and thin and some bread is square ...*

KEY TERMS

Grapho-phonic, orthographic and phonological clues	Clues concerning both the patterns of letters in words and the sounds or rhymes they make.
Lexical clues	Clues concerning the word and the company it keeps, for example, knife and fork not powder puff.
Syntactic clues	Clues concerning the structure of language.
Semantic clues	Clues concerning the meaning behind the words (within the culture or within the text).
Bibliographic clues	Clues concerning the type of text read, for example, a novel, a car manual and so on.

In this chapter, new language learners from various backgrounds provide an insight into their strengths and weaknesses in learning to read. A framework is provided by presenting each knowledge centre or set of clues (each 'finger' in our hand image used in Chapter 4) in turn and focusing on three issues: its strengths, weaknesses and a brief summary of questions for pedagogy. These questions will be the springboard for constructing classroom reading programmes which is the focus for Part 2 of this book.

As these clues are unpicked, readers might consider the following questions:

- Which clues appear most useful to different children?
- Can we see links between the mental and the social context of reading?
- How do children use some clues to compensate for others which are still lacking?

Deciphering letters and sounds: grapho-phonic, orthographic and phonological clues

Nine-year-old Saida has recently come to Britain from Bangladesh. She speaks and understands only a few words of English. However, it is obvious that she has attended school regularly in Bangladesh as she is literate in Bengali and quickly completes mathematical tasks once they have been explained to her in Sylheti. Her teacher is at a loss to know how best to help her. So that she should not appear different from the other children, she gives her an easy reading scheme book, which depicts children at the fairground. To her amazement, Saida says almost every word correctly. She stumbles only over the word 'dived' which she pronounces 'deeved' and 'climbed' which she says as 'climb-ed'. Upon questioning, it is obvious that she has understood virtually nothing of the text, yet she has successfully decoded comparatively difficult and very culture-specific words, such as 'roller-coaster'.

Later, Saida explains in Sylheti how she is able to do this. She has already successfully completed Class 5 (the final primary school year) in Bangladesh and has learned to read in Bengali and English. 'But how did she manage this if she couldn't understand the words?' asks her teacher. Saida explains that she learned all the sounds, then how to put the sounds together into syllables which she then practised. She explains earnestly that she only got as far as learning to say the words and that understanding was to follow, but at that point, she had left for England. Saida's approach does not seem unusual to her. After all, it parallels the way she is learning to read the Qur'ān in Arabic where she is already on her second reading of the Holy Book and is progressing towards understanding. Learning to read the Qur'ān is, of course, an excellent example of the separation of 'reading' and 'meaning'; 'reading' (reciting) comes first, followed by 'understanding' as one learns the the content and significance of the prayers. But is Saida actually reading? Not as far as our teachers in Chapter 2 were concerned, where 'understanding' figured as an intrinsic part of their definition of 'reading'. However, Saida has had an excellent start, one that results from her early biliteracy. Her teacher is now able to use Saida's decoding skills as a means towards learning English. She makes picture sequences for each story and discusses appropriate sentences for each. Saida is also making her own dictionary and her lists of objects, each written in a sentence, are increasing rapidly. Saida's 'reading' highlights both the strengths and weaknesses of grapho-phonic and phonological clues as new language learners make sense of the reading task. Both are outlined further below.

LOOKING AND LISTENING CAREFULLY: THE STRENGTHS OF GRAPHO-PHONIC AND PHONOLOGICAL CLUES

Nicole's use of phonics when she reads French in some ways mirrors that of Saida. She is now confident in knowing how to 'sound words out' in French and her success leads to her claim that French is easy to read. The power of her French tuition is strong. When shown a word which can be either French or English (for example, double), she will first try the French [du:bla], saying that 'ou' always says 'u' in French. 'French is always like that … Only there are some "secret" letters, like 'souris', but I know the rules for them'. When asked, 'But what if it were an English word?', she immediately pronounces it correctly. 'But it's not always like that,' she adds and cites 'cloud' and 'touch' – 'that's why French is easier than English'. She illustrates her point by citing 'read, lead and heaven' and stresses 'that's why it's hard!' She prefers to transfer another strategy from her French school to her English reading: that of dividing words into syllables. 'Like if I see "tired",' she says, 'I divide it into "ti-r-ed".' She demonstrates with a previously unknown word, clapping at the same time: 'gua-ran-tee'.

Saida, Lina (whom we met in Chapter 4) and Nicole show how grapho-phonic and phonological clues can assist the emergent bilingual to read and even speak a new language. First, learning to match symbols to sounds is a confined task. It does not demand the sophistication of needing fluent or colloquial English and consequently gives children confidence. Both Nicole and Saida are already in the habit of consulting dictionaries and very quickly look up words independently. Second, many new language learners are familiar with phonic clues from reading tuition in their first language or from learning the Qur'ān in Arabic. In Chapter 2, we saw Husanat's skill in using his knowledge of the phonic principle in English to learning to read the Qur'ān. Although both sounds and symbols are obviously very different, he is in a strong position to transfer learning into a new context. Third, new language learners are often more able to play with the sounds and rhyme of words regardless of their meaning. Listen to 6-year-old Maria from Portugal standing on a cold railway station platform in London with her father just after Christmas:

Lawyer, lawyer, lawyer.
Daddy, I want to be a lawyer when I grow up.
(no response from father)
Lawyer, lawyer,
Gloria,
Gloria, in excelsis deo. (she begins to sing this)

Maria was playing with the sounds of new English words she had heard in quite different contexts in her English school. In this way, like many new language learners, she is using rhyme to both practise and extend her repertoire of English words. Maria's skill in rhyming is also reflected in Lina's acute ear when dealing with new sounds. She sounds out 'h-i-s' correctly, but using a voiceless 's' (as in 'snake'). When her teacher repeats the word but uses a voiced 's' (as in 'zoo'), she asks: 'Why 'zz', not 's'?'

Nicole also shows how carefully she dissects words and focuses on individual or groups of letters. Of course, she is at an advantage because French uses the same *orthography* (alphabet system) as English. However, although it is clearly more demanding to learn two separate orthographies, Saida and other new language learners show that formal mother-tongue tuition of a different script gives them both an eye and an ear for detail. This is particularly true of children learning to read in Mandarin where there is a symbol/meaning rather than a symbol/sound association. As soon as he enters his English school at just under 5, Tony is able to copy writing and drawings meticulously. His eye for detail is not surprising when we consider the work that he and many other Hong Kong origin children are engaged in at their Saturday schools. The Mandarin script contains six sub-groups, three of which are of particular importance to the early reader (see Figure 5.1):

The child, therefore, needs to focus very carefully on both the constituent parts of *characters* as well as how they can be used as parts to create a new character which holds a different meaning.

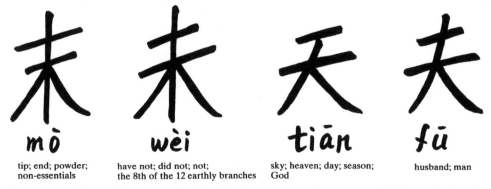

mò	wèi	tiān	fū
tip; end; powder; non-essentials	have not; did not; not; the 8th of the 12 earthly branches	sky; heaven; day; season; God	husband; man

Figure 5.1 *Chinese classes emphasize the importance of accuracy. It is important not to confuse characters which look similar but have very different meanings*

1. Pictographs

(Derived from pictures of the object)

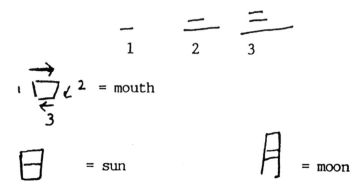

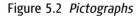 = mouth

= sun

= moon

Figure 5.2 *Pictographs*

2. Ideographs

(Representing ideas like 'up' and 'down')

= up

= down

Figure 5.3 *Ideographs*

3. Compound ideographs

(Based on metaphorical extensions or associations of constituent parts; 'bright' is derived from the combination of 'sun' and 'moon')

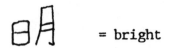 = bright

Figure 5.4 *Compound ideographs*

PROBLEMS OF PRONUNCIATION: THE WEAKNESS OF GRAPHO-PHONIC AND PHONOLOGICAL CLUES

The mishearing of 'gosh' and 'dosh' by Husna and Naseema and their teacher as they read *Each, Peach, Pear, Plum* and Lina's problems with pronunciation symbolize the difficulties experienced by new language learners in utilizing phonic clues. New language learners are likely to have considerable difficulty in distinguishing and pronouncing certain sounds or combinations of sounds which do not exist in the same way in their first language. The combination '-sps' is particularly difficult for children speaking most Asian languages. Many teachers recall searching desperately for 'crips' which have disappeared or even more desperately for 'wops' which refuse to disappear from their classrooms. Similarly, it is often difficult for speakers of Asian languages to distinguish between the sounds of 'v' and 'w' as they begin English. The difficulties of other sounds are more subtle, for example:

walked	jogged
slapped	sobbed
passed	fizzed

Saida's mispronunciation of 'climb-ed' and Lina's of 'look-ed' and 'help-ed' illustrate the first rule (do not stress the -ed). In addition, they must learn that '-ed' after *voiceless* consonants (for example, 'k', 'p' and 's') will be pronounced as 't' and after *voiced* consonants (for example, 'b', 'g' and 'm') will be pronounced as 'd'. Lina has a problem (as many new English speakers) with 'th-'. She pronounces it as 'dd' and, although learning 'the' and 'these' as sight words, continues to write them as 'dd' (the) and 'dies' (these). Japanese children will often have difficulty with distinguishing 'l' from 'r' and consequently not be able to sound them out or spell them accurately.

But pronunciation difficulties are only one aspect weakening phonic clues. Consider the following words:

ptak	thole	hlad
plast	sram	mgla
vlas	flitch	dnom
rtut	toasp	nyip

All of these phonemes are found in English, but it is not difficult for a first language speaker to recognize that 'thole', 'plast' and 'flitch' could actually be English words, whereas the others could not. Speakers of a language learn at a very early stage that certain sounds can occur together (for example, in English, thr-, cr-, spl-, and so on), whereas others cannot. Similarly, they learn about the position of certain sounds (for example, in English, -ng must come at the end although it can occur initially in some African languages).

These examples highlight how important it is for understanding the meaning of words to parallel the learning of phonic clues. Without this understanding, it is very difficult to know where sounds end and words begin. When is a 'pea' a 'p' for example? Is a 'bzzz' an object or a sound? Even Nicole, whose phonic tuition was extremely effective, recalls her early problems at school:

> 'Learning to read in French was a bit hard at first – like, if you have the word "chantais" where the "-ais" is pronounced) and "chant<u>ent</u>" (where the "-ent" is silent). I wanted to pronounce the "-ent" and say the whole word!'
> 'Why was that, do you think?'
> 'Because I couldn't understand it.'
> 'Does that ever happen in English?'
> 'No.'

In any case, Lina has already shown us that 'sounding out' a word will not get you far unless a word is understood. Six-year-old Artur, recently arrived in London from Poland, also illustrates this dilemma as he struggles through 'Mr (pronounced 'Mirr') Pizza' and continues reading 'do' (rhyming with 'toe'), 'make' (as 'muck'), 'made' (as 'mad') and 'night' (as 'nig'). Artur is making very good progress with his phonics but he has a very limited idea of what (or, indeed, why) he is reading. Even Nicole (whose French is very good but her English is still stronger) epitomizes this as she attempts to read an adult book, *A to Z Gastronomique*, which mixes the names of dishes written in French with descriptions written in English. She comes to the recipe for 'colin' (hake) and pronounces it in the French way (kôlé). When asked if she knows what it is, she shakes her head. Then she reads the brief description of the fish in English. A flash of recognition comes, 'Oh, I know now. It's Colin (pronounced in English) the cod, isn't it!' A neat summary, perhaps, of the advantages of reading in a language you can understand.

GRAPHO-PHONIC AND PHONOLOGICAL CLUES: IN SUMMARY

Phonic, phonological and orthographic clues are both strong and weak for children during the first stages of new language learning. They are strong since their signal is much easier to pick up than those of learning a whole new language; they are weak because, in themselves, the clues do not get you far in the whole process of meaningful reading. There is no doubt, however, that children who are using a phonic approach to learn to read in another language are more able to capitalize on these clues in English. In Chapter 2, Dineo from South Africa showed us that 'the meaning was in the performance' as she practised reciting her story in Sesotho perfectly. In Arabic, learning to *read the Qur'ān* involves learning complex phonic rules where the use of accents changes the pronunciation of a symbol. A whole set of these will need to be learned before a child is ready to begin the Qur'ān. Although the sounds will be learned using different orthographies in different languages, it is clear that the principle itself of sound/symbol association will make sense to both children and families who will support them. Even writing systems using symbol/meaning rather than sound/symbol associations, such as Mandarin, equip the child with the skill of focusing precisely on parts of words and noticing the way a tiny alteration will change the meaning.

Nevertheless, there are two distinct hurdles to be overcome before beginner biliterates can benefit from their headstart: the problems of pronunciation and the 'feel' for what sounds are 'allowed' in a language. The first is a relatively confined task to work upon. The second hurdle involves understanding words and their contexts and is much more difficult. It is the topic for Part 2 of this book. To make the most of children's phonic and orthographic clues, teachers and other educators will need to ask:

Questions for reflection: (grapho-phonic, orthographic and phonological clues)

- Are children familiar with phonic approaches through learning to read in their first language or in Arabic or are they learning a different writing system such as Mandarin? If so, how can their knowledge best be utilized?
- How can the use of phonics be incorporated into a family reading programme where parents read only in other scripts?
- In what ways can pronunciation be practised using interesting and imaginative approaches?
- Is it possible to ensure that the teaching of phonics always includes teaching the meanings of words? If so, how?

Memorizing important words: lexical clues

Here is a snippet from Tony, our Cantonese speaker, whom readers have met in the introduction to Part 1:

(*'Reading' Mr Fussy by Roger Hargreaves a few weeks after starting English school*)

Tony: *What's his name?*

Teacher: *Mr Fussy.*

Tony: *Mr Fussy.* (repeats four times with different intonation) *Mr Fussy is in the house.* (turns page)
          Mr Fussy   … What's that?

Teacher: *It's a glass … Oh no, it's a jar of marmalade.*

Tony: *Jar marmalade?*

Teacher: *Yes … to put on your bread … you know, in the morning.*

Tony: *Here's …* (mumbles)
          What's his name?

Teacher: *It's Mr Fussy's hand, I think.*

Tony: *That's Mr Fussy's hand. What's he touch … his hand?*

Teacher: *It's an iron.*

Like Ah Si and Curtis in Chapter 2, who are also of Chinese background, Tony is storing up a bank of words. Their insistence on hearing words correctly, asking for repetition and then repeating them after the teacher shows how important lexical clues are for them in the reading process. A practical example makes this more explicit. Readers might like to imagine looking at a picture-book in an almost unknown language and being expected to make some sense of it. The eye is drawn to important nouns (naming words) in the illustrations. In this case, the eye goes to the beautiful lady on the cover (see Figure 5.5). Even without being able to say 'What (or who) is it?' it is easy enough to point to it and look questioningly. The teacher replies 'La Ventafocs' and points also to the words. Both the oral and visual labels give the beginner something to hang on to and to pick out in a stream of sounds. As the teacher reads, it will probably sound something like this: 'La Ventafocs blah blah blah La Ventafocs blah blah, etc.' It makes sense for the beginner to point to every other illustration which looks as if it might be 'La Ventafocs' and to keep repeating it until certain it is correct and stored away in the memory. This process is exactly what Tajul is doing as he focuses on the question marks earlier in this chapter. His eye is drawn to the written symbol, but the teacher then links sound to symbol and includes the word in her reading, pointing to it every time. In this way, Tajul will gain an automaticity of important sight words both individually and in context. We shall return to 'La Ventafocs' as other clues are examined later in the chapter.

Tony, Ah Si and Curtis show how actively they are building on this strength. Yet, paradoxically, what is potentially their strongest set of clues as new language learners begin reading is also in danger of being their weakest. This is epitomized by Husna and Naseema reading *Each, Peach, Pear, Plum* (see p. 114) as they sadly fail to understand the meaning of 'plum pie'. Examples of early 'reading' help us analyse more precisely the nature of both the strengths and weaknesses of lexical clues.

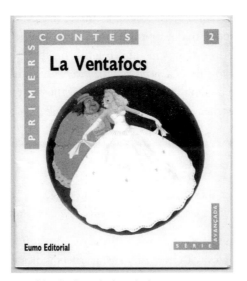

Figure 5.5 *The importance of lexical and visual clues.*

THE POWER OF WORDS: THE STRENGTH OF LEXICAL CLUES

I scream	*Fuzzy Wuzzy was a bear*
You scream	*Fuzzy Wuzzy had no hair*
We all scream	*Fuzzy Wuzzy wasn't fuzzy*
For ice cream	*Was he?*

Many children's rhymes and songs contain *oronyms* like those above, highlighting how strings of sound can be carved into words in two different ways. Steven Pinker (1994: 159–60) neatly summarizes the place of words in speech:

> *All speech is an illusion. We hear speech as a string of separate words but unlike the tree falling in the forest with no one to hear it, a word boundary with no one to hear it has no sound. In the speech sound wave, one word runs into the next seamlessly; there are no little silences between spoken words the way there are white spaces between written words. We simply hallucinate word boundaries when we reach the edge of a stretch of sound that matches some entry in our mental dictionary. This becomes apparent when we listen to speech in a foreign language. It is impossible to tell where one word ends and the next begins …*

Many young children enter school aware of speech only as a seamless string of sounds. Learning to read will show them how this flow can be divided up into words, phrases and sentences. In what ways might becoming bilingual help children to put in the 'seams' needed for beginning reading?

In Chapter 2, we saw how children as young as three, like Ah Si, were able to keep two languages apart and to respond to the appropriate one. Her mother's flash cards with a word and illustration in Mandarin on one side and English on the other made this particularly clear for her. We referred to this as a *metalinguistic awareness*. This awareness often leads to children using similes and metaphors in their search for the right word. For example, here is Tajul 'reading' with his teacher after a few weeks in school:

Teacher: (reads from *Meg at Sea*) *That's the magnifying glass … There's the fire. Can you see?*
Tajul: *Yes. There?*
Teacher: *Yes.*
Tajul: *There's the window.* (points to the magnifying glass)
Teacher: *That's the magnifying glass. It's nearly the same as a window, isn't it?*

Is Tajul trying out the boundaries of words as he learns to distinguish 'window' and 'magnifying glass'? Similar examples with new language learners indicate this may be so. A second task in boundary demarcation will be to realize that the boundaries of words and their meanings will differ according to the language spoken. The single word 'cousin' in English needs many different words in most Asian languages (according to whether on the mother's or father's side, and so on). In reverse, the strict demarcation of gender (he/she, his/her, and so on) in European languages will be covered by one word in most Asian languages. With all this to consider, new language learners learn from the start that reality can be divided up differently according to the language spoken and that they must operate within a double set of rules.

The awareness that language is arbitrary, together with a lack of knowledge of the 'conventional' word in the target language, may enable children to play with words and experiment with them. Teachers of new language learners can provide lists of imaginative experiments with words, such as 'necklace man' (a mayor), 'a kissing lady' (a bride), 'Happy Wu Year', 'a ghonster' (ghost/monster), 'a polly' (kettle), 'a bzzz' (a bee). Lacking the word used unconsciously by their monolingual peers may force children into a conscious search for the real meaning behind a concept in order to find an appropriate synonym. Tajul uses a number of strategies to get the appropriate English word out of his teacher. For example, he points to a lion in an illustration and says 'That tiger?' to which his teacher replies 'No, it's a lion'; or he points to an illustration and uses a negative 'That's not Daddy' to which his teacher replies 'No, it's the milkman'. At 6, Artur, whose mother tongue is Polish, is able simply to ask 'What's the opposite of "up" in English?'.

These examples reinforce results from more formal tests conducted mostly with older children which show how slick they become at attending selectively to words and their boundaries. Working with 4- to 9-year-old bilingual English/Afrikaans children, Ianco-Worrall (1972) found that bilinguals excelled in ability to state the principle that words are arbitrarily assigned to things. Tests such as the following symbol substitution games have shown that even children new to a language are two to three years ahead of their monolingual peers:

Researcher: *This is named 'plane', right?*
Well, in the game, it's 'turtle'.
Can the turtle fly?

Similar tests conducted in different countries have all shown superior performance by children speaking more than one language. Learning a second or additional language thus gives children greater flexibility in separating words and their meanings, a useful tool for becoming literate and developing abstract thought.

A DOUBLE-EDGED SWORD: THE WEAKNESS OF LEXICAL CLUES

> The teacher is reading *Rosie's Walk* to a group of 5-year-old new language learners ... As she comes to the page with the bumble bee, she makes the sound 'bzzz' in order to try to make the meaning of the word 'bee' clear. After she has finished, the children turn over the pages of the book, looking at the pictures. Suddenly, one child points to the bee and says, 'Bangla say "bumbla", English say "bzzz"!'. Realizing her mistake and anxious to avoid misunderstandings, the teacher quickly says, 'No. English say "bumble bee" too, but it makes the sound "bzzz"!'

This example highlights the complexity involved in matching the right word to the appropriate object as new language learners set about learning the new language. Teachers can add their own examples to the 'bee' story and may become paranoid about their language use when they hear certain of their own 'key words' appearing in the most inappropriate places in the mouths of the children! One story, told by an older teacher, comes from the days when a single reading scheme ('The Happy Venture') was often used in British schools, featuring Dick and Jane and Fluff the cat. An important indication that her reading programme was somewhat limiting was made clear by the insistence of some children on referring to all cats as 'fluffs'!

During the early stages of second language learning, a major task is to sort out 'real' from 'nonsense' words. Tests have shown that monolingual children perform better at reading words in context, but new language learners better at reading a list of nonsense words. Such tests highlight differences between mono language and new language learners which Lina and Artur, whose phonic knowledge is developing rapidly have already shown us. New language learners tend to rely on their superior memories whereas monolingual children are able to draw upon the meaning of the text. It is clear that prediction of a word will be very difficult if its meaning is not understood and the syntax (grammatical structure) of the language is not at the command of the child. As Tajul reads with his teacher, he pinpoints this difficulty and shows how he is trying to work it out for himself:

(Tajul's teacher is reading *The Tiger who Came to Tea* (Kerr, 1968) and Tajul is joining in wherever he can)

Teacher: (reads) *'And tiger started eating all the sandwiches.'*
Tajul:　　*You know, lion …*
Teacher: *They're like tigers, aren't they?*
Tajul:　　*Yes.*
Teacher: *But tigers have got stripes.*
Tajul:　　*Yes.*
Teacher: *Lions haven't got stripes.*
Tajul:　　*And tiger … And lion is tiger's friend.*
Teacher: *Yes, that's right.* (reads) *'And ate all the buns.'*

Tajul is showing remarkable dexterity for a beginner in trying to work out the double meaning of the word 'like'. In the hubbub of the classroom, it is impossible for the teacher to pick up on this. Nevertheless, we see how he manages to make sense out of the situation and continue the discussion.

Lexical clues are also weakened for new language learners by the sheer abundance of words. When children read in a familiar language many non-content words such as *prepositions* (on, off, up, down, under, and so on), *conjunctions* (and, but, and so on) and *possessive pronouns* (his, her, and so on) are *redundant* as they can be predicted in the context of the sentence; for example:

He fell (down) flat (on his) face.

Other lexical clues also help words become almost redundant for young children reading in a language they are familiar with. Words often restrict the company they keep. A few examples make this clear:

A knife and (plate or fork)?
A cup and (spoon or saucer)?
A handsome or a pretty prince? A wicked or a bad witch?
To wipe or to clean your nose?

This mutual expectancy is known as *collocation* and it will be important when we study bibliographic clues. Knowledge of these 'partner words' comes easily when speaking a first language. Nevertheless, anyone speaking another language knows only too well that words differ in the company they keep. In German, the term *putzen* can be used for cleaning shoes, brushing teeth or wiping your nose. In Mandarin, the same word is used for 'seeing' a film, 'watching' television and 'reading' to oneself (or a newspaper). 'Reading out loud', on the other hand, needs a different word. One theory on beginning reading, 'the verbal efficiency theory' (Perfetti, 1984), proposes that there is something akin to a cake for all the clues needed for beginning reading. In other words, the more taken up by one slice (in this case, word identification), the less there is left for others (phonic, syntactic, semantic). Although we have no evidence to prove this, it would make sense that the huge demand made on memory if every word must be read equally is likely to make beginning reading more difficult.

But the most important lexical clue for children and adults as they read in any language must be the extent to which the word carries deep personal meaning (its 'sense', using Vygotsky's definition). Readers can probably draw upon their own experiences as illustrations. Perhaps there springs to mind the name of a station in Cyrillic script (in this case Russian) which is memorized out of fear that one will disappear forever into the depths of the Moscow underground system or even the name of a delicious Greek cake in order to buy it again. We cannot underestimate the value of 'one-sight' words in early reading. This term was coined by Sylvia Ashton-Warner (1963) to mean words which are close to children's hearts or deep in their personal experience, sometimes referred to as their 'organic' vocabulary. Ashton-Warner worked as an early years teacher during the 1950s with Maori children in New Zealand. Realizing that the 'Janet and John' reading scheme in use in school bore no resemblance to the children's lives, she devised an approach whereby children thought of personal words they wanted to learn to read, which then became their first reading material. We learn more about Ashton-Warner's work in Chapter 6 of this book where we focus on her practical approach for the classroom. What is important here is the role of 'one-sight' or important words as vital lexical clues in early reading.

It is not too difficult for teachers to predict some of these words for monolingual children. 'Mum', 'dad', 'television' (and favourite programmes), 'McDonald's' as well as emotive terms, such as 'kiss', 'cry', 'scream', 'terrified', 'hate', and so on are likely to figure high on children's lists. These words will call up an experience or *schema* (abstract knowledge structure) which may trigger off a whole web of words:

But what about children for whom *schemata* follow a different pattern and 'one-sight' words are in other languages? In her book, *The Woman Warrior*, Hong-Kingston (1977), whose family emigrated from China to the US, describes poignantly ways in which the new language (English) 'does not fit on my skin' (p. 53). As monolingual teachers (or teachers unable to speak our children's first languages) it is obvious that important emotional words in the lives of our new language learners outside school will remain inaccessible to us. The question, then, must be: In what ways can we create together 'one-sight' words in the new language for children either at home or in the classroom?

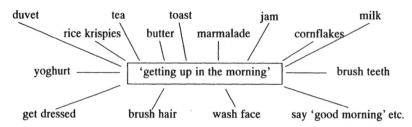

Figure 5.6 *Clues for learning to read in a new language: A typical schema in young children's lives*

LEXICAL CLUES: IN SUMMARY

This section shows us that young new language learners are potentially able to call upon a wealth of lexical clues, but that these are of a different nature from those at the fingertips of children learning to read in their first language. They have an advanced metalinguistic and analytic awareness in that they are able to see the arbitrary nature of words as labels and can detect and compare the boundaries of words in their different languages, and, usually, they have excellent memories. At the same time, they cannot call upon experiences or schemata to call up a network of words in the new language nor can they depend upon the redundancy of words to assist prediction. To make the most of the children's lexical clues as they plan a reading programme, teachers will need to ask:

Questions for reflection: lexical clues

- How important is lexical knowledge in learning to read for new language learners?
- What approach to lexical knowledge might children bring from home or their community language or religious classes?
- In what ways can this be accommodated in a home reading programme?
- How can we build upon children's metalinguistic skills in classroom practice?
- In what ways can we both ensure automaticity of certain key words and expand children's knowledge of collocational expressions in English?
- If 'one-sight' words are intimately linked with important experiences, how can we provide such experiences and the language belonging to them in the classroom?

'Chunking' useful sentences: syntactic clues

Tajul is reading *Meg's Car* (Nicholl and Pienkowski, 1972) and breaks off to practise 'Do you like – ?' in the middle of reading:

Tajul: *You know, milk.*
Teacher: *Milk? Mmm. What?*
Tajul: *Do you eat milk?*
Teacher: *Drink?*
Tajul: *No. Milk.*
Teacher: *Do I drink milk? Yes. Sometimes. Do you?*
Tajul: *Yes.*
Teacher: *Do you like milk?*
Tajul: *Do you like ... (teacher understands 'driving')*
Teacher: *Driving? ... a car?*
Tajul: *No. Ribena.*
Teacher: *Yes. I like Ribena. Do you?*
Tajul: *I like. Do you like Coca-Cola?*
Teacher: *Yes. I like Coca-Cola. Do you?*
Tajul: *Yes. Do you like sweets?*
Teacher: *Sweets? Do you?*
Tajul: *Do you like big sweets?*
Teacher: *Mmm. Do you?*
Tajul: *Do you like that big* (shows huge) *sweets?*
Teacher: *Big. big sweets! Yes. And cakes.*
Tajul: *You can't eat big, big sweets!*
Teacher: *Well, perhaps if my mouth were bigger, I could!*
Tajul: *And long.*

We are left uncertain as to how far Tajul is really interested in finding out about the likes and dislikes of his teacher and how far he is simply trying out and practising a grammatical structure. Whichever may be the case. he is very successfully doing both. His teacher notes that this type of repetition is a well-used strategy by Tajul and some of his peers who seem to be more concerned with the structure of the language than collecting words like Tony, or using phonics like Saida. New language learners have simply not yet had enough experience in the new language to be familiar with the grammatical structures likely to appear in many early reading books. The dilemma for the teacher lies in trying to provide a high quality of dialogue for children like Tajul, yet in a language simple enough for them to understand.

COPYING OTHERS: THE STRENGTH OF SYNTACTIC CLUES

When Tajul uses the word 'window' to refer to the magnifying glass in an illustration, he is using the same strategy of overgeneralizing employed by much younger monolingual children. Teachers of new language learners have a store of examples similar to our 'cats = fluffs' example cited earlier as well as evidence of overgeneralizations of past tense verb forms such as 'he hitted me', and so on. Many researchers bring evidence showing that reading miscues made by young second language learners tend to be predominantly *intra-lingual* (arising from the structure of the target language) rather than *inter-lingual* (arising from interference from mother-tongue influence). Catherine Wallace's (1986) detailed miscue analyses of the speech and reading of a variety of second-language learners from age 10 to adult in West London shows them searching for appropriate new rules rather than transferring from their first language. Teachers and educators working with new language learners see evidence of both intra- and inter-linguistic interference which will differ from one child to another as well as reflect the stage of their learning. Inter-lingual interference is generally more common when children are very new to the language or the first language is very different from the target language, such as Chinese or Japanese. However, both Tony and Tajul had first languages that were very different from English (Chinese and Sylheti/Bengali), yet interference for Tony was inter-lingual and for Tajul intra-lingual. Generalizations are, therefore, problematic and not very useful.

Children who *are* able to take over first-language learning strategies have obvious advantages. In Chapter 3, we saw how very young children can internalize and use whole expressions in appropriate contexts in their first language long before they are able to understand them word for word. Close observation of young new language learners who learn a new language rapidly reveals that they also take over 'chunks' of speech during interaction with first language speakers. The important thing about this strategy (referred to by Hatch, 1974, as 'chunking') is that the chunks of language do not need to be understood by the child. They are attached to a specific context and can be called up whenever the same context recurs. This often happens in play situations: 'I'm gonna beat you up …', 'Oh no, you're not', and so on. They can also happen between child and teacher, particularly during book-reading sessions. Tajul is expert at this. Notice the way he models his reply on the structure used by the teacher:

(A few months after practising 'Do you like' in the Meg and Mog story, Tajul and his teacher are looking at a Ladybird book *The Fireman*)

Tajul: *Look, they're gonna find gold!* (pointing to the picture of firemen entering a burning house)
Teacher: *(laughs) Do you think so?*
Tajul: *Yes.*
Teacher: *(laughs) I don't know. They might be.*
Tajul: *And there might be fish and water.*
Teacher: *Do you think so? Might be.*
Tajul: *In there, there's water.* (points to bubbles under the fire-hose)

Teacher: *Underneath, you mean? Under the bubbles?*
Tajul: *Yes.*
Teacher: *Could be.*

The same pattern occurs on numerous occasions: the teacher 'models' a certain structure; the child copies it immediately afterwards and then goes on to practise it repeatedly. Tajul continues using 'and there might be' throughout the book in the same way as 'Do you like …?' a few months earlier.

A year older, 6-year-olds Lina, Artur, Konrad (also from Poland), Anna-Maria (from Rumania) and Melanie (from Ecuador) illustrate well Ben-Zeev's (1977) point that learning a second language promotes an early analytic awareness of language. The children are acting out the nursery rhyme 'Jack and Jill' and experiencing considerable difficulty with *preposi- tions* (over/under, on, into, up, down, after, and so on). Their teacher plays a game of 'guess- ing the opposite' which includes nouns and adjectives as well as prepositions. Very quickly, the children use the idea for expressing what they want to say: 'It's the opposite of enormous, Miss …' (meaning 'tiny') or 'It's like "down" …' (meaning 'under').

WUGS OR WÜGE: THE WEAKNESS OF SYNTACTIC CLUES

Syntactic clues are probably the most useful and the most reliable for children who are learning to read in their first language. Children have a 'feel' for the syntax or structure of their language from a very early stage. A much cited example by linguists is the 2-year-old English speaker who is told an object is a 'wug', then shown two of the same object and asked to label them. Invariably, the children will refer to them immediately as 'two wugs', not only applying the correct rule for forming plurals, but using the appropriate *voiced* 'zz' rather than *unvoiced* 's' sound. But for new language learners, syntactic clues are unquestionably weak. Lina questions why 's' is not always voiceless in English. Speakers of other languages react differently when asked to make plurals. A German infant might correlate the word with 'Zug' (train) and form the plural in a similar way 'Züge' or 'Wüge'. We see, then, that learn- ing to read in a familiar language aids prediction of a text enormously.

Research tells us (Adams, 1995) that reading demands much more syntactic sophistication than listening as the syntactic structure of the written text must be discovered by the reader whereas it is largely given to the listener by the speaker through the context, for example, 'Haven't I — you somewhere before?' at a party or 'Pick it — — the floor' in a classroom. Young first language readers have a range of syntactic clues as they approach a text. They are able to call upon many *cohesive devices* (devices which link one sentence or part of a sentence to another). Some of these are: *pronominal reference*, for example, 'I saw John yesterday. *He* was ill'; *synonyms*, for example, 'sick/ill'; *superordinates*, for example, 'apples, oranges = fruit'; and *collocational expressions*, for example, 'toast with butter and jam'. Teachers in multilingual classes know how easily young children who are confident in a language can predict a word to complete sentences in popular, yet structurally difficult, texts, for example, 'Mirror, mirror, on the wall, Who is the fairest of us all?' Syntactic clues also facilitate automaticity and enable some words to become redundant (refer back also to the section on lexical clues). Until a sufficient supply of chunks have been built up, new language learners will need to compensate by reading every word, posing great demands on both memory and concentration.

How important are weak syntactic clues for new language learners? Common sense tells us that prediction of a text must be difficult if we cannot speak the language. Tony shows how difficult book-reading can be if children cannot 'chunk' language:

Tony: *What's his name?*
Teacher: *That one's called Mr Impossible.*
Tony: *Mr Inpossible.* (looks at cover and repeats four times) *What's his name?*
Teacher: *Mr Impossible.*
Tony: (turns page saying nothing) *Mr Inpossible talking a boy.*
              Mr Inpossible. He fall down <u>shes</u> hat. There's a girl and a boy ... that's girl and boy.

'Shes' is undoubtedly an interlingual error (interference) from Cantonese where gender is not marked by *possessive pronouns* as in European languages. A few months later, Tony and his teacher are reading a counting-book *Over in the Meadow* (Wadsworth, 1986) together:

Teacher: (reads) *'Over in the meadow where the stream runs blue ...'*
Tony: *Blue.*
Teacher: *'Lived an old mother fish ...'*
Tony: *Fish.*
Teacher: *'And her little fishes two ...'*
Tony: *Two.*

This continues except where Tony interrupts, for example:

Teacher: *'... lived an old mother cat and her little catties four ...'*
Tony: *What she eating?*
Teacher: *I think they look like strawberries to me.*
Tony: *I like strawberries.*
Teacher: *So do I.*
Tony: *I like, I like ... strawberries.*
              (this is obviously not the word he wants)
Teacher: *Do you?*
Tony: *Mmm.*

The important question for teachers is: what enables some children, like Tajul, to learn 'chunks' of the new language very quickly while others, like Tony, seem to find this so difficult?

SYNTACTIC CLUES: IN SUMMARY

Syntactic clues are undoubtedly weak as new language learners learn to read in a new language. In contrast with monolingual or fluent speakers, these children are unable to narrow down the choice and predict words through a knowledge of the structure of the language. They also find it difficult to draw on discourse devices for cohesion, for example, 'it' referring back to 'the dog', and so on. On the other hand, they often have a strong and early analytic awareness and know that a structure actually *exists*. We can trace ways in which successful young second language learners go about practising both specific structures and 'chunks' of language during play and book interactions with their teachers and more fluent peers. To assist children in making the most of syntactic clues, we shall need to consider:

Questions for reflection: syntactic clues

- What types of 'chunks' of language will be particularly helpful for the early reader to practise and which activities will help them do this?
- How can automaticity be acquired?
- In what ways can children practise the syntax of a new language at home if their parents have limited English?
- What pattern of errors (if any) can be detected in the learning strategies of successful and less successful beginner readers? Does the child who is less successful in learning the target language generally make more errors of an interlingual nature?

Matching experiences to texts: semantic clues

Tony, Husna and Naseema illustrate well the nature and importance of semantic clues in early reading. Even at the moment in which Tony's teacher explains that the stylized illustration in his 'Mr Men' book is 'toast and marmalade ... you know, like you have for breakfast in the morning', she realizes that her words may be senseless for Tony. Later, she learns that Tony's family usually has soup for breakfast. As members of the same cultural group and speakers of the same language, we automatically rely on shared understandings. In his work, *Language, Culture and Personality* (1970: 8), the anthropologist Edward Sapir puts this succinctly when he says that language 'does not ... stand apart from or run parallel to direct experience but completely interpenetrates with it'. Later, he illustrates the importance of a shared language as groups interact and where 'He talks like one of us' is equivalent to saying 'He is one of us' (1970: 17). Learning to speak a language and consequently to predict that language when reading a text, therefore, is intimately linked with the experiences gained in the language.

In her book, *Purity and Danger* (1970), Mary Douglas uses examples from many cultures to illustrate the importance of different rituals in each society and how expectations of these will be different across cultures. However, we know that cultural routines within Europe, the US and Australia are likely to share much more in common with each other than with those in Asia or Africa. Moving to France, Nicole and her family have few difficulties in this respect. Although she also finds comprehension texts linked with specific cultural practices (particularly those linked with eating and food!) difficult to understand, her family's lifestyle and expectations are largely similar to those of her French peers. She knows the same traditional folk and fairy stories, watches the same television programmes and listens to the same music. But what if children's cultural routines are very different from those in the host community? With apparently all the odds against them, in what ways might new language learners benefit from semantic clues as they learn to read in the classroom?

THE STRENGTH OF SEMANTIC CLUES: THE POTENTIAL ADVANTAGES OF BEING A 'STRANGER'

At first, it seems sad that Husna and Naseema read the words of *Each, Peach, Pear, Plum* without knowledge of the experience of the magnificent plum pie. They have not yet assisted in the long ritual of making it, smelling it as it cooks and eventually having the pleasure of eating it with their family and friends. If they had, they would most certainly have been able to remember its English name. Yet as we saw from their analogy of 'gosh' with 'dosh', they have a flexibility regarding words and are prepared for adventure as they use them. Lambert (1967) refers to this as a 'cognitive flexibility' where children are learning double sets of lexical and syntactic rules. It may be that this extends to a cultural flexibility', an openness towards learning the new routines of the host culture.

It is obvious that children such as Husna and Naseema who enter school from a very different cultural orientation are faced with a bigger learning task from those who share the culture of the teacher. However, these 'strangers' may be able consciously to inquire into the 'what' and the 'why' of every situation. Tajul seems to be doing this as he shares stories with his teacher:

Teacher: (reading from *Meg at Sea*)
      That's the fish.
Tajul: *And that?*
Teacher: *That's the octopus. That's an octopus.*

Tajul: (points) *That's the fish.*
Teacher: (reads) '*A present for you …*' (out of text) *Yes, there's the fish.* (reads again) *Meg cooked the fish …*
Tajul: *And, do you like?*
Teacher: *Mmm. And they like to eat octopus, too, I think. Do you like octopus?*
Tajul: (hesitantly) *No. Do you?*
Teacher: *No. Some people do.* (Reads) '*Meg and Mog had a rest.*'
Tajul: *English do?*
Teacher: *Well, some English do. Not many …* (reads) '*Chopper ahoy! They saw a helicopter …*'

Tajul is eager to learn about the new language and culture he is entering. The enthusiasm and inquisitiveness shown by these children give us reason to believe that attitudes and social experiences in the new culture will be a major influence on the speed with which they learn the target language and are able to utilize semantic and syntactic clues. Similar findings have been made by Wong-Fillmore (1982) who argues that sociable, outgoing children tend to learn the target language more efficiently because they quickly learn appropriate language 'formulae' for different events. 'Formulae' are similar to Hatch's 'chunks' discussed in the previous section. We saw in Chapter 3 how young children go about mastering these formulae in their first language. Tajul shows us that successful new language learners do something similar, but, unlike monolingual infants, they are aware of what they are doing.

In his detailed study of 63 young Turkish children learning to read in Dutch, Verhoeven (1987) found that the degree to which children were able to identify with both their language and culture of origin and with the new culture paralleled their reading progress. He cites Lambert's (1967) notion of four patterns of identification with a new culture: (a) identification with both cultures; (b) identification with the majority culture and rejection of the culture of origin; (c) identification with the culture of origin and rejection of the majority culture; and (d) failure to identify with either culture. Lambert argues that learning a new language will, of course, be possible, simply by living in the country and using it entirely for instrumental purposes. Nevertheless, learning is likely to be much more successful if the new group is taken as a reference point and if new lifestyles and values are grafted onto old. Where families have recently arrived in a new country, it may be the children's responsibility to mediate the new language and culture to their parents. The task for the teacher, then, will be both to initiate the child into the host culture of the country and jointly to negotiate a classroom culture of reading.

STRAWBERRIES OR STRAWBERRIES? THE WEAKNESS OF SEMANTIC CLUES

Tony's positive responses as he read *Over in the Meadow* with his teacher in the last section were to count carefully from one to ten, pointing to the numbers as he did so and to pick on a detail in one illustration, saying 'I like strawberries'. But he does not manage to get his meaning across to the teacher. He wanted to add something else that he liked, but realized he did not know the name and, rather than risk complications, he simply repeated dejectedly 'strawberries'. Does he want to tell his teacher but does not know the English word and is loath to risk saying something that might be wrong? Or does he feel that what he wants to refer to will be outside the experience of his teacher and he would rather keep it to himself? The teacher's experiences when meeting his family lead her to suspect the latter.

Undoubtedly, new language learners will be at a disadvantage when calling upon semantic clues to predict words and texts. Their difficulties are likely to be on two levels. First, children may have difficulty in predicting a text because it describes something outside their experience. Many teachers recall tackling an explanation of 'plum pies' or even simpler fare with children to whom such dishes are inconceivable. Of course, we all meet unknown or culturally strange items in texts. Nevertheless, if it happens frequently enough and is combined with the whole text being in a new language, learning to read will obviously be made more difficult. Teachers, themselves, recall how much more difficult it is at first to remember the names of bilingual pupils in comparison with familiar ones. In a study with fluent adult biliterates, Steffensen et al. (1980) show how familiarity with an experience makes a difference to reading. They gave American and Indian readers two letters about a wedding in each culture and found that each group read the passage relating to their own culture faster and more accurately. The familiar occasion made sense to them and consequently they could predict what was likely to happen. Looking back to the section on lexical clues, we saw how a network of words is linked to a particular schema (in this case 'getting up in the morning'). The schema itself enables us to call up a range of experiences and corresponding lexis and expressions. Tony obviously gets up in the morning too, but parts of the experience are very different from those of children like Lina and Artur whose experience is a European one.

The second level is wider. For Tony's family, literacy is seen as mediated through obedience and training and 'the book' is the reward rather than the medium for learning to read. Dineo's family in South Africa, whom we met in Chapter 2, also showed us the importance of learning to read 'correctly'. Scollon and Scollon (1981) suggest that particular discourse patterns and forms of literacy are related to personal and social identity. Important questions for teachers are: how are 'learning' and the role of the learner conceived by families? Are experimenting and risk-taking part of their understanding of formal education or do they view learning as taking place initially through copying and repeating? If views of home and school are very different, how will home/school reading programmes take account of this?

SEMANTIC CLUES: IN SUMMARY

During detailed observations of monolingual children in an East London nursery class, Valerie Walkerdine (1981) noticed how effectively monolingual children used dialogue in certain role-play situations in the dramatic play area. Particularly, she identified the context of 'watching' and recorded how children seemed able to interact together, calling upon 'chunks' of speech which were quite specific to that context but would otherwise have been inaccessible to them. In some ways, the children were re-enacting the 'modelling' and 'scaffolding' we saw taking place between the caregiver and young child in Chapter 3. Rather than relying on adults, they were using a familiar context to support each other. Where young first and second language learners are in classes together, fluent speakers will be able to help new language learners 'situate' themselves in contexts and the pre-packaged routines of the target language at the same time. Hatch et al. (1979) give examples comparing how effective this sort of language can be for children at a very early stage in second language learning. They describe a 5-year-old Taiwanese child playing with a first-language speaker during the first two months of beginning English:

First language child:	*I got a real gun.*
Second language child:	*I got a real gun.*
L.1:	*You gotta parachute?*
L.2:	*Yeh. Gotta parachute.*
Adult:	*What's a parachute?*
L.1:	*It has a man go down.*
L.2:	*Yeh? go down, down, down.*

Using semantic clues effectively will inevitably involve a blending of new ways of life onto the home culture. Young new language learners will often be in a stronger position to do this than their parents. They are surrounded by all types of exciting oral and written language initiating them into the new culture. Even in classes where almost all children are second language learners, they are unlikely to escape a variety of crisp, chocolate and biscuit wrappings, street and bus signs and probably (though not inevitably) television programmes. Children's cultural flexibility will be a strength upon which to build in the classroom. Grosjean (1982) develops this idea and stresses an integrated or holistic view of the bilingual whereby we realize that children combine a unique blend of two cultures and languages rather than being two monolinguals with separate languages and cultures. To assist children in making the most of semantic clues, we shall need to consider:

Questions for reflection: semantic clues

- How can teachers provide new language learners with opportunities for developing experiences and corresponding language routines in the target language?
- How and in what ways can teachers themselves develop cultural flexibility?
- In what ways might the 'scaffolding' and modelling given by the teacher differ from that offered by the first language child? How might both complement each other?

The world in a story: bibliographic clues

Until then, I had thought each book spoke of the things … that lie outside books. Now I realised that not infrequently books speak of books; it is as if they spoke among themselves. It (the library) was, then, the place of a long … murmuring. an imperceptible dialogue between one parchment and another, a living thing, a receptacle of powers not to be ruled by human mind, a treasure of secrets emanated by many minds. (Eco, 1980: 286)

How can young children whose new language is so limited begin to use the complex language of books? It would be a mistake to believe that children who have no experience with written stories cannot offer bibliographic knowledge of a different sort.

WRITTEN LANGUAGE AS A CODE: THE STRENGTH OF BIBLIOGRAPHIC KNOWLEDGE

Alif has been sent to the headteacher accused of hitting someone in the playground. The expression on his face is very serious as he denies the offence. Asked why his opponent should be crying if he has not been injured, Alif replies: 'I was just looking and then the tears came into his eyes …'

Alif has taken a chunk of literary language from his reading and is using it in speech. Artur does the same when, also being accused of hitting someone in the playground, he says, 'he struggle me and then I did go …'. Books are important teachers of the target language to new language learners and may enable them to step straight into academic 'school' language. Dineo, Sanah and Pia in Chapter 2 showed us how they were becoming aware of the importance of books and the special language they contain from an early stage in their biliteracy. Annie, too, read her book in Thai using a 'story intonation'; Ah Si was learning English nursery rhymes. An immersion programme in Canada whereby native English speaking children completed their first two years' schooling in French (Lambert and Tucker, 1972) revealed that the children achieved almost as well on English reading tests and better on mathematical tests than their monolingual peers. The researchers proposed that the new language was being used as a sort of 'code' attached directly to new concepts. There are a number of reasons why new language learners may be able to learn the language of books easily. First, as in the Canadian experiment, these children learn 'chunks' of book language from listening to the stories where they are used. There is no problem that they might mix features of spoken and written language as first-language speakers, for their two languages will be totally different. Then, we know that new language learners are particularly sensitive to the language used by the teacher, who acts as a role model. Together with their usually excellent memories, children may well take 'book' or academic language on board simply as the new 'school language'.

To recognize the bibliographic strengths of new language learners, we cannot restrict our definition of 'book knowledge' to 'story-book knowledge'. All our children in Chapter 2 possess books, but not necessarily 'story-books', at home. That these contain the alphabet, exercises, short reading texts, and so on, and may sometimes be of flimsy material or in black and white does not diminish their validity or value for the children and their families. Quite the contrary; for most families, these books are seen as preparation for reaching important texts (for Julializ the Bible and for Hasanat the Qur'ān or, for Tony, the book itself). In addition, the children are aware that books can be written in different scripts and can be read from right to left or sometimes from top to bottom. All this sort of knowledge is not of the traditional story-book variety but is important book knowledge just the same. In her study of dual-language books, Edwards (1995) shows how easy it is to become 'culture-bound' when defining a 'good book'. She contrasts the views of children and their teachers when choosing dual-language books. Teachers preferred glossy 'Western'-looking dual-language dictionaries, whereas some children preferred the rather faded Indian dictionaries with traditional illustrations on the grounds that they were more 'adult' and 'serious looking'.

Our children in Chapter 2 also show us that even the term 'book knowledge' is not sufficient and that we need to include knowledge of all types of written materials. Research studies on both indigenous and immigrant origin families who do not share the reading practices of the school show that they participate in a whole variety of literacy activities, albeit not linked with children's story books or books themselves. In Chapter 2, Pia showed us how important letter writing was for her. Muijtaba's facility with the computer which we saw in Chapter 4 came from home. When Tony links the Queen's appearance on television with her photograph in the newspaper shown by the teacher in school – 'Princess ?... She in Hong Kong. I see in the television' – he shows us the important step he has made in realizing the purpose of both in conveying information through image or print.

'STICKING DOORS' AND 'WINNING HANDS IN MARRIAGE': THE WEAKNESS OF BIBLIOGRAPHIC CLUES

> Lina, Artur, Konrad, Anna-Maria and Melanie are learning about rhymes with their teacher in London. Their aim is to read the rhyme 'Jack and Jill went up the hill to fetch a pail of water. Jack fell down and broke his crown and Jill came tumbling after. Up Jack got and home did trot as fast as he could caper. He went to bed to mend his head with vinegar and brown paper', then act it out. The teacher reads the rhyme and asks the children questions. 'Where did they go together?' 'Seaside' says Anna-Maria. The children are then encouraged to read the words using their knowledge of phonics. This proves very difficult. 'Hill' is read correctly, but did not appear to be understood (in preference to 'seaside'). Lina reads 'pile' for 'pail'. 'F-etch' is managed but the meaning seems unclear to all. Finally, the teacher suggests they use 'get' for 'fetch', 'bucket' for 'pail'. They get as far as acting our the first verse – which they really enjoy.

New language learners are likely to have three main weaknesses when calling upon bibliographic clues: (a) they may well be unfamiliar with traditional and well-known European stories and nursery rhymes; (b) the language used in many books will be even more complex than spoken language and, therefore, very difficult to understand; and (c) the use of story books for beginning reading may not correspond to their families' interpretation of what 'counts' as valid material for learning to read.

Reading the words of a story is much easier if the plot is familiar

---

Nicole's parents buy her traditional European fairy-tales in French. The whole family laughs together over 'Cendrillon' which they are already so familiar with as 'Cinderella'. Just a few pictures from *La Ventafocs* is enough to tell her that it is the same story and she is able confidently to learn a few key words. Other new language learners receive the same clues when they listen to traditional stories with their families in their first language before tackling them in English in school. Of course, the stories need not necessarily be from the families' country of origin. Nevertheless, a familiarity with names, items of clothes, food and other cultural practices represented will all assist prediction and remembering the relevant words to attach to items. A good way to test the importance of familiarity is to try learning to read the text in Figure 5.7. How much easier is it than learning the text of unfamiliar and unrelated pictures?

La Ventafocs

Tu, a la cuina, Ventafocs

-Què tens? Per què plores?

I el príncep i la Ventafocs van ser molt feliços i van menjar molts anissos.

Figure 5.7 *The importance of illustrations, simplicity and context when reading in a new language. What differences does it make that the story and the script are familiar and the language is of European origin?*

The language of stories and books can be very difficult

A glance through children's story books reveals just how complex structures and decontextualized language can be for the emergent bilingual. Here are just a few examples from well-used books:

Your daughter is indeed clever if she can do as you say. (Grimm, 1993)

Captain Crab rushed out, ranting and roaring, and STREAK went the brush, right through

Jethro's work. Down came Jethro to give Captain Crab a piece of his mind. (Don't Blame Me!,
Rogers, 1990)

Inversion of language may add to difficulties:

In came two little elves. (The Elves and the Shoemaker, *Ladybird*)

Idiomatic language can be hard, too:

He picked it (the golden apple) *up in a flash and rode away like the wind.* (A Second Story-
Teller's Choice, *E. Colwell*)

There are many similar examples. It is important that children hear and learn the language
of books and Alif above shows how he has taken this into his spoken repertoire. Part of the
magic of books is the sound of words and not understanding them all (abracadabra, open
sesame, Rumpelstiltskin). Nevertheless, children will need time, repetition and practice
before some book language makes sense to them and becomes a useful clue as they set about
learning to read.

Education systems have different ideas as to what is appropriate material for beginner readers

Tony's Chinese class and his grandfather for whom the book is seen as the reward for learning to read show how one particular reading practice (in this case the story-reading practice)
cannot be seen as 'natural'. Nicole and Pia's French schools also use very different materials
from their home reading. Julializ's family too, are accustomed to very different books from
those in their daughter's American school. The example of these families underlines the
danger in assuming that parents will automatically understand school teaching methods and
highlights the importance of dialogue between home and school.

BIBLIOGRAPHIC CLUES: IN SUMMARY

> *Gemma: Porridge was too hot and they set off in the woods. Long time ago. Her name was*
> *Goldilocks … Too sweet, said Goldilocks, Daddy bear … too hot. Tries mummy bear. Too lumpy*
> *… Tries mummy bear … tries baby bear … the best, so baby bear now just right. So she ate it*
> *all up … Tries baby bear's bed. Just right. (Minns, 1990: 104)*

This excerpt highlights the importance of bibliographic clues as new language learners learn
to read. Gemma has already grasped the narrative in that her story has a beginning 'Long
time ago …', a middle and an end 'Just right'. Although still at the early stages of learning

English, the book has provided her with complex 'chunks' of language. She is comfortable with the past tense of the verbs 'to be', 'to eat' and 'to say'; she can say that something is 'too sweet, too hot, too lumpy' and she has mastered the superlative 'the best'; she knows the conventional opening 'Long time ago ...' and she can use the complex verb 'they set off'. Margaret Meek (1988) points out the importance of illustrations in explaining a story and assisting prediction for young readers by using the example of the chicken followed by the fox in *Rosie's Walk* (Hutchins 1968) to show how excitement, fear and anxiety can be awakened in children in spite of a very simple text. Books such as this will be especially important in enabling new language learners to make sense of texts. Story books may act as a catalyst in developing new language learners' other clues as they set about learning to speak and read a new language together. In Chapter 7, we shall trace how this can take place in the classroom. As they assist children in developing bibliographic clues, teachers will need to ask themselves:

Questions for reflection: bibliographic clues

- What types of 'written knowledge' do children bring to school from home?
- Which story books best enable children both to make sense of text easily and 'chunk' important pieces of book or story language?
- Which stories are likely to present emergent biliiiguals with difficulties and why?
- Is there a dialogue between family and school on the place and use of different types of materials in early reading programmes?

Suggestions for teaching and learning

- Think of ways, including games, in which children's lexical strengths can be developed without becoming simply strings of individual words.
- If syntactic and semantic clues depend upon 'welding' language onto experiences so that phrases become automatic, how can such experiences be provided within the confines of the classroom?
- If children learn English through reading itself, consider what sorts of texts we need for this.
- How can phonics be used in a *meaningful* way in a reading programme?

SUMMARY

◆ New language learners draw upon the same clues as their monolingual peers but use them in different ways, reflecting different strengths and weaknesses.

◆ Children are often able to transfer strategies used in one language and literacy to another.

◆ Strength in one set of clues can partly (but never wholly) compensate for another. Lexical clues are particularly useful to new language learners because they have often developed excellent memories.

◆ The social, interpersonal and mental contexts constantly interact: children's home and community language class experiences are likely to influence their view on what counts as valid approaches to beginning reading as well as the strength of particular clues; the strength or weakness of syntactic, semantic and bibliographic clues will depend upon children's knowledge and acceptance of the host culture and the sharing of new cultural practices.

◆ Spoken language and reading development are inextricably linked with experiences gained in the language itself.

These are topics for the second part of this book.

Further reading

Donaldson, M. (1978) *Children's Minds*. Glasgow: Fontana.

Edwards, V. and Walker, S. (1995) *Building Bridges: Multilingual Resources for Children. Multilingual Resources for Children Project*, Clevedon: Multilingual Matters.

Goelman, H., Oberg, A. and Smith, F. (eds) (1984) *Awakening to Literacy*. London: Heinemann Education.

Meek, M. (1991) *On Being Literate*. London: Bodley Head.

Part 2

From theory to practice

Introduction: making sense of words and worlds

A krinklejup was parling a tristlebin. A barjam stipped. The barjam grupped 'Minto' to the krinklejup. The krinklejup zisked zoelly.

What was the krinklejup doing?
What stipped?
What did the barjam grup?
How did the krinklejup zisk?

To the ... question – is this reading? – a Year 4 child (and a fluent reader) gave an interesting response: 'Yes, because I could work out the answers.' Then he added, 'But it's not really reading, because I just went from here,' indicating the questions, 'to here,' indicating the text. 'It didn't go through my head.' (Gibbons, 1995: 70–1)

KEY TERMS

Alphabetic	A term used to refer to languages that use a standardized set of letters (graphemes or written symbols) of which each roughly represents a phoneme (or sound) in spoken language.
Syllabic	A term used to refer to languages that use syllables to denote different sounds. For example, Thai is referred to as a tonal monosyllabic language. It has 44 basic consonants, each with an inherent vowel and 18 other vowels. There are five different tones for each syllable, the tone being determined by a combination of the class of consonant, type of syllable, the tone marker and the length of vowel.
Ideogram/ideograph	Terms used to refer to Chinese logograms whereby one character represents a whole word or idea. Sometimes these are pictograms (that is, derived from pictures of the objects they denote), sometimes ideograms (that is, symbols representing not the object but idea), sometimes they are compound indicatives where pictograms or ideograms are arranged together (that is, bright = sun + moon).
Convergent/divergent	Terms used to describe ways which typify the way children think and approach tasks. Convergent thinkers generally prefer a systematic approach, are neat and tidy and prefer not to make mistakes; divergent thinkers tend to be creative, flamboyant, less tidy and prefer to experiment, even if this means making mistakes.

Part 2 of this book moves from educators *learning* to educators *doing* and presents a reading programme for new language learners that can be used in both homes and classrooms. Although the programme is designed for new learners of English, the principles are relevant for learners of any new language. It is also just as relevant for children learning to read in their home language. Underpinning the programme is the belief that decoding and under-standing are mutually dependent and are learned together at every stage. Paradoxically, *understanding* does not necessarily entail knowing the *dictionary meaning* of every single word in a text, but the ability to *make sense* of it through *personal meaning*. All the children we met in Part 1 showed how important *meaning* was from the earliest stages of learning to read. In fact, as we observed children learning to read at home, we saw that reading was never an end in itself but was always a way of gaining meaning. For example, we saw how Julializ and Elsey read the Bible in order to learn about the word of God and how one should live one's life; Dineo and Hasanat were also preparing to read religious texts, making sure they pronounced the text as beautifully as possible. Pia saw her letter writing as a way of commu-nicating with friends (or her parents when they were busy) or listening to stories. Sanah, Annie, Elsey, Ah Si and Curtis saw learning to read as part of the challenge of learning a very new language and culture. Throughout Part 1, the argument was made that decoding and meaning should be intimately linked. The child opening this chapter puts it neatly: decod-ing alone means that words 'don't go through one's head'. For new language learners such as Lina, decoding alone also means that the words often cannot be accurately pronounced since she cannot tell whether they make sense or not!

Part 2 provides a programme that builds upon the argument central to this book: that new language learners are simultaneously making sense of words and worlds. The programme, therefore, links decoding and meaning at every step. Important to the programme is the belief that , although I propose a common perspective there can be no universal *method* where every part works equally well for all children. The children in Part 1 of this book have shown how different aspects of literacy learning may be difficult or easy, and that this is likely to be determined by a number of factors. Some of these are as follows:

1 *The language of origin*: children where the family language is alphabetic (for example Lina, Artur, Dineo, Julializ, Pia, Nicole, Sanah, Elsey) may well find phonics easier than those whose mother tongue is syllabic (Annie) or ideographic (Ah Si, Tony) who may find learning syllables or whole words respectively easier than individual sounds.
2 *The literacy level of the child in the language of origin*: if children are already literate in the mother tongue, literacy in the new language will be easier (see Chapters 1, 2, 4 and 5).
3 *The learning style of the child*: convergent learners are likely to make faster progress in a highly structured reading programme; divergent learners may benefit more from a flex-ible and less structured approach.

4 *The personal and cultural view of what 'counts' as reading*: whether the view of the family matches that which counts in school (for example, the excellent pronounciation and intonation patterns of Dineo, the accurate Bible and Qur'ānic reading of Julializ and Hasanat, the story-reading of Pia, the functional literacy knowledge of Elsey and the skilled memories of Ah Si, Tony and Curtis) may or may not be seen as important by their school.

Many countries will have mandatory reading curricula which teachers may find difficult to reconcile with the approach presented in Part 2 of this book. However, it is important to realize that all educators actively interpret curricula and also constantly construct and reconstruct their own work. Like children, they need to make sense of what they are being asked to do. This book asks teachers to consider ways in which the perspectives and principles presented can be interwoven with the mandated curriculum. The approach may be used with small groups of new language learners who need extra tuition (as in Europe, Australia, New Zealand, Canada, and some classes in the US) or with whole classes where all the children are new language learners and beginning literacy in more than one language at the same time (as in China, Singapore, South Africa, bilingual classrooms in the US and some classes in Thailand), as well as international, British or US schools throughout the world. Many of the ideas may also be used by caregivers at home. Thus, although materials used will be different, the same principles of teaching and learning as presented in the programme may be applied. For this reason, the programme does not refer to particular reading schemes or computer software, since these are likely to be different in every country. All the ideas offered have been used successfully with both groups and whole classes of new language learners in London classrooms. The home reading suggestions have also been used with parents whose written and spoken English was very limited.

The programme described has two parts which I call the 'Inside-Out' and the 'Outside-In' approaches. These do not adhere entirely to either the 'bottom-up' nor the 'top-down' views of reading outlined in Chapter 4. Phonics (analytic and onset-rime as well as synthetic where appropriate) are used as long as the *meaning* of the words is explained concurrently and children are then asked to use them appropriately in their own sentences. Stories, songs and nursery rhymes are an important part of the programme, since they enable children to 'chunk' refrains and whole phrases in the new language and also provide access to the culture to which they belong. Children do not need to understand every word of these (who really knows the meaning of the 'tuffet' upon which 'Little Miss Muffet' sat?) but will become confident in calling up the phrases and refrains learned both for singing *and* in other situations when appropriate. The 'Inside-Out' and 'Outside-In' approaches are described more fully in Chapters 6 and 7. Chapter 8 briefly presents ways in which both may be combined in classroom settings.

SUMMARY

♦ Part 2 moves from educators *learning* to educators *doing* and presents a reading programme for young children learning to read and speak in a new language simultaneously.

♦ The programme is supplementary to a main reading curriculum and may be used with both groups of new language learners or with whole classes in countries where two or more languages and literacies are being learned simultaneously. Ideas may also be used by caregivers at home.

• There is no universal method that works equally well with all children. Children learn in different ways according to their personalities and their cultural background as well as the life and literacy experiences of their families.

♦ The *Inside-Out* and *Outside-In* approaches adhere to neither the 'bottom-up' nor 'top-down' theories.

♦ The programme proposed puts *meaning* in the middle and assumes the interdependency of decoding and understanding at all times.

6 Starting with the word: the 'Inside-Out' approach in action

Tajul, our Sylheti-speaking child, is sharing a book in English with his teacher:

Teacher: (reads from *The Hungry Giant*)
        '… and got the giant some bread.'
Tajul: (points to bread) *This not bread.*
        These are finger.
Teacher: *It's supposed to be bread, actually.*
        Some bread looks like that. It's not supposed to be fingers. It's supposed to be bread.
Tajul: *It's not bread.*
Teacher: *Well, if you go into Tesco's supermarket, you can find some long thin bread like that. What does your bread look like? Does your bread look different from that?*
Tajul: *My bread is square.*
Teacher: *Oh, your bread is square, is it? Well, some bread is long and thin and some bread is square …*

KEY TERMS

Language-Experience approach	An approach to teaching reading that starts from children's experiences and words describing those experiences. This may be as simple as one important word or may be a whole story or event important to the child. A key factor is the belief that experiences can be described in speech and that speech can be written down.
Inside-Out approach	An approach that draws on the Language-Experience approach but focuses on *new* experiences in the target language and culture represented by that language.
Generative words	Words chosen for both their semantic importance and phonetic richness to beginner readers in the approach used by Freire, for example, 'fa-ve-la'

Continues over

	(shanty-town) which is first discussed in terms of meaning, then broken down into syllables from which other words can be formed, for example, 'fa-, fe-, fi-, fo-, fu-; ve-, va-', and so on.
One-sight words	Words chosen for their importance to children in the approach used by Ashton-Warner. Such words are those 'never-to-be-forgotten', regardless of phonic difficulty or irregularity.
Modelling	A term used to describe the important task of the educator or child more fluent in the target language to 'model'(present/use) new language structures or phrases.
Socio-dramatic play	Play crucial to new language learning whereby children 'make-believe' with others, using their imagination and creativity to take on different roles and practise the talk associated with them.

We have met Tajul before and noted how interested he was in questioning his new 'world' of the English language, its literacy and ways of living. At first, he was keen to participate in reading in the only way he could with 'full stop' or 'question mark' as his teacher read to him; later he guessed 'window?' as he pointed to the magnifying-glass in a 'Meg and Mog' book. Later still, he tried to get information from his teacher by his deliberate use of negatives. He would point to a picture of a milkman or a fireman and say 'That's not Daddy' and received the appropriate label 'No. That's the milkman (fireman).' In the excerpt above, he also points but goes on to contribute three short sentences: 'These are finger. It's not bread. My bread is square.' In response, he manages to receive back a considerable amount of detailed information and complex sentence structures from his teacher, a fluent English-speaker. Most of us use similar strategies of 'saying what we can' as we learn a new language. Returning to our Catalan story *La Ventafocs*, we see how much easier it is for a beginner to label objects or people, like *'Ventafocs'* or *'dama'* and gradually build upon these to *'Mira … aqui Ventafocs'* and so on rather than master long sentences like *'Mira, aqui teniu la Ventafocs!'* or *'Si haguessis vist qiiin vestit duia aquella dama!'*

In Chapter 5, we saw that lexical (word) clues are likely to be an important resource as young children begin reading in a new language. Different research studies showed us that children have an early understanding of one-to-one correspondence as well as an excellent memory and a sensitivity for words should they slip into the wrong language. At the same time, we saw that children are likely to be held back particularly by two factors: (1) they lack personal 'key' or meaningful words in the target language, and (2) they are forced to remember every individual word until they have enough 'chunks' of language at their fingertips. This chapter suggests a programme which starts from the child's own knowledge and experience and gradually moves outwards into the new world; it starts from the smallest units of meaning, the letters and words, and gradually links these into complete texts. The approach outlined in this chapter shares a number of common features with 'Language-Experience' approaches to beginning reading. But its crucial feature is not to tie children into known experiences. Rather, it has in mind the countless experiences of the new world to come. I call it an 'Inside-Out' approach. It is but one half of the programme, complemented by the global or 'Outside-In' approach based on the life and language of literature, which we shall meet in Chapter 7.

The chapter is divided into three sections: the first examines the theory behind the approach and explains the principles upon which it is based. The second section outlines ways in which similar principles are illustrated in different practices taking place at different times and in different countries. The third section presents practical ideas for a programme in classes of new language learners today. In Chapter 2, we asked how far teachers can 'scaffold' the learning of young new language learners in the classroom. This chapter outlines ways in which explicit 'scaffolding' may take place when working with very young children either in the classroom or in the home context.

What does an 'Inside-Out' approach to reading mean?

INFLUENCES FROM PSYCHOLOGY AND LINGUISTICS

During the 1950s and 1960s important parallel developments were taking place in psychology and linguistics. In psychology, the work of Piaget (1959) and in linguistics the work of Chomsky (1964) were influential in providing evidence to show that children do not learn simply by copying the actions and language of adults. Instead, they actively construct their own view of the world and use language both to represent and extend experiences made. In his book, *A Theory of Personality*, the American psychologist George Kelly (1955) outlines a view of 'personal constructs' which conveys vividly the active nature of human learning. He uses the metaphor of humans working as 'scientists'. Like scientists, we are constantly making hypotheses in order to predict what awaits us. If our hypothesis proves to be correct, the experience is stored within our 'construction' of reality to be used as a template for generalizing and predicting in similar circumstances. If wrong, it is discarded and a new hypothesis tried out. A simple example to illustrate this is 'waiting at the bus-stop'. We soon learn to predict that a bus will stop, especially if we hail it. However, it is essential to realize that our learning is specific to our cultural group. Although the bus-stop might be common to many cultures, knowing whether or not to queue, whether to get on at the front or back or whether to pay the driver or a conductor, is not.

Our language learning takes place in a similar way. We know that an infant learning the word 'dog' will generalize and predict that all four-legged animals are dogs until the prediction proves inadequate and a new word is learned. Young monolingual children are often still over-generalizing the past tense in nursery school when they tell us they have 'sticked their picture on', and so on. Language prediction can be extremely useful. In Chapter 5, we saw how even very young children were able to predict 'two wug-s' from their knowledge of English syntax. Imagine being at a party where loud music blocks out much of the conversation. If the talk is in a language we understand, we have little difficulty in predicting the sentence 'Haven't I – you – before?' We are able to do this first by understanding the context of the situation. Our conversation partner was hardly likely to be presenting complex medical findings. If this had been the case, and if we had been unfamiliar with the world of medicine, prediction would probably not have been possible. Then, our knowledge of syntax or the structure of the language enables us to complete what we cannot hear. Assuming our partner knows the language, he or she is hardly likely to be saying 'Haven't I mix you sun before?'

It takes little imagination to draw parallels between predicting life experiences and language structures and predicting words as we learn to read. Obviously, other 'clues' such as phonics will be useful, but, in the end, *meaning* will be paramount. In other words, it is better to predict (wrongly) 'Haven't I *met* you somewhere before?' if the text says 'Haven't I *seen* you somewhere before?' than 'Haven't I *sent* or *sand* you somewhere before?' which may contain a number of appropriate sounds but completely bypass the meaning. We are back to our 'Mir (Mr.) Pizza' example from Chapter 5. The key question then is: what enables learners to take the step from speaking to understanding writing on a page or screen, to realize that knowledge of life and language can help them make sense of words and texts?

'Language-Experience' approaches across the world

It was two inspired teachers working in very different circumstances during the 1950s and 1960s who showed how ideas from psychology and linguistics could be translated into practical reading programmes for both adults and children. Both shared a common approach, yet their interpretation was very different, for their learners were worlds apart. Their common starting point was that traditional learning materials simply did not make sense for their pupils. The teachers were Paolo Freire and Sylvia Ashton-Warner. Their approach teaches us much about a way into reading based upon personal and group experiences and their ideas are still inspirational to work now taking place in many parts of the world. How and why they abandoned traditional methods of teaching and chose radical alternatives is explained in more detail below.

'GENERATIVE WORDS': ADULTS LEARNING TO READ IN BRAZIL

Paolo Freire was a literacy teacher in Brazil where, during the 1950s and 1960s, few rural workers had been able to attend school. His innovatory literacy programme (translated into English in *Education: The Practice of Freedom* in 1973) was based on two interlocking principles:

1   Learning is not simply a passive memorising of letters and words but a creation on the part of the learner who is involved in self-transformation. Learners must actively take learning into their own hands and become agents of their learning. This means that learning becomes a dialogue between teacher and learner, symbolized by the words of the teacher who refers always to 'we' rather than 'you' as tasks are undertaken.
2   Learning does not, therefore, successfully take place where texts are meaningless for the life of the learner (Freire quotes the first sentence of a traditional reading primer 'Grace eats the grapes' where his learners have neither known anyone called Grace nor eaten a grape in their lives). Instead, learning must take place through 'generative words' or words which enable communication between the pupil and the world so that the content is identified with the learning process.

The programme takes place in five phases:

Phase 1: The teacher researches the vocabulary of the group of learners to find out which words are most weighted with meaning. These might be words linked with work, emotions or even colloquial phrases.

Phase 2: These generative words are sorted and ordered according to (a) their phonemic richness and phonetic difficulty (the simplest first – this becomes clearer below); (b) their semantic flexibility (some words can be used more frequently and flexibly than others); (c) the importance of the emotional content of a word (how far it triggers common emotions in the group).

Phase 3: The teacher builds 'codifications' around the generative words (stories or typical situations into which these words can be set).

Phase 4: A timetable or sequence of reading activities or lessons is designed which must be flexible.

Phase 5: The reading sessions take the following form: first, the situation involving the generative word is discussed and only after this is the word shown; the word is then broken down into 'phonemic families', for example:

'tijolo' (brick): ti – jo – lo

The family of the first syllable or 'piece' is shown:

ta – te – ti – to – tu

This is followed by the others:

$$ja - je - ji - jo - ju$$

$$la - le - li - lo - lu$$

A problem is posed by the teacher: do the pieces have something that is the same and something different? The students point out very quickly what is the same and what is different. The teacher then asks: can they therefore all be 'ti'? Again, the answer is not difficult. The same question is asked of the other syllables. Freire stresses that since it is preceded by a problem, the information is not a gift. The most important moment comes when the three families are presented together:

$$ta - te - ti - to - tu$$
$$ja - je - ji - jo - ju \quad \text{(the discovery card)}$$
$$la - le - li - lo - lu$$

At this moment, the group all begin to make words with the combinations available, for example: tatu (armadillo); luta (struggle); jato (jet); juta (jute); lula (squid); tela (screen), and so on. On the same first evening, the participants write the words. On the following day, they bring with them from home as many words as they were able to make with the combination of phonemes they have learned. Mistakes are unimportant at this early stage; what matters is the discovery of phonemic combinations. Finally, the group discuss which of these words are 'thinking' and which are 'dead' words.

Freire asked: 'How can one explain the fact that peope who were illiterate several days earlier could write words with complex phonemes before they had even studied them?' He offers an explanation: the use of 'thinking' or generative words plus learning the mechanism of phonemic combinations or being able to express themselves graphically in the way they spoke. A simple example illustrates this clearly: on the fifth day of discussion in which simple phonemes were being shown, one of the participants went to the blackboard to write (as he said) a 'thinking' word: *'o povo vai resouver os problemas do Brasil votando conciente'* ('the people will solve the problems of Brazil by informed voting'). As with other sentences, the group discussed the text, debating its significance in the context of their reality.

Like all approaches where phonics play an important role, Freire's generative words approach is easiest and works best with other phonically regular languages like Spanish and German. Nevertheless, the same principles can be used with phonically irregular languages such as English. For example, by using onset and rime (see Chapter 4), children began with the generative word 'gr-an' and went on to find 'gr-owl, gr-unt, gr-ip, gr-umpy' and so on, as well as 'r-an, p-an, c-an, D-an, f-an, m-an', and so on. Lina looked at her name and made up others for girls in her stories 'D-ina, M-ina, T-ina, N-ina', and so on. In each case, the crucial point is that new language learners also learn the *meaning* of the words they make and can use them appropriately in their own sentences.

'KEY VOCABULARY': MAORI CHILDREN READING IN NEW ZEALAND

At about the same time, yet on the other side of the world in New Zealand, Sylvia Ashton-Warner was making similar discoveries about the reading of the young Maori children in her infant class. Frustrated by their lack of progress using the 'Janet and John' readers from England, she realized that the texts these books were offering were as meaningless as 'Grace eats her grapes' to Brazilian illiterates. Within the framework offered in Part 1 of this book, we can explain the children's difficulties as follows: they were unable to 'situate' themselves in the social context of the classroom since their home language and culture and in particular their highly developed oral and musical culture from home were not recognized as relevant to school learning; nor could they 'situate' themselves in the mental context of the reading task, since they were not able to draw upon appropriate clues in a new language.

In the same way as for Freire's Brazilian adults, 'reading' using traditional primers did not make sense for Maori children in the New Zealand classroom. Ashton-Warner's action was radical for her time. She abandoned the textbooks and devised what she termed an 'organic approach' to learning to read. The principle of her approach was simple: children will immediately learn to read their own personal 'key words', words that have great personal meaning to them. Like Freire's 'generative words', she found that a bank of these special 'one-sight' words provided a stepping-stone into reading. In her classic book *Teacher* (1963: 28–9), she explains how and why she developed her approach:

> *Back to these first words. To these first books. They must be made out of the stuff of the child itself.*
>
> > *First words must have an intense meaning.*
> > *First words must already be part of the dynamic life.*
> > *First books must be made of the stuff of the child*
> > *himself whatever and wherever the child.*
>
> *The words, which I write on large tough cards and give to the children to read, prove to be one-look words if they are accurately enough chosen. And they are plain enough in conversation. It's the conversation that has to be got. However, if it can't be, I find that whatever a child chooses to make in the creative period may quite likely be such a word. But if the vocabulary of a child is still inaccessible, one can always begin him on the general Key Vocabulary common to any child in any race, a set of words bound up with security that experiments, and later on their creative writing, show to be organically associated with the inner world: 'Mummy', 'Daddy', 'kiss', 'frightened', 'ghost'.*

She explains in detail the mechanics of working with the key vocabulary approach. Its focus is at the beginning of the school day when children's energy is at its highest. The teacher needs just a supply of cards, about a foot long and five inches wide and a big black felt-tip pen. The cards which are already written on are kept in a plastic folder or cardboard container. Each morning, they are held up and claimed by their owners (names are written in small letters in a corner). While the children work in pairs reading to each other, the teacher calls one pair to read to her and to tell the new word each wants to learn. Any words unread are discarded for the moment. In this way children realize the importance of choosing only important words. After the morning break, the new words are taken out to see which ones are remembered. Those forgotten are immediately discarded. Later in the day, the children use their words as a bank as they go about their writing. Only when children have about 40 words in their collection do they start reading 'transitional books' which are the texts of older primary children who have written books on traditional Maori life and customs.

'WHOLE LANGUAGE' AND 'LANGUAGE-EXPERIENCE' APPROACHES

From 1964 to 1970, a major Schools Council research and development project in Britain known as the Programme in Linguistics and English Teaching, directed by Michael Halliday, set out to draw upon relevant findings from linguistics and other fields in developing materials for the teaching of English. Within this project, a smaller initial literacy team was created and led by David Mackay which became known as the 'Breakthrough' unit. Although the approach promoted by the team had its roots in theories of language development, rather than aiming to hand control over to children, ultimately it shared much with the instinctive notions of Paolo Freire and Sylvia Ashton-Warner that reading must above all *make sense* for the child and that the reader must take control of the learning. In Britain, this way of teaching early reading became known as the 'Language-Experience' approach; the US, New Zealand and Australia adopted the term 'Whole Language' approach, to indicate the relationship between listening, speaking, reading and writing as well as experience itself in learning to read. 'Whole Language' approaches in the US, Australia and New Zealand also drew many of their ideas and principles from Freire and Ashton-Warner's work as well as the the work of Chomsky and Piaget outlined earlier in this chapter.

In a similar way to the 'organic reading' approach, children learning with a 'Language-Experience' approach draw individually upon past experiences to compose their first written texts and join together to share these with others in a group or the whole class. But there are differences between Breakthrough and both Ashton-Warner's and Freire's approach. The focus of the 'Language-Experience' approach in Britain and the 'Whole Language' approach in the US, Australia and New Zealand is on the structure of language, on syntax rather than lexis. The starting point for the child is the composition of experience sentences rather than recognizing personal key words. For example, instead of simply 'possessing' a personal key word like 'tigers', if Ashton-Warner's Maori child had been learning with the Language-Experience approach, s/he would have learned to put the 'tiger' in a sentence from the start, for example, I stick my knife in the tiger (from Ashton-Warner's own example) and to go on and refer to the individual words, the sentence and, probably, the full stop at the end of the sentence. The aim, therefore, is to build upon a child's knowledge and awareness of language and metalanguage (for example, by understanding and using terms like 'full stop', 'question mark', 'sentence', and so on). Although overtaken by a revival of interest in phonic methods without relating them to children's own vocabulary or experiences in Britain and the US during the early twenty-first century, 'Language-Experience' and 'Whole Language' approaches hold their own as an important element in classroom reading programmes and are recognized in many parts of the world as an invaluable tool in introducing young children to literacy in both their first and a new language.

Questions for reflection

- In what ways did ideas from linguistics and psychology during the twentieth century underpin new approaches to teaching reading?
- What do 'Language-Experience' and 'Whole Language' approaches share in common?
- In what ways do those approaches differ from phonic methods which do not relate to children's own language or experience in teaching reading?
- Describe the role of the teacher depending largely on (a) 'Language-Experience' or 'Whole Language' approaches; (b) phonic methods. How might these be similar or different?

The 'Inside-Out' approach in action

The 'Inside-Out' approach to beginning reading draws principally upon theories of learning which the reader has already met in Part 1 of this book:

- that language and experience are inextricably linked (Sapir, 1970). Effective use of semantic clues in reading a text will depend upon understanding or 'feeling' for the experiences described in the language in which they are described
- that learning to read and write promotes a greater consciousness of language structure and that bilinguals already have a headstart in this (Vygotsky, 1962)
- that the teacher's awareness of the child's home culture and an explicit introduction to the

new culture of school are prerequisites for the 'joint culture creation' (Bruner, 1986) important for successful classroom learning.

Although the 'Inside-Out' approach builds upon children's existing knowledge and experiences, it looks firmly towards the new language and culture which the child is about to enter through literacy. The child's cultural knowledge is used rather as a springboard for comparing differences and similarities between languages and cultural practices, for showing children that stepping into a new world provides access to exciting experiences but need not mean abandoning the language and culture of home. Within this framework, the educator plays a vital role as mediator, understanding as much as possible about family funds of knowledge and the children's home reading practices, while providing a bridge to the new culture, knowing that the children in turn may well act as mediator for parents and later for younger siblings.

In classes where new language learners are a small minority, we know that fluent target-language peers do a much more efficient job than teachers at helping young children relive experiences in a new language through play. Later in this chapter we see in what contexts this 'teaching' most successfully occurs. In classes where the teacher may be the only (or almost only) target-language speaker, s/he will need to be constantly alive to his/her role as language model, carefully considering vital 'chunks' of language needed, initiating and practising them in a variety of spoken and written contexts. For this reason, more whole-class or teacher-directed discussions are likely to take place than in a mixed mono-lingual/bilingual classroom. The 'Inside-Out' approach differs from Language Experience programmes in that the teacher aims to recognize reading experiences brought from home by the children but explicitly to model and discuss different types of reading in different contexts. In other words, the teacher introduces children to the host culture and language by comparisons with others or making it 'strange'. The approach is also only one half of the complete programme which also depends upon the 'Outside-In' approach outlined in Chapter 7.

WORKING FROM THE INSIDE-OUT: AN OVERALL PLAN

By its nature, any approach based upon the knowledge, experiences and emotions of individual or groups of children cannot be contained within a rigid programme. Each classroom culture will reflect different adventures, different classroom stories. Ashton-Warner and Freire both illustrate clearly how 'generative words' or 'key vocabularies' will be specific to different cultural groups and the programme must, therefore, be flexible. Some words are likely to be tied to the language in which they are experienced. In the Maori culture, for example, certain words awakened deep emotions in the child's first language; to have translated them would have rendered them meaningless. 'Pa', the name given to a Maori village, was one such word and it remained as 'pa' on the children's cards. These key words can be discussed with children and parents and form an excellent basis for discussion which draws upon the knowledge of new language learners: 'How can we say "mummy" in Mandarin?'; 'How many different words can we find for "mummy"?'; 'Do they all sound nearly the same or are some very different?' 'Can we write "mummy" using different scripts?' 'Can we make a collage using them?' The only Chinese child in a multilingual class then becomes a source of wonder as she writes what sounds very similar to the English 'mum' ('ma') but looks very different in print.

What follows below are some classroom suggestions on beginning an 'Inside-Out' approach with young new language learners entering school. The framework is divided into three headings:

- First things first: starting with questions
- Resourcing the 'Inside-Out' approach in the classroom
- Working from the 'Inside-Out': a simple procedure.

FIRST THINGS FIRST: STARTING WITH QUESTIONS

An essential first step in the 'Inside-Out' approach is to find out about the knowledge and strengths of the children, families and communities represented in the classroom. Although the questions below will not all be relevant in every situation they are examples for the early years teacher's repertoire:

Home languages and literacies: questions to ask

- Was the child born in the host country?
  What is the country of origin/religion of the family?
  What is the child's mother tongue?
  Is this the language the child uses at home?
  To whom and in what contexts?
  Does the child use the target language at home?
  To whom and in what contexts?
  Does the child watch English television/videos?
  Does the child watch videos in any other language?
  Can the child speak/understand any other language(s)?
- Is the child (or older siblings) learning to read/write the mother tongue in community language/other private class?

Continues over

Are any other community classes being attended (for example, Mosque class) and do they involve reading and/or writing in additional language(s)?
If so, how often do children attend and for how long?
What standard has the child reached?
What materials does the child use in these classes?
What approach does the teacher use?
Is there a pattern of tuition the children are accustomed to?
If so, what form does it take?
Can community class teachers be invited to talk with the staff?
What other reading materials are available in children's homes?
- What skills/funds of knowledge are available in the community and in families?
In what ways can they be utilized?
Do parents understand how reading is taught at school?
How does the school explain its approach to parents?
Are community class teachers involved in parents' meetings?
- What type of reading activities do children take home?
How are these explained to parents?
Is there a dialogue with parents on the nature of tasks given?
What efforts are made to ensure that parents with limited English understand tasks?
How is the help of siblings enlisted?

Finally, but most importantly:

- How can the school go about finding out all of this?
Will it need reorganization of timetables, duties of ancillary staff, and so on?
Can the assistance of education departments at universities or colleges of education be called upon?
Can the work link with teacher in-service or advanced degree work where teachers adopt the role of teacher/researcher in the classroom?

RESOURCING THE 'INSIDE-OUT' APPROACH

Ideas for resourcing the classroom are not difficult if we remember the aims of this approach. The questions to ask are: how far do resources chosen both build upon children's home and community knowledge and enable them to enter a new world? Do they foster children's awareness of what they already know, skills they already have? Do they show children that 'reading' means different things to different people in different contexts, takes place in different languages and can be used for different purposes?

The resources suggested below differ very little from those used in every good early years classroom across the world. After all, to a certain degree, every child enters a new world and a new 'language' when walking for the first time through the school gates. Margaret Donaldson opens *Children's Minds* (1978) with the memorable quote from Laurie Lee which tells us how upset a 5-year-old was on his first school day, waiting for the 'present' which never came (his teacher told him to sit where he was 'for the present').

Nevertheless, the differences will be quite different in nature and scope for children who do not recognize their language and ways of life in the classroom or for those countries where all children are learning in a new language. Consequently, although the resources themselves may present few surprises, in predominantly multilingual or bilingual classes as well as in classes where all the children are learning in a new language there will be more teacher-direction in their use. This is because teachers will need to provide carefully planned experiences tied to the spoken and written language currently in focus.

Below are the most important resources proposed for the 'Inside-Out' approach. Obviously, classrooms in different countries will vary enormously; the items listed below demand a minimum of expensive equipment.

The basics

For 'Inside-Out' class and group reading sessions, the teacher has a literacy area which houses permanently the materials needed on a daily basis. These may be some or all of the following: card (may be recycled or the reverse side of packaging) or stiff paper cut into strips, somewhere on which to display recent sentences and words of the children so that they can be seen clearly (additionally, the whiteboard, blackboard or a large magnet-board might also be used if available), containers to store familiar words cards and sentence strips from past weeks, a thick pen, a sentence stand into which the words can be inserted or magnets to display them on the magnet-board, scissors, and word banks (either teacher or child produced; for example, a large card picture of a face with words slotted into appropriate places – nose on nose, and so on). These take their place beside old and current Big Books made by the class, a tape recorder with tapes where the texts of Big Books are recorded, alphabet books and computer software to practise the alphabet and so on (if available). Aside, but close to hand, is a camera to record drama or other experiences for the class Big Books. This area will be in addition to the book and story area attached to 'Outside-In' sessions which are outlined in Chapter 7.

The puppets

We have only to reflect back to the examples in Chapter 3 to remind ourselves of the myriad of experiences and corresponding complexity of language gained in the first language at home before a child enters formal school. Consequently, teachers are going to need to structure their time carefully to maximize children's experiences and to tie these experiences to essential chunks of the target language needed. It may, then, be a relief to discover that they have extra 'magic' teacher assistants waiting to be called upon. The only criterion is that teachers, themselves, must believe in them.

The assistants are small, may be scruffy and cheap (or self-made) and rely for life upon the teacher. Yet, used well, they will teach far more than the teacher within her own skin. Glove puppets are an integral part of an 'Inside-Out' approach in early literacy tuition for new language learners. At least two puppets are needed; one girl and one boy who also represent children new to the language and culture of the school. Preferably, a collection should be built up of boys and girls from the different linguistic backgrounds of all the children in the class. Different members of their families may also be added. Gradually, puppets from well-loved traditional tales (see also Chapter 7) will also become part of a collection. However, a kernel of these, perhaps two or at the most six, are likely to become the key figures in every class reading session. The puppets become 'real' people, have names which are meaningful to the children, and have their own voices and their own personalities which are constant over time. Importantly, they are not available for the children to play with – otherwise their magic disappears. They live separately, hidden from view but easily accessible for the teacher (their dwelling may be as humble as a plastic bag) and need to be awakened or called by the children in a particular way (practising a particular point – perhaps a song a child sings or a greeting given). They are excellent language teachers; they use simple language which is carefully structured to practise the known and extend the 'child's repertoire to new expressions' and they model a particular chunk of language or a language structure which the children unselfconsciously repeat over and over again.

Like the teacher, the puppets serve as mediators, introducing children to the new language and culture, while being familiar with those which the children bring from home. Shy children are able to empathize with a quiet and timid puppet, while gaining courage to speak for the first time in a new language themselves. At the same time, a naughtier, more extrovert puppet enables children to practise well-known reprimands. Through their incipient bilingualism, the puppets reflect the children's own position and encourage them to tackle the learning of a new language arid culture. Their role as members of a culture with which children identify together with their adventurousness in entering a new world allow children 'a security which experiments' (Meek, 1979); the love of being scared as they enter dangerous situations, yet having the comfort of knowing that they, themselves, remain safe and sound. Of all the resources needed for the 'Inside-Out' reading classroom, the puppets are the most important. Later in this chapter we see how they come to life and animate beginning reading sessions.

The socio-dramatic play area

The socio-dramatic play area is a focal point of the 'Inside-Out' approach to early literacy. As in every early years classroom, the area must be imaginatively planned and well-resourced according to the experiences the teacher aims the children to enact. Where there are a number of native speakers in the class, much can be left to their teaching skills. In a study of a 5-year-old Taiwanese child's first two months of English learning in a linguistically mixed pre-school environment in the US, Hatch and her colleagues (1979) made some interesting observations. They found that 46 per cent of the child's comments were imperatives, 40 per cent 'Wh-' questions and only 14 per cent statements. What the child seemed to be doing was 'chunking' formulae contained in the input from other children, for example, 'What's that?' often became 'What is this aeroplane?' In other words, the child was able to derive rules combined from the question/ answer patterns of conversations. A little later, the child began memorizing large chunks of the target language which he used appropriately in conversations regardless of whether he understood it or not. Hatch and her colleagues trace ways in which the Taiwanese child does this:

First language child: *I can beat your brother up. I can beat him up.*
Second language child: *You can beat him up, huh. I can beat him to my party 'n you can beat him*
                            'n you can beat my brother. I'll beat you up.

Very early first language learning also takes place in this way. In his study of a child's language between the ages of one and two, Ron Scollon (1979) described how much is learned in the form of 'pre-packaged routines', language which is incorporated from adults' speech without being internally analysed. This type of approach in second-language learning appears to take place only during early childhood, since older children and adults are constrained by the fear of having to make a relevant reply in conversations. Play, then, provides an ideal opportunity for young children to learn formulae which can be used as 'chunks' of appropriate language. The language during play is predictable, repetitious and well contextualized which contrasts sharply with the 'Wh-' questions children are likely to meet from an adult.

Nevertheless, socio-dramatic play areas in classes where either all or the large majority of children have a limited understanding of the target language need particular planning which recognizes that the teacher provides the only or one of very few role models for the target language. In some countries, this situation occurs frequently. In Spain, since the death of General Franco in 1975, the Catalan language has gained enormously in importance until now all children in Catalonia receive their early years schooling and early literacy tuition in the heritage language. However, a number of children still enter school speaking only Castilian (Spanish); an increasing number of new language learners largely speak Moroccan. Early years classrooms are geared to 'immersing' these children in the Catalan language and role-play in the socio-dramatic area plays an important part in this. The teacher works with native language speakers or more fluent children if they are available (or herself and the puppets if they are not) 'modelling' the language of specific situations or practices in the new language and culture, such as making a paella, and so on.

Our socio-dramatic play area will, therefore, be resourced for children to enact situations which will often be geared to the 'adventure' of the lesson. The area will be equipped with resources reflecting the theme of the moment. For example, if the theme is 'Food' (see Chapter 8) and the 'Inside-Out' sentences 'I love-' (crisps and so on), one half of the socio-dramatic area may represent a traditional sweet/tobacconist shop while the other becomes a Turkish/Indian, and so on sweet shop/bakery. In this way use of an appropriate language in each situation becomes clear to the children. Dressing-up clothes will also be geared to the theme or specific reading sessions within it. For example, if the theme is 'My family' and the 'Inside-Out' sentences 'My – is sick', clothes and resources might be geared towards the doctor, patient and 'parent' in the song 'Poor little – (the name of a puppet –) is sick' (to the tune of 'Miss Polly has a dolly who is sick, sick, sick'). Separate dressing-up clothes for drama will be related to specific stories focused on during 'structured stories' (see Chapter 7).

Cooking

We saw in Part 1 of this book that eating and drinking habits are very particular to different cultural groups. Understanding the rituals and language surrounding food is a big step forward for the novice to a new culture. It is clear that predicting a text will be so much easier if children can relate what is happening to their own experience. Living within a Hong Kong kitchen at home in Northampton, Tony was probably as dumbfounded by toast and marmalade for breakfast as Europeans might be by eating soup first thing in the morning or by finishing off a meal with soup instead of ice cream. It is impossible to glance along a row of children's books, traditional tales, songs and rhymes, and so on without seeing how often different items of food figure (plum and cherry pies, jam tarts, bacon, porridge, gingerbread men, turnips, pasta, dumplings, ice cream, pickles, cheese, salami, and so on). Food is an excellent medium to show how language is intimately linked with experience. We may all recall how effortless it is to remember even difficult names of exotic foods when abroad in comparison with other lexis which cannot be related to such pleasant experiences.

Cooking and eating are also an excellent means of drawing children's awareness to words in different languages and showing how the name of a dish in one language simply cannot be translated and allowing children to use 'key words' in their first language meaningfully in sentences in the new language. Language used while cooking is purposeful and can easily be linked with songs and rhymes (either existing ones or with texts invented by the teacher, for example, 'This is the way we roll our dough ...', and so on to the tune of 'Here we go round the mulberry bush'). Although not as essential as the puppets or socio-dramatic play, easy and frequent access to cooking facilities is a great advantage for a teacher working to an 'Inside-Out' beginning reading approach. Preparation of food or having tea parties does not have to entail actual cooking; rituals can also be learned through sandwiches, biscuits and squash. Nevertheless, all these activities will mean engaging the assistance of extra adults in the classroom – an excellent way of accessing the different funds of knowledge held by members in the community.

'Playing school'

In monolingual classrooms, a 'playing school' area is often viewed as part of socio-dramatic play provision in the early years. In multilingual classes or in classrooms where all children are learning in a new language it receives a special status. Like the puppets, 'playing school' provides a bridge for children from their home and community to the new culture because it recognizes that 'school', 'the classroom' and 'classroom learning' may be interpreted very differently by children regularly attending very different classrooms (for example, community language classes to learn the mother tongue and the state school). This is where the teacher as researcher is important. The 'playing school' resources should provide utensils to which the children may be accustomed from both worlds (perhaps lined exercise books, pens, simple primers, a blackboard or slate and chalk for handwriting practice, a computer, if available, as well as alphabet books and simple dictionaries, the sentence and key word cards, simple word banks for themes covered in reading sessions, rough paper for practice writing, different thicknesses of pencils and the computer which represent the host classroom). Different 'teaching' methods will be played out by the children in formal and informal situations. When a drama is enacted before the class, it provides an excellent opportunity for fostering children's awareness of 'reading' in different contexts, and signals that both approaches are valid, simply different.

Songs, poems and rhymes

A collection of songs, poems and rhymes relating to the theme of each reading session is essential to assist children in 'chunking' the target language. Nursery rhymes are particularly important and can be illustrated and dramatized by a class or group of children. The tunes of these rhymes can then be adapted to practise whatever new language structures are being taught. Children who are at the very earliest stages of language learning will often be able to sing perfectly songs containing difficult language structures. These are important for a number of reasons: they enable new language learners to practise with others the pronunciation of difficult sounds which means that they do not have to 'perform' alone (the difficulty of pronunciation for new language learners can often be underestimated); they give children large chunks of language which can gradually be used in conversations. For example, 'Pussy cat, pussy cat where have you been? I've been to London to see the Queen' can be used as a song to question a puppet or a child, 'Shahina, Shahina, where have you been …?', or as a game to practise spoken and written language whereby one child either picks a card with a place name (London, Bangladesh, India, home, school, hospital, park, and so on) hides it and asks the others to guess 'Where have I been?' From these large units, children learn to abstract sets of rules for the new language (from our 'Pussy cat' example 'Wh-' question + form of present perfect for the verb 'to be' + to + place name + to + infinitive). Obviously, the child masters all of this unconsciously. Nevertheless, automaticity will facilitate the use of both syntactic and lexical clues during early reading.

Songs are an integral part of the 'Inside-Out' approach where they are used in purposeful situations. For example, the class sings 'Good morning' to the puppets in order to wake them, (see Chapter 8) to sequence the day's routines with corresponding times: 'This is the way we wake up …' (sung to the tune of 'Here we go round the mulberry bush'), or to act out a drama where a puppet is sick: 'Poor little Dina is sick, sick, sick …' (sung to the tune of 'Miss Polly had a dolly who was sick, sick, sick'). These songs are written out in large print so that a child, teacher or puppet can point to each word as the texts are sung. Classroom rhymes also provide a meaningful context for the class to chant together, practise pronunciation and gain confidence (for example, 'Who put the cookie in the cookie jar?' 'We're going on a bear hunt' or 'Pop!' by Michael Rosen). The teacher must innovate freely inventing new texts for well-loved tunes. These often become the most popular songs as the melody is well-known and easily learned. Again, the puppets are always at hand to encourage children in their singing.

Linking home and school: taking the school culture home and bringing other cultures into school

Considerable evidence is available from numerous projects in English-speaking countries which points to the increased progress made by children when they are able to read at home with caregivers. Yet a dilemma has always existed: how can parents who cannot read the target language themselves go about helping their children? Below are ideas for beginner readers to use with caregivers who do not write the target language but are literate (as almost all are) in their mother tongue. A main principle is to recognize both the knowledge held by caregivers as mediators of the home language and culture to the child and the incipient knowledge of the child in mediating the host language and culture to the parents. A dynamic two-way process is, therefore, set in action. Parents will be 'expert' in the home language; children in the target language. A second principle is that children take home reading which the parents *understand* and with which they can *assist* as well as *learn* from the child. They are not 'deskilled' by a lack of understanding of what is expected of them. Even if the child needs to translate the word, the caregiver can discuss the home language translation and, at the same time, learn the target language word.

How does this take place? Each school will devise its own programme in the light of findings from 'initial questions' rather than adopting a programme which may have been devised for fluent target language speakers. Ideas are explained at a parents' meeting which is likely to be well attended if parents know exactly what is on the agenda. A possible programme for the very first stages is as follows: children take home 'key words' from classroom reading sessions, practise 'matching' them to words and pictures on a card and spelling them (the alphabet is usually familiar to all). If possible, the caregiver writes the word in the child's mother tongue on the back and discusses the word with the child, encouraging him/her to use the word in sentences. With this kernel of key words, the child practises making sentences and completing a variety of word games. The child writes the sentences made in an exercise book which, like the books used in many community classes, is specifically for this purpose (see Gregory, 1995, for a fuller description of work with linguistic minority parents).

It is important that any homework expected of parents should all be demonstrated explicitly at the parents' meeting to which interested siblings should also be invited. Caregivers who do not manage to attend the session will almost always respond to a home visit by the teacher. At the same time, parents are invited into the class to complete this work with a group of children in their mother tongue. If all (or almost all) the children speak the same mother tongue and bilingual support is available, an ideal opportunity arises for a bilingual approach using the same 'key words' and sentences in both languages, for evidence available indicates that even incipient biliterates have advantages over new language learners who have no tuition in their mother tongue (Fitzpatrick, 1987). Some projects using this approach have been undertaken in Germany, where a Turkish community class teacher works along-side the German teacher so that children complete work in German and the mother tongue (Holscher, 1995). Home–school links depend upon the energy and perseverance of teachers and take a long time to establish. Only in retrospect and over the long term does it become obvious that every minute was one well spent.

WORKING FROM THE 'INSIDE-OUT': A SIMPLE PROCEDURE

With information from the initial questions in mind and with essential resources in place, a simple framework links practice with theory. Within this framework, the teacher considers the following:

- How can the child be made to feel 'a reader' from the very start?
- Which themes are closest to the child and the family?
- Which key experiences from the host culture should be explicitly introduced and how?

- Which emotions are important in the child's life and how can they be linked with early reading?
- Which key words might be essential in each of the above?
- Which chunks of language will be vital?

The plan below provides an example showing how teachers can begin to provide new language learners with lexical and syntactic clues in the new language and how these are embedded in the semantic knowledge of the host culture. The starting point of the plan is to introduce experiences which excite children and to recognize their fears upon entering an unknown world in a new language while showing that the classroom is a safe haven in which to experiment and where fears can be reconciled. Each theme, therefore, sets out with an adventure which is based upon experiences from the home or school culture. Themes are endless, but there are common key interests as children begin school: loves, hates, new babies, accidents, illness, fears, journeys and other adventures.

A DAILY 'INSIDE-OUT' READING SESSION

1 Start with an 'adventure' or drama which draws upon the child's emotions: fear, love, hate, sympathy or simply the excitement of guessing the unknown, for example, Dina (a puppet) is in hospital following an accident.

2 Initially, 'model' the experience through the puppets. They use (sometimes hesitantly and sometimes needing the children's help) essential chunks of the target language which are to be introduced and practised. This explicit modelling is particularly important where most of the class are beginners to the new language. The chunks (or structures) of language practised will form the basis for early class 'Big Books' (large books visible to the whole class which may also be self-made) for reading together. As the theme is developed together orally, children are encouraged to experiment and the language used is less controlled.

3 After the scene has been enacted by the puppets, the children offer their own parallel experiences and key words are noted by the teacher. They then re-enact the scene shown by the puppets. Sometimes, the teacher will use a song she has found or invented which practises these particular language chunks. The children will act out the song, often using the dressing-up clothes or other props as they do so.

4 During the early stages, one or two sentences (later more) are written on strips of card using the language chunks which the teacher wishes to practise and containing the children's key words. Two copies of each sentence are made: one is cut into separate words which fit into the teacher's word stand or can be attached to the magnet-board;

the other remains intact as a sentence and is stored with a collection of past class sentences.

5 The class reads the sentence cut into individual words in chorus after the teacher first and then individually. As the teacher changes children's key words, the child who originally 'owned' the word is given the chance to read the sentence first. During the early stages, one or two replacements are sufficient, but these increase rapidly as the children gain in confidence as readers. The teacher is careful to refer to terms like 'word', 'sentence', 'full stop', 'question mark', and so on as the children work and, where relevant, calls children's attention to letters which recur.

6 The children play games with the words, for example, one child removes a word while the other children close their eyes and then guess which word is missing or the words are jumbled by a child and need to be reordered.

7 Finally, the sentence is entered in the class news-book and illustrated by the child whose key word it contains. These big sturdy books, together with the class sentence, past sentences, word cards and plastic stand are easily accessible for the children to practise with each other during free moments in the day.

8 At odd moments during the day when the class is assembled together, take the pile of key words. Choose a word and ask the child to whom it 'belongs' (or any child who volunteers) to read the word first and then to use the word in a sentence or question. This is very important in helping children to both 'chunk' the language and to pick out individual words in the chunks.

9 Wherever possible, draw the children's attention to the phonic make-up of key words and find words following a similar pattern (for example, s - ick, p - ick, l - ick, and so on) and practise these in sentences.

Throughout the reading sessions, some points to remember:

• Do allow children time to respond. The temptation to assist a new language learner quickly is great, but sometimes reduces children's confidence in trying to pronounce words themselves.

• Do recognize the value of reading in chorus before asking a child to read alone. Imagine again the 'Ventafocs' example and the difference between joining in with friends and having to pronounce strange words alone.

• Do understand the child who is too shy at first to take part actively in class reading. Listening is an essential part of early second language learning and some children need much longer than others before beginning to speak.

• Do remember the 'magic' teacher-assistants, the puppets: they will succeed where 'normal' mortals fail.

Questions for reflection

- How does an 'Inside-Out' approach differ from other 'Language-Experience' or 'Whole Language' approaches?
- What key words do you think children in your school or community might have?
- What classroom resources will be most appropriate to your classroom or setting?
- Can you add other questions to the list on children's 'Home Languages and Literacies'?

SUMMARY

In this chapter, we have seen ways in which the teacher may explicitly 'scaffold' and 'model' the learning of children using an 'Inside-Out' approach to beginning reading in school. From the framework offered, we see how explicit 'scaffolding' takes place through:

- ◆ recognizing children's existing linguistic skills and cultural knowledge and building these into both teaching content and teaching strategies

- ◆ limiting the size of the reading task by introducing explicitly common new lexis and language 'chunks'

- ◆ modelling chunks of language orally and in an idealized way through the puppets and/or songs and socio-dramatic play

- ◆ devising home–school reading programmes which recognize the role of both parent and child as mediator of different languages and cultures and which families feel comfortable with.

A final unique feature of the 'Inside-Out' approach is that it is not designed to be used in isolation but to be only half of the reading programme. It is the other half, looking from the 'Outside-In', to which we now turn.

Further reading

Ashton-Warner, S. (1963) *Teacher.* London: Penguin (reprinted in 1980 by Virago Publishers, London).

Cochran-Smith, M. (1984) *The Making of a Reader.* Norwood, NJ: Ablex.

Freire, P. (1973) *Education: The Practice of Freedom.* London: Writers' and Readers' Publishing Co-op.

Gibbons, P. (1995) *Learning to Learn in a Second Language.* Newtown, Australia: Primary English Teaching Association.

Starting with the world: the 'Outside-In' approach to reading

Six-year-old Sunit and Kamlyit are studying a crab which they have brought back from a trip to the seaside.

Sunit: *We went in our rocket.*
              We saw a giant crab in the sky.
Kamlyit: *The claws were open.*
              It was crushing the sun.
Sunit: *But the sun was too hot.*
              It burned the crab.
              Crab breathed out onto sun.
              And it turned colder.
              And the crab could hold the sun.
Kamlyit: *And crush it.*
              And eat it.

KEY TERMS

BISC (basic interpersonal communication skills)	Natural informal communication, for example, conversation, home or playground language.
CALP (cognitive academic language proficiency)	Academic language used for school learning or the language of books.
Onomatopoeia	A word that imitates the sound it is describing, for example, click, buzz, moo, quack, meow.
Metaphor and simile	Both terms that describe a comparison. A metaphor describes something as if *it is* something else, for example, You <u>are</u> my sunshine; A good book <u>is</u> food for thought. A simile describes something as if it is <u>like</u> something else, for example, Your eyes are <u>like</u> the sun; A good book is like a good meal.
Collaborative reading/ structured story	Terms to describe structured programmes of reading whereby children work together with a teacher or more experienced adult to explore written stories. Collaborative reading is suitable in classrooms where only some children are new language learners; structured story is designed for groups or classes where all or most children are new to the target language.

Excited from their trip into an unknown world of shells, waves, seaweed and jellyfish, Sunit and Kamlyit (above) are imagining an even more adventurous journey they might make. Eighteen months ago, they appeared unable to understand simple instructions given by their teacher in the new language; now, they have a range of lexis and syntax at their fingertips and are able to 'map' these onto new experiences taking place in the target language. Sometimes, experience and language might narrowly miss each other as when Sunit saw the sea for the first time and shouted excitedly to the others 'Look, that big puddle!', but he was soon able to relate all the illustrations and stories he had seen and heard about the sea to its reality.

How are these children now able to use a new language so impressively? Let us focus more closely on their achievement in terms of the lexis and syntax the children use. They both realize that the past tense is usually used for story-telling and they can use both regular (burned, breathed, turned) and irregular forms (went, were, saw, was, could) as well as the past continuous form (was crushing). They have also mastered the comparative forms of adjectives (colder) and are comfortable with some prepositions (in, onto). Finally, they have a fascinating array of lexis suitable for dramatic story-telling (rocket, giant crab, claws, crush, burn, breathe, eat, and so on). Kamlyit particularly loves 'crush' which he uses twice. A glance at these words shows how they are likely to fit into Ashton-Warner's 'key vocabulary'; they belong to a world of fear and violence, yet the children know that it is all imagination and that they are in the security of the classroom. Yet how might the children invent a story so confidently using suitable lexis when we know from Chapter 5 that story language demanding CALP (cognitive academic language proficiency) is so much more difficult than everyday talk or BISC (basic interpersonal communication skills)? According to Jim Cummins (1979) this can take many years to learn in a new language, yet these children have been learning English formally for only a year.

The answer might lie in their classroom experience with a wide range of books and stories. Looking closely at the children's text, some features seem familiar to their teacher. She knows that they have often entered the world of giants; 'Jack and the Beanstalk' was a favourite story. They certainly have 'chunks' of language containing comparatives and superlatives in their repertoire from 'Goldilocks and the Three Bears' and 'The Three Billy Goats Gruff', and so on. Yet, their story seems even more familiar to their teacher. Suddenly, she remembers that a longer theme of work the term before centred on the Anansi Spider stories from Africa. Remarkably, the children have used the lexis and syntax of one spider story (*Anansi the Spider* by Gerald McDermott, 1972) which they had listened to many times on a tape with dramatic sound effects and had woven their own meanings into it.

Sunit and Kamlyit are not unusual. What they show us is the immense influence of the written story heard time and time again in enabling new language learners to make a new language and new world their own. In a book called *Coming to Know* edited by Phillida Salmon (1981), Margaret Meek writes of the value of reading or telling stories as 'handing down the magic' from one generation to the next. This chapter examines the magic whereby written stories can provide a unique 'scaffold' for new language readers in building up graphophonic, lexical and syntactic clues. The chapter is divided into three sections. The first asks: what is an 'Outside-In' approach to reading and what is the magic which story books are able to feed into all the clues new language learners draw upon as they begin reading? The second section presents an 'Outside-In' approach for classes where all (or almost all) the children are early stage new language learners. The third part of the chapter offers the same approach for use in multilingual classrooms with a number of mother-tongue speakers or more fluent new language learners. Each of these two sections presents both ideas for resources and suggested procedures for teaching. In each section, we see ways in which modelling and scaffolding can guide our teaching strategies when working with an 'Outside-In' approach to reading with emergent bilingual children.

What does an 'Outside-In' approach to reading mean?

Hearers of folk fairy tales, without being aware of it, experience a sort of initiation not unlike that in the customs of some primitive peoples … the folk fairy tale transposes the initiation process into the sphere of the imagination. (Lüthi, 1970: 103)

An 'Outside-In' approach to early reading with new language learners works through the vehicle of stories and narrative. It provides teachers with a framework for teaching the following:

- the structure of a story (beginning, middle and end)
- the language of story (metaphors, similes, onomatopoeia, and so on)
- the 'chunking' of story language, for example, 'Once upon a time …' 'happily ever after …'
- an initiation into universal truths, morals across cultures while recognizing the differences between them
- the linking of different clues needed for reading (semantic, syntactic, bibliographic, lexical and grapho-phonic, see Chapters 4 and 5) in a meaningful way.

Unlike most spoken conversations, written stories are structured. This structure is often referred to as a 'story grammar' (Lüthi, 1970). Put simply, texts have beginnings, middles and ends, identifiable 'chunks' of texts which act together as parts. Luke shows how 'Goldilocks' can be 'parsed' using a story grammar template:

Three bears at home (setting/main characters) » Bears leave home; Goldilocks arrives (initiating event/main character) » Goldilocks is hungry (problem #1) » Father Bear's porridge (attempt

#1) » too salty (outcome #1) » Mother Bear's porridge (attempt #2) » too sweet (outcome #2)
» Baby Bear's porridge (attempt #3) … (Luke, 1993: 36)

Carol Fox (1988) and Henrietta Dombey (1988) show how a familiarity with this 'grammar' transforms the language of young children who store story-language from books in memory for retellings of their own stories. In this way, they are able to call upon 'chunks' of language which will later help them in predicting written versions of the same texts. When 5-year-old monolingual Josh declares in his telling of a story 'What was his dismay when he got up there? There was gnashing of teeth', he shows that his language repertoire is ready and waiting to predict the texts of books he cannot yet read. The contrast between 'conversation' and 'stories' is apparent even with new language learners' simplest retellings. Compare, for example, the conversation between an adult and 5-year-old Parag, who is new to the language of school. As they look at a fish in a tank together their talk might run something like this:

Child: *This, (pointing to fish)*
Adult: *What? Fish?*
or: *What's this?*

Other questions by the adult wishing to continue the conversation are plausible, such as: Where's the fish? Whose fish is that? Is it yours? How many fish are there? What colour is it? What's the fish doing? Little reflection is needed to show that the child's answer is likely to comprise a single word and that the conversation will, at the very most, be limited. In contrast, 5-year-old Ikhlaq is glancing through the story of *Topiwalo the Hatmaker* (Harmony Publishing) and making his own story:

Night-time
I see a monkey
On the roof of my house
He was eating a banana
Monkey eating banana
Banana eating monkey
I said
Why are you eating that banana?
And I kicked him off
into the water

Even in such a simple narration, the book supports Ikhlaq in setting the scene and giving his story a structure (a beginning, middle and end). Edie Garvie (1990) refers to stories as 'vehicles' for teaching about a new language and culture. A story, she says, is 'going somewhere and the learner wants to reach the end' of the journey' (Garvie, 1990: 31) and this is precisely what distinguishes Ikhlaq's story from Parag's conversation starter above.

Traditional tales simultaneously transcend and unite cultures by depicting universal morals and truths. In *Stories and Meanings* (1985), Harold Rosen neatly coins stories as being 'the common possession of humankind – part of the deep structure of the grammar of our world'. Within the 'security which experiments' provided by the classroom, world-known traditional tales help all children develop not just linguistic, but sensory and emotional acuity. For example, Perrault's 'Cinderella' (or was it, perhaps, first of Chinese origin? We simply do not know) not only invites children into the world of cinders, hearths and poverty as well as that of the glamour of the ball, but also gives hope to the lonely child. Likewise, the 'Ugly Duckling' story gives hope to many a child who cannot express fears openly. In contrast, children who lead only safe, secure and protected lives vicariously learn of fear, want and pain, and so on. In this way, there is for all children a two-way process, whereby children both bring their own experience to the book and at the same time, take what the author and illustrator have to offer. What they take is believed to be permanent and 'for ever'. Children's words show us that the fact that stories are inscribed in books gives them an immutability they might not otherwise have.

The process of initiation into a new culture offered by important tales will be of a special kind for young children encountering them in a new language. Of course, certain experiences must be first-hand for them to become meaningful. It is not easy to replace a real experience through illustrations, or even text. Remember Tony and his difficulty with toast and marmalade for breakfast? Tony may eventually learn the rules and corresponding lexis for a European breakfast, but a thousand story-readings will not replace the experience of trying it himself. Likewise, Sunit's joy at realizing that the sea is something different from a 'big puddle' had to wait until he saw it for himself. Nevertheless, we know that the classroom cannot begin to provide real-life experiences for everything young new language learners will meet in their new world. Gradually, the stories Tony and Sunit will learn about in books will fill the gaps and allow them vicariously to gain access to new and sometimes strange experiences and practices. Stories, then, act as mediators of language and culture to children entering a new world in the classroom.

Tajul shows how he uses story-books as a springboard to find out about the eating habits of the new culture when he can speak only a very few words of the host language. Reading *Meg at Sea* with his teacher, he asks 'English eat octopus?'; *The Hungry Giant* (Storychest) gives him the opportunity to ascertain that 'stick loaves' can also be bread rather than big 'fingers' which is his first hypothesis. None of this would be possible without the story book as support or 'scaffold' in Bruner's (1986) terms. The 'Outside-In' approach to beginning reading, then, takes the world of story books as its starting point. Figure 7.1 summarizes ways in which story books act as the key to developing the vital knowledge centres as children begin reading.

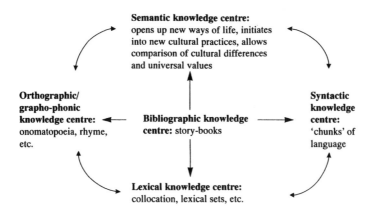

In practice, this may look as follows:

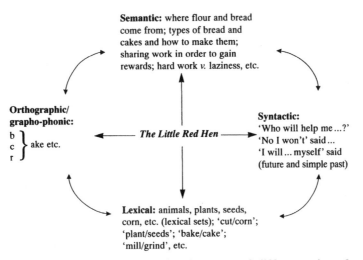

Figure 7.1 *Story books are the key to development of different clues for learning to read.*

An analysis of other important tales using this framework would show how they feed immense funds into the different clues needed by young readers. *Semantically*, they introduce children to different ways of life, to new experiences and cultural practices, yet they draw upon universal morals and values (greed/generosity; cruelty/kindness; cowardice/courage, and so on). *Syntactically*, they provide difficult yet memorable chunks of language which are often reinforced by rhymes and repetition ('Run, run, as fast as you can …'; 'Mirror, mirror on the wall …'; 'Fee, fi, fo, fum …', and so on). *Lexically*, they reinforce difficult collocations and lexical sets (plough/field; sow/corn; scatter/seed, and so on)

Orthographically/grapho-phonically, they draw children's attention to patterns of letters and sounds through rhymes ('run as fast as you c<u>an</u> … gingerbread m<u>an</u>'; 'b-ake/c-ake', and so on) as well as through onomatopoeia. So how might teachers foster this knowledge with both groups and classes of new language learners? We turn first to settings where all children are at the beginning stages of a new language.

The 'Outside-In' approach and structured story

In this section, the teacher is introducing a group of very new language learners to 'The Three Billy Goats Gruff'. It is the first of a series of traditional folk and fairy tales they will read and study during their second year in school. In this case, all the class has the same language background (Sylheti Bengali) and for this particular group of children English is generally not used at home. Consequently, the children's spoken English is still very limited. In this example, the teacher speaks the children's mother tongue as well as being a fluent English speaker. If this had not been the case, she would have asked a classroom assistant or invited a parent or other family or community member to work with her. She has several versions of the story which will be read to the class at storytime. She has chosen the cheapest but most robust version for the structured story sessions (in this case the Ladybird 'Read it Yourself'). There are various reasons for her choice: it will be used for her home reading packs; its sentence structure is simple and clear, moving purposefully through the story using rhymes and repetitions; last, she can cut up a second book for magnet-board figurines. She knows, however, that her oral work must focus on the past tense, since this is the tense normally used as we retell stories. She is interested to see how far the children will distinguish the two tenses as they tell the story and read the text.

The teacher first tells the story in English using the figurines as she does so. She tells it a second time hoping the children will respond to an oral cloze 'Trip, trap, trip, trap, over the —'. She learns from this and her questions that the children can say very little from the story in English. She tells the story in a similar way in Sylheti. The children's faces come alive. The teacher is surprised, however, that none know the word for 'goat' and only some the word for 'bridge' in their mother tongue. Nevertheless, their interest is lively and they actively join in retelling the story and talking about the text.

After ten sessions, each of about one hour, the children's retelling in English is transformed. They are also able to read the story and have made their own small books using a talking computer programme and rewriting the text. What does the process of coming to know a story in a new language look like?

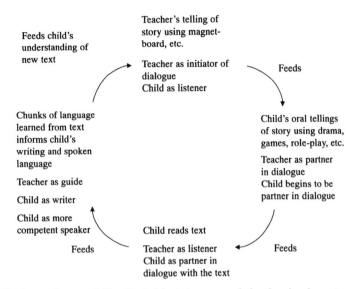

Feeds child's understanding of new text

Teacher's telling of story using magnet-board, etc.

Teacher as initiator of dialogue
Child as listener

Feeds

Chunks of language learned from text informs child's writing and spoken language

Teacher as guide

Child as writer

Child as more competent speaker

Feeds

Child's oral tellings of story using drama, games, role-play, etc.

Teacher as partner in dialogue
Child begins to be partner in dialogue

Child reads text

Teacher as listener
Child as partner in dialogue with the text

Feeds

Figure 7.2 *The inner layer of the 'Outside-In' approach is circular in nature.*

In this section, we study:

- Choosing books and stories for this approach
- Resourcing 'structured story' in the classroom
- Working with 'structured story': a simple procedure.

FIRST THINGS FIRST: CHOOSING BOOKS AND STORIES

A number of stories with simple, clear repetitive texts are available in every country and culture. Traditional folk and fairy stories and fables are particularly valuable for affective, cognitive and linguistic reasons. They introduce children and their families into a new cultural heritage, yet contain familiar morals and values the world over. In *The Uses of Enchantment* (1975), Bruno Bettelheim gives us a comprehensive analysis of the deep moral questions contained in fairy tales which appeal to all children. Why should the queen want to kill Snow White? Why does Hansel and Gretel's stepmother hate them? And so on. We know that fables (for example, 'The Hare and the Tortoise', 'The Lion and the Mouse') appear in different guises ('Kaluli the Hare' in Zambia, 'The Hunter and the Deer' in India) and are well known and loved across cultures.

Nevertheless, it must be remembered that the aim of 'structured story' is for new language learn-ers actually to read the texts and that some of these will form the basis of home–school reading packs. This means that teachers will need to adapt some excellent but difficult stories (*The Hungry Caterpillar* by Eric Carle is likely to fall into this category) by making their own versions (perhaps 'Big Books'). Original complex texts (which will include more difficult versions of traditional folk stories) will be read by the teacher during class story-reading sessions.

Questions to consider when choosing books for 'structured story'

Teachers and other educators may find it helpful to consider the following questions when choosing a book upon which to base 'structured story' work:

- How memorable and appealing is the story for young children?
  Does it have a repetitive element?
  Is the plot easily understandable?
  Will it introduce children into valued (whether old or new) stories?
- Does it already exist as book, audio and/or videotape or computer disc version?
  Are dual-language versions already available (texts and tapes)?
  Is a suitably simple written version already available?
  If not can one be made?
  Are more complex versions available for use during class story-reading sessions?
  Can parents or other members of the community be invited to make illustrated dual-language versions of traditional tales from across the world?

Once a book is found or one has been written:

- Is the language accessible and suitable as early reading material in a new language?
  Is the text of a good size to be seen by the children?
  How much text is on the page?
  Are the illustrations clear?
  Can magnet-board figurines be made easily?
  Will it provide children with useful 'chunks' for their spoken language development?
  Does it have a memorable rhyme or refrain?
  Can songs be linked to it?
- Will it provide links with the 'Inside-Out' approach? (Use of 'key words', such as those relating to fear, and so on, and experiences, which can be expressed through dance, music, cooking, and so on.)
- Will it be accessible to parents and be familiar to siblings? (Does it have a moral which is important in both cultures; can links be made with stories known by parents?)
- Generally, how much potential does it have in developing different clues for learning to read as outlined in Chapter 5?

RESOURCING 'STRUCTURED STORY' IN THE CLASSROOM

We must remember that the 'Outside-In' approach is but half the suggested reading programme. All the resources needed for the 'Inside-Out' approach outlined in Chapter 6 should be available for use during this work. However, some will take on a special importance during 'structured story'. A key addition is the story-pack upon which the approach rests and which I describe below.

The basics

The 'basic' is a story-pack of resources with work and ideas relating directly to each story. Depending upon the size of book, it will probably be contained in a plastic folder. A second and different pack will be available for children to borrow. There are no strict rules on the contents of the pack and dual-language versions may on occasions prove impossible, but packs will usually contain the following:

1 An outline of suggested sessions for teachers as well as a list of focus lexis and syntax for children (see the section 'Structured story: a simple procedure' below).
2 Figurines for a magnet- or flannel-board. These depict the story and may be self-made or cut out from a second version of the book.
3 An audio-tape of the spoken version of the story in English and the children's mother tongues on one side and the story as it is read (using a sound to mark off where a child turns the page) in English and other languages if dual-language stories are used on the other.
4 A second tape I refer to as the 'Listen, discuss and do' tape. On this tape, the teacher tells the story and pauses frequently asking the children to draw something from the story. The children have a worksheet either with six empty squares for their drawings or items which they need to discuss in some way with others in the group.
5 Possibly a video of the story or relevant computer software. A video of children acting the story might be included.
6 The story itself. Dual-language versions using the children's mother tongues should be included wherever possible.
7 Word cards for the magnet- or flannel-board with focus lexis from the text.
8 Simple 'cloze' cards with sentences from the story where children need to find the appropriate word and letter/sound search cards for grapho-phonic/orthographic focus.

Drama resources

In being who we are not, we can call upon a whole set of features we would not normally have ...
In play we are one head taller ... (Vygotsky writing about play in Mind in Society, *1978: 102)*

Drama is a type of play and like play it involves a kind of learning about self which results in a change of the self (Bateson, 1955). Drama takes on a special importance during 'structured story'. At first, children find it difficult and need to repeat phrases after the teacher. With practice they become more adventurous and experiment with the new language in ways where they would otherwise not dare. For each story, devote a lot of time to drama, for it takes many 'rehearsals' before children say confidently what they mean. For each story, provide a set of props and dressing-up clothes. Video practices for discussion with the children and final performances if possible.

Community resources

'My favourite story is "Heidi". I think I'll write that.' Jeanette has three young children in the school where she is an active member of a writing group set up by one of the teachers. Her friend talks about 'The Little Mermaid' and the group discovers that Nilmani, the Gujarati-speaking member of the group, also knows the story. Both work together to produce an illustrated dual-language version for the school. Jan chooses 'The Hare and the Tortoise' (see Figure 7.3). The story is also familiar to her husband, a Twi speaker from Ghana, and he works at home with her on a book and audio-tape. She illustrates the story herself. After a short time, the group are working together on simple dual-language versions of traditional tales, supported by audio-tapes, for use by both themselves and the teacher during 'structured story' sessions. Within a year, the group have received funding to cover the costs of their work and one afternoon per week of a teacher's time to work with them.

The above vignette comes from a group of parents who decided to work on packs of dual-language materials which they later used with groups of children in the classroom and in the school's Parents' Room. The community is an invaluable resource for 'structured story' with new language learners. Benefits for both children and the community (often, but not always, a group of mothers) are mutual (see Figure 7.4).

Book corner

As in any early years classroom, this should be an attractive and comfortable area for children to sit and browse or for 'collaborative reading' and/or 'structured story' to take place. Fewer, more carefully chosen books are better than a disarray of numerous books which the children never use. A display of books by the same author/illustrator or on the same theme (see 'collaborative story') together with children's self-made books should regularly change to reflect the current story which is presented. By limiting the number of books displayed, children quickly become familiar with their stories and recognize the value each individual book holds.

The Hare and the Tortoise
in English and Urdu.

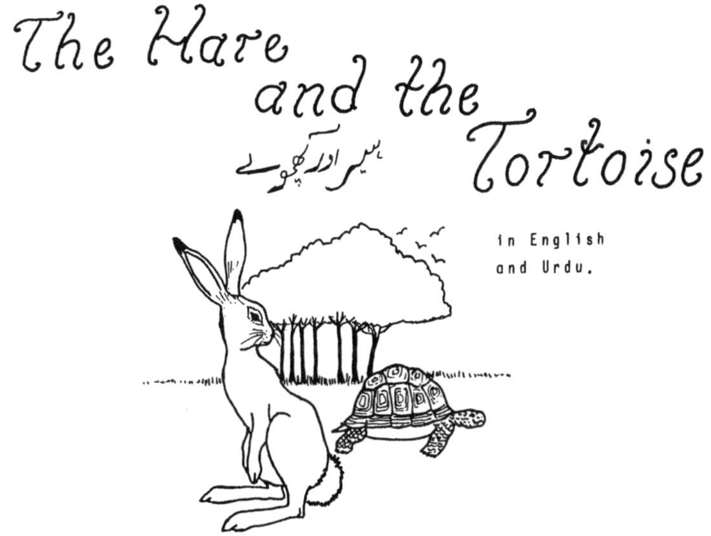

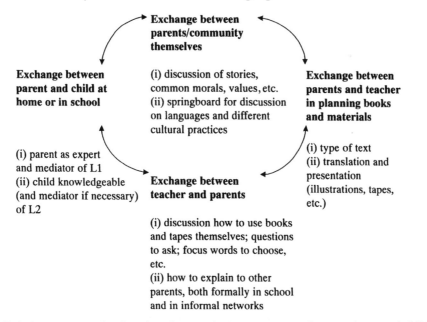

Figure 7.3 *Community work on children's dual-language stories.*

Exchange between parents/community themselves
(i) discussion of stories, common morals, values, etc.
(ii) springboard for discussion on languages and different cultural practices
Exchange between parent and child at home or in school
(i) parent as expert and mediator of L1
(ii) child knowledgeable (and mediator if necessary) of L2
Exchange between parents and teacher in planning books and materials
(i) type of text
(ii) translation and presentation (illustrations, tapes, etc.)
Exchange between teacher and parents
(i) discussion how to use books and tapes themselves; questions to ask; focus words to choose, etc.
(ii) how to explain to other parents, both formally in school and in informal networks

Figure 7.4 *Language and cultural exchanges between community, teachers and children.*

The listening area

The 'structured story' packs are housed in the listening area which has a tape recorder and the magnet- flannel-board. It will be close to the computer and writing area where children compose their own stories. Children are encouraged (using headphones) to listen to the spoken stories in their mother tongue and English, to follow the text using the book and to tell the story to their classmates using the figurines and the board. They may also complete the 'Listen, discuss and do' work in this area, although this may sometimes be completed as a whole-class activity first. In the writing or computer area, they make their own books based on the 'structured story' they are discussing.

Art, music and cooking will all be included in the storywork wherever possible.

WORKING WITH 'STRUCTURED STORY': A SIMPLE PROCEDURE

'Structured story' aims to build upon strengths brought by new language learners into school as well as recognizing their specific weaknesses. What might this look like in practice?

Stage 1: Telling the story

1 Tell the story using the past tense to narrate (other tenses as appropriate) and clear simple language with the help of the figurines and magnet- flannel-board. The story is taped for the children's later use and kept in the story-pack.
2 If possible, tell or play a tape of the story in the children's mother tongues (this is obviously easiest if all the children have the same mother tongue). If not, the tape can be heard at home or with classroom assistants who speak the child's language.
3 Tell the story in English again, asking the children to fictionalize themselves as the characters ('and little Billy Goat Gruff said …') or using oral cloze ('I'm going to eat you — !'). If this is difficult, let the children repeat in chorus or invite the children to speak in their mother tongue. Participation is important here rather than accuracy.

Stage 2: Acting the story

1 With the children, make various props/costumes for the story, referring to the language of the story as these are made.
2 Narrate the story. Individual children play different characters and everyone joins in with a refrain (trip, trap … over the bridge; Grannie, what big eyes you've got! and so on). It may well take three or four sessions before children are confident in their role and contribution. Video a final version if possible.

Stage 3: Listen, discuss and do

1 Prepare the children for listening sessions on the tape in the story-pack.
2 Complete the listening work, having simple or more difficult versions of the task if possible.

Stage 4: Across the curriculum

Extend oral work into other curriculum areas if possible, for example, music and dance or cooking ('Hansel and Gretel'), taking photographs of the children to make a class/group book on what they are doing. Cooking can be especially valuable (cakes, biscuits, and so on for both 'Little Red Riding Hood' and 'Hansel and Gretel') and the results used during drama sessions.

Stage 5: Reading the story

1 *Providing the context*: read the story from the book highlighting individual key words which are attached in turn to the magnet-board (these words are kept in the story-pack). The children read the words (after the teacher if necessary). After reading, ask the children to spell some of the words. Point to similarities in meaning, for example, below and under; small and little, as well as orthographic and phonic likenesses between the words, for example, sm-all and t-all; ch-icken l-icken, pl-ate and g-ate, kn-ife and w-ife, and so on.
2 *Word focus*: remove all the words from the board. Then either give a description of the word chosen or ask a question to which it is the answer, for example, What is under the bridge? (showing the word 'water') Can you spell it? How does the Big Billy Goat Gruff sound? (show 'loud') What does little Billy Goat Gruff like to do? (show 'play') This is to prepare the children for the 'Guess the word' game.
3 *Guess the word game*: (this is to fix the word in coil text in spoken language). (a) The words are placed face down. (b) A child secretly chooses a word. (c) S/he gives the other children a clue without saying the word, for example, goats like to eat this (grass) or this feels wet (water), and so on. (d) The others try to guess the word. This is difficult and needs practice with the whole class and the teacher taking the first few words before children can work in groups.
4 *Opposites game*: (focuses the children on important adjectives and prepositions in the story). The 'opposites' word cards are placed face down on the table. One child picks a card and says 'it's the opposite of "little"'. The other children guess the word and go on to use it in a sentence, for example The wolf was *big* and bad. The children repeat using other cards (wet/dry; dirty/clean; big/little; under/over; up/down, and so on). You may need to give several examples at first, but once children understand the term 'opposite' there should be no difficulty.

5 *Emphasizing intonation*: the children read the story sentence by sentence after the teacher, first in chorus as a group and then individually. The choral reading is important when children are very hesitant in a language as even the shyest gain confidence. This stage is important to enable the children to gain correct pronunciation and intonation patterns without having to concentrate on the reading itself. If possible, support this through songs and rhymes using the text of the story.

6 *Building up a text*: the children are asked to read one word in a sentence and then read the whole sentence, for example, 'goat' – 'Big Billy Goat Gruff goes over the bridge'. During this, build upon the children's knowledge of metalanguage, for example, use terms like 'word', 'sentence', 'letter', and so on. 'How many sentences are on that page?' 'What makes a sentence?' 'Read me the second sentence on that page.' 'How many full stops are there on that page?'

7 *Picture description*: only at this late stage are the children confident in describing different pictures. Begin by asking 'Show me …', then ask 'Tell me what is happening in this picture'.

8 *Story-reading*: ask the children to read the whole story individually or in pairs (or groups if work is completed with the whole class). Try to tape some of their readings so that you can pick up on individual or group difficulties to give extra practice.

9 *Final story-telling*: ask children to tell the story using only the figurines. Tape their tellings. Notice whether forms of language read accurately can be carried over into their tellings. Notice also their use of tenses, adjectives, pronouns (s/he; his/her; him/her, and so on), which are difficult for children who have Asian languages).

10 *Story-telling in other languages*: if you are able, ask children to tell the story in their mother tongue using the figurines (you may need to tape this and ask colleagues or parents for assistance). Compare children's capabilities in both languages.

Stage 6: Writing the story

(Children are only asked to write the story when they have adequate 'chunks' of the target language to enable them to approach the task confidently.)

1 *Cloze cards*: these are at various levels of difficulty and aim to familiarize and reinforce the structures of English syntax before children go on to write their own story. Some will also provide grapho-phonic and orthographic practice.

2 *Story-writing*: use photographs from drama and so on to make a class/group 'Big Book' or make individual story books. You might try using computer software programmes if available. Use key word cards or an exercise book as a simple dictionary as a basis for a wordbank for the children.

Stage 7: Extension into collaborative reading and class story-reading sessions

Search for different versions of traditional stories to use during class story-reading (for example, Paul Galdone's 1973 version of *The Three Billy Goats Gruff* and various other traditional tales, Anthony Browne's 1983 version of *Hansel and Gretel*, and so on).

The 'Outside-In' approach and collaborative reading

This approach assumes either a reasonable grasp of the new language or a multilingual classroom where some children will be either mother-tongue speakers or competent users of the language of the stories to be read. It is designed to be used with whole classes where the teacher reads the story to the class first. Below, we look at:

* Choosing stories
* Reading the story
* Working with 'collaborative reading': a simple procedure.

FIRST THINGS FIRST: CHOOSING BOOKS AND STORIES

Questions to consider when choosing books for 'collaborative reading'

Some questions relating to the text and illustrations:

* Will the story interest the children? Is it *memorable*?
* Will the story motivate the children by drawing on their personal experience or emotions? Will it *develop their imagination and/or appeal to their sense of humour*?
* Is there a *strong and exciting or appealing storyline* which will hold the children's interest in spite of not understanding all the language used?
* Will the story *arouse their curiosity* and help them respond positively to the target culture, language and language learning? If there are specific cultural references, are they clear?
* Is the language level *appropriate*? Is it *clear and unambiguous*? Does it make sense without relying on children's ability to understand complex structures and/or colloquialisms? Is it *memorable*, that is, does it contain features such as *rhyme, onomatopoeia, rhythm* and *encourage appropriate use of intonation patterns* which will help children's pronunciation?

Continues over

- Is there any *natural repetition* to encourage children to participate in the text, facilitate memorizing and provide pronunciation practice? Does the repetition enable children to predict what is coming next in the story? Is the amount of key lexis and syntax which will need to be introduced and practised manageable?
- *Do the illustrations relate to the text* and support children's understanding? Are they clear and attractive? Do they lend themselves to discussion about the story? Are they big enough for all the class to see if necessary?

Some practical questions:

- Is the story available in *different versions*, so that a more difficult version can be used for storytime and a simpler version for the children to read themselves in 'structured story' sessions?
- Is there an *audio-tape and/or videotape or computer program* available for use with the story which children can listen to alone in the listening area or borrow to take home?
- Is the story available in *dual-language* versions and are all the languages spoken in the class available?

Finally, some general questions:

- Does the story have a *high learning potential* in terms of learning about universal morals, truths and values, about the target culture and customs, about the world, and learning about learning generally?
- Does the story provide a *starting point for related language or cross-curricular activities* and lead to follow-up work such as role play and drama, art and craft, and so on in order to reinforce lexis and syntax in a meaningful way?
- Do you like the story yourself? Do you find it memorable and enjoy reading it? If not, discard immediately.

READING THE STORY

We require an education in literature … in order to discover that what we have assumed – with the complicity of our teachers – was nature is in fact culture, that what was given is no more than a way of taking. (Howard, 1974, in Heath, 1982: 49)

Howard's words originally introduced Roland Barthes's volume *S/Z*. Here, Barthes describes the way in which readers use their knowledge of the world (their codes of knowledge) to frame their understanding of written narratives. In Chapter 2 of this book, we saw how easy it is wrongly to assume that our own codes of knowledge and ways of taking from texts are 'given', that is, 'natural' rather than learned. Tony, Julializ, Pia, Dineo, Ah Si, Curtis, Sanah, Hasanat and Elsey showed us that families of emergent bilingual children across the world interpret 'reading' and 'getting meaning from books' in very different ways.

The simple framework offered below is drawn from close observation of teachers whose story-reading sessions are particularly successful and where new language learners are making remarkable progress.

- *Overall rule*: explicitly 'model' what reading actually is and what the fluent reader does. This will mean showing what the reader can bring to and take from the text, but above all it will mean making clear to children the difference between what is actually written on the page and what is teacher/child comment on the text.

How might this be done? Divide the reading into stages:

Stage 1. Setting the story in context: this may be talking to the children about the place where the story is set, why you like the story, other stories by the author, introducing one of the characters or the theme and relating it to your own or the children's lives, and so on. The aim is that children are on tenterhooks to hear the story. As one monolingual child pleaded to his teacher, 'I'm really dying to hear the story now'.

Stage 2. Reading the story: tell the children 'Now I'm going to read the story …'. The story should then be read as well as possible (slowly and clearly yet with lively intonation). There are to be no interruptions during this time. The teacher may point to items in the illustrations, but she does not leave the text.

Stage 3. Talking about the story: after reading the whole text, tell the children clearly that what is to follow is *talk* about the story, not reading it. Show the illustrations, asking the children to relate text-to-life and life-to-text. Ask how they feel about the characters, and so on.

Stage 4. Rereading the story (if required).

'COLLABORATIVE READING': A SIMPLE PROCEDURE

> We become literate by behaving as the literate do, making efforts under their instruction, at home, at school and in our encounters with writing in the world. (Meek, 1991: 6)

'Collaborative reading' is based on the belief that literacy learning is a social process and that children's ideas on reading are built from the practices they observe and participate in as members of a community. In Part 1 of this book, we became aware of the wealth of community literacy activities which young children engage in and bring with them into school. Within the 'collaborative reading' framework, it is the teacher's responsibility to provide access to socially valued literacy practices which may be very new and different from those found within the child's own community. In their role as expert, as mediator of what for many children may be a new cultural practice, teachers must balance explicit teaching with allowing opportunities for children to think independently and to become experts themselves. 'Collaborative reading' builds upon the idea that what counts as reading in each classroom will be constructed by teacher and pupils working together on a common understanding of the reading task.

In 'Beginning reading with children's literature' (1993) Len Unsworth and Mary O'Toole explain that the origins of their programme, first used in Australia, lie in their aim to learn 'more about "the teaching role of the text and its writer"' (Meek, 1982: 20); the ways in which adults '"scaffold" young readers' interactions with texts; the successive approximations which characterize young children's oral reading development; and the essential relationship of these aspects of learning to read' (1982: 95). They stress how important it is for teachers to examine the social processes whereby children become early independent readers and to take these as a starting point for classroom work. Important aspects of these processes, they maintain, are:

- the incorporation of appropriate written language in an enjoyable, functional manner into the normal social routines that a child experiences
- the collaborative exploration of written language with an experienced reader in these routines
- the provision of recurrent, enjoyable and supportive contexts where the same texts may be 'revisited' over time
- access to quality children's literature.

Obviously, resources will be important – from a dynamic classroom library, a reading corner, listening area, a 'publishing' (writing) area to links with parents and the wider community. However, the key to successful collaborative reading lies in careful planning within a structured framework. They offer a planning outline for 45-minute daily sessions over about two weeks for children who are well into their first year or at the beginning of their second year in school. The theme is a selection of books by Pat Hutchins. What follows below is a summary of the overall design of each session followed by a brief summary of one reading session to illustrate how this design works in practice.

The design

Unsworth and O'Toole decided upon using classic texts by excellent authors (in this case Pat Hutchins) because they are supportive of novice readers yet at the same time offer multi-layered meanings which invite different interpretations. These included *I Hunter*, *Goodnight Owl*, *Don't Forget the Bacon*, *The Wind Blew* and, of course, *Rosie's Walk*, a tale of timeless brilliance, thoughtfully analysed by Margaret Meek in *How Texts Teach What Readers Learn* (1988), a tale which, she says, 'has taught hundreds of children that stories include what the reader knows and what the text needn't say' (Meek, 1991: 122). One longer text (*The Very Worst Monster*) was also chosen to emphasize that children's reading development can benefit significantly without them necessarily being able to read all of the text in every book which is the focus of the lesson. However, the authors suggest that themes such as 'bullying' (*Willy the Wimp* and *Willy the Champ* by Anthony Browne), illustrators, books without words, poems, and so on may comprise similar units.

They are careful to stress that the stages within each session should remain flexible and not become rituals. Generally, however, they will fit into the following pattern:

- orientation to collaborative reading
- introduction of the new book
- collaborative reading of the new book
- exploration of text meanings
- consolidation of text processing
- extension reading/writing activities.

Orientation
This stage calls upon material which is very familiar to the children (rhymes, chants, poems, songs). Gradually, these can be displayed in large print and a child points to the words appropriately. The aim is for maximum participation in a group and to give confidence to less fluent speakers. Later, familiar stories can be retold or briefly dramatized or children's writing shared. This stage occupies about 5 minutes of the session.

Introduction of the new book
The aim in this stage is to arouse children's interest in the book by drawing attention to its external features such as the cover design, name of author, and so on. Children use picture or title clues to guess what the book might be about. The teacher also builds upon the children's developing sound–symbol knowledge in identifying the name of the author and the title, for example, whose name begins with the same letter as the author? Where have we seen that word before? The teacher may write the author's name and the title may be written large on the black/whiteboard sounding it out as she does so. This stage also needs about 5 minutes.

Collaborative reading
There are five steps in this section:

1 The teacher's initial reading of the book (to provide a model for the children).
2 Initial discussion with the children about the story (teacher poses some general questions and then asks the children to listen again for answers and see what else they notice).

3 A second reading with informal participation by the children as a group (teacher pauses in appropriate places for children to join in reading).
4 Follow-up discussion drawing on further observations about the story to scaffold-directed participation in a third reading, planning of systematic participation by children in third reading – different groups read different refrains or choruses (trip, trap … and so on) or sound effects.
5 A third reading with teacher-directed participation by the children chorally in small groups or as individuals as appropriate.

The object is to engage children in the reading of the story in a supportive context. This section takes about 15 minutes.

Exploration of meanings

This is 'talk around text' time. It is to encourage children to question texts, pose problems, and so on; for example: 'Did Rosie the hen know that the fox was following her?' (*Rosie's Walk*); 'Was there really a monster?' (David McKee, *Not Now, Bernard*). The first steps in this stage will no doubt be taken by fluent target language speakers, but each of their comments offers a model to others. This stage lasts about 5 to 10 minutes. Children may also work in groups or pairs.

Consolidation

Here children are given structured opportunities to deal directly with print. Work for small groups is designed to develop grapho-phonic, lexical and syntactic clues. One group is targeted for intensive teacher interaction each day. This section lasts about 15 minutes.

Extension

There should always be a 'bank' of activities for children to choose upon completing their work. Harder activities should have been practised by the teacher with the whole class before asking individuals to complete alone. Unsworth and O'Toole suggest 'captioned collages', for example, depicting the scene where a mass of objects are flying in the sky (Pat Hutchins, *The Wind Blew*), by drawing the background, pasting on relevant articles and labelling them using captions from the book. Other extension activities might include constructing and inserting 'speech balloons' into stories, recording stories or a storyboard (matching illustration and text and sequencing photocopied pages from the story).

The session summarized below is an adaptation of the fourth in their series. It takes place towards the end of the first week.

Orientation

Ask the children the names of the three other Pat Hutchins books which have been read (*I Hunter*, *Rosie's Walk* and *Goodnight Owl*) and vote on the favourite. This is then read again and the children are encouraged to join in. Then simple poems on 'wind' are read out ('Dark, windy night' by Anne English, 'Wind song' by Lilian Moore in *My Very First Poetry Book*, Oxford University Press).

Introduction

Ask the children to find *The Wind Blew* from the display. Read and discuss the title and ask children to predict the story from the cover illustration and the title.

Collaborative reading

Mention the dedication. Upon the second reading, use the repetition and rhyme as a way into *oral cloze* (pause just before the end of the second line for the children to complete).

Exploration

Encourage the children to notice how the illustrations tell the story before the text and compare with the illustrations in *Rosie's Walk* and *Goodnight Owl*.

Consolidation

The children are divided into four groups:

1   The children listen to a tape of the story and follow with the book. On some pages, the text has been affixed on a card leaving spaces to forrn a rhyming cloze:

> 'It grabbed a shirt left out to dry
> And tossed it upward to the —'

The reader waits a moment for the child to respond and only then carries on reading.

2   Labelling: a group has a photocopy of the third last page of the book with arrows from the objects to boxes. Children either look through the book or use word cards made from the book to label the object.

3   Similar to the group above but labelling the characters of the story.

4   A captioned collage (see description in the general section above on 'Extension').

Extension

Provide the children with the text for each page on separate cards and invite them to sequence differently so that the story will still make sense.

Questions for reflection

- What special features of language are contained in traditional stories? List some special phrases and discuss how these might be transferred into the everyday language of young children
- Choose two traditional stories. Using the plan in Figure 7.1, how might these link the different clues needed for reading?
- How might families and members of your community become involved in 'structured story' and 'collaborative reading'?
- Which stories might be used from the children's own traditional heritage? Can one story be found from all the language backgrounds in the class and a dual-language version produced?

As he begins his volume of traditional Jewish stories, I.B. Singer (1966: 2) writes, 'The present is only a moment … Today we live, but by tomorrow, today will be a story. The whole world, all human life, is one long story …'. Five-year-old Derrick Wu closes this chapter with a story of his journey to rescue Abeli the monkey with the aid of his kite:

In Hong Kong there are lots of kites
I had a butterfly kite in Hong Kong
A bird did eat it
I told my grandmother
She say 'Go next door'
I make another kite
In secret
Out of paper and wood
If it hasn't got a tail, it can't go high
I could make a kite
And go to Hong Kong
And fly it
I could go in a helicopter
You come into the playground and you
Say 'Good-bye'
I go to Hong Kong and fly kite
Then come back

How much of Derrick Wu's 'story' is from life and how much comes from the many stories he has heard read? We shall never know, nor, perhaps, do we need to.

SUMMARY

Through good stories, especially if dual-language versions are available, new language learners learn to:

♦ **match new words to new cultural practices and ways of being in a new world**

♦ **'chunk' phrases and expressions in the new language and learn to use them appropriately**

♦ **extend their use of metaphor, simile and onomatopoeia in both the new language and the mother tongue**

♦ **share new stories with their parents through dual-language versions.**

For this to happen, educators need to consider:

♦ **linking spoken and written language through the use of drama, music, cookery, art, and so on**

♦ **defining the rules of class story-reading sessions so that children begin to realize the difference between 'reading the words' and 'talk about text'**

♦ **'modelling' reading and enabling children to repeat manageable 'chunks' of text in chorus first**

♦ **increasing the language demands on a child gradually.**

Further reading

Datta, M. (ed.) (2000) *Bilinguality and Literacy: Principles and Practice.* London: Continuum.

Edwards, V. and Walker, S. (1995) *Building Bridges: Multilingual Resources for Children.* The Multilingual Resources for Children Project, University of Reading. Clevedon: Multilingual Matters.

Garvie, E. (1990) *Story as Vehicle.* Clevedon: Multilingual Matters.

Gregory, E. (1996) Learning from the community. A family literacy project with Bangladeshi origin children in London, in S. Wolfendale and K. Topping (eds), *Parental Involvent in Literacy – Effective Partnerships in Education.* London: Croom Helm.

Whitehead, M. (2004) *Language and Literacy in the Early Years.* London: Paul Chapman Publishing (Ch. 7).

8 Linking the 'Inside-Out' and 'Outside-In' approaches: ideas for groups and classes

And the wild things roared their terrible roars and gnashed their terrible teeth and rolled their terrible eyes and showed their terrible claws … (Sendak, 1963)

This short chapter presents a plan for a series of lessons linking the 'Inside-Out' and 'Outside-In' approaches. They should be read alongside Chapters 6 and 7 where general resources and plans are detailed. Since so many lesson plans (and an increasing number daily) are now available for those who have access to the Web, the suggestions are meant only to convey the essence of the approach rather than being in any way comprehensive. The ideas build upon a young child's fascination with fear, danger and excitement (see back to Sylvia Ashton-Warner's ideas in Chapter 6) but at the same time show the child that all is well in real life. In other words, they present a security which experiments: adventure, fear and safety.

Figure 8.1 *Plan for a series of lessons*

The suggestions below are for work related to each of these areas. They are designed for lessons with classes or groups where a majority of children are at the early stage of new language learning. The lessons may stretch over at least a week, much longer if they are the starting point for a curriculum theme. To return to our child opening the introduction to Part 2 of this book, the aim of each activity and session is that the words must pass 'through the head'. Since only then will children make sense of both words and their future worlds.

Example 1: A very early stage – names

AIMS

Conceptual

- To show children that meaning can be represented symbolically through print.
- That streams of sound can be divided into words and syllables and that there may be a one-to-one correspondence between sound and symbol.
- That print is purposeful.

Linguistic

- That the children should use the following lexis and syntax actively: 'My name is —; His/her name is —; What's your/his/her name?; Good morning; How are you today?; Very well, thank you; I see. I can see —; under, over, around, between' (or most important lexis of stories chosen).
- That the children should understand the texts of the books read, even if unable to use all the words in speech.

'INSIDE-OUT'

Key words

Children's names; names of puppets (plus others suggested by the children of those they want in their book).

Resources

- A photo of each child, the teacher, assistant, headteacher, puppets and anyone in the school who is important in the child's life. Duplicate photos of each child and the puppets – one photo per page to be stuck into the large Class Reading Book and one on the front of each child's personal first reading book. Under each photo in the large book, she has written 'My name is —' (for the children to complete). The teacher also has a 'book about herself' which she completes alongside the children. A child is chosen each day to 'help' the puppets do their work.

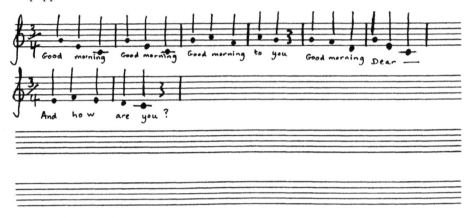

Figure 8.2 *The 'Good morning' song*

- the 'Good morning' song (Figure 8.2) (a very simple introduction to an important 'cultural recipe' of English speaking countries).
- The puppets and their abode (a bag, and so on).
- Name-cards for each child plus 'My', 'name', 'is' and either a stand into which these can be inserted or a magnet-board and magnets.
- The sentence 'My name is (name of 1 puppet)' ready on stand or board but concealed.
- The 'Good morning' song.

Plan

1 The teacher introduces the 'Good morning' song simply by singing it to one child. Gradually all the children join in. Then one child sings to another s/he has chosen, and so on.
2 The teacher tells the class/group she has two friends who have recently arrived in the host country and are very shy. She tells their names and asks children to sing to them to entice them out of their home. Slowly, the puppets emerge and the teacher models 'What's your name? My name is —' (for each puppet). As the puppets gain confidence, they ask the children their names too.
3 Straight away, the teacher shows the large class book, finds her own photo, reads the text pointing to the words and then writes her name in the appropriate place. The children go through the book and each child reads a page inserting his or her name.
4 The name-cards are introduced (usually familiar), called out and games played (for

example, all in the bag and one child picks one for the others to guess 'Is it my name?'). The puppets' name-cards are introduced (these should both begin with the same letter – Dina and Dabir – to initiate sound/symbol correspondence between other names).

5   The sentence with 'My name is (puppet's name)' is shown. The puppet cannot read it (too shy or unable) and needs to be helped by a child. The teacher then takes different names from the bag and the children read 'their' sentence. A game is played where the words are muddled or one is removed. One child is the teacher and the others must guess.

6   The class book is completed by each child and becomes the first Class Reading Book. It is taken to others (headteacher, etc.) to complete and someone 'helps' the puppets. The individual book will also be completed (children copy below teacher or computer to write from the class book or cards). (Handwriting practice will be in a separate book.)

'OUTSIDE-IN'

Resources

• Suggested key books: *Rosie's Walk* (Hutchins)
                        Brown Bear (Martin)
• Other good choices: *Goodnight Owl* (Hutchins)
                        Mr Gumpy's Outing (Burningham)
                        Come Away from the Water, Shirley (Burningham)
                        Bear Hunt (Burningham)
                        Granpa (Burningham)
                        Billy Goats Gruff (Hunia)
                        Where the Wild Things Are (Sendak)
                        Rumpelstiltskin (Hunia)
• Tapes of the stories (dual-language versions if possible); figurines for magnet-board; puppets, dressing-up resources.
• Word cards with 'I', 'can', 'see' put together into 'I can see (child's name)' onto a stand or board (concealed).
• A large class book with 'I can see —' written on each page.

Plan

The children read both with and after the teacher. *Rosie's Walk* is acted out as the teacher reads and is accompanied by a song 'Little (name of puppet) dances …'. The puppet dances 'on', 'under', 'around', and so on different parts of the body and the children 'make' the puppet by using their finger (s/he also goes and dances on individual children).

After reading *Brown Bear*, the teacher 'makes' a telescope with her hand and 'spies' through it saying 'I can see (child or object)'. The children imitate and each says what s/he can see. A guessing game is played where children guess 'Can you see —?' and one child is 'teacher'. A song is learned, to the tune of 'Frère Jacques' (Can you see me? (repeat) Yes, I can. (repeat) Look at how I (actions, for example, 'brush my teeth'). (repeat) Just like this. (repeat)

The sentence card is shown 'I can see (puppet's name)' and many others are made using children's names. The guessing game (mixing and removing words) is played. Different children complete the pages in the class book by drawing a picture of a child and inserting the appropriate name.

Example 2: Food

AIMS

Conceptual

Change of state (involved in cooking and food preparation) – melting, dissolving, thickening, rising, and so on. Sense of taste (might be linked with other senses). Possibly link with 'growing' (typical vegetable and so on).

Linguistic

Lexis and syntax linked with particular cooking, food preparation and serving activities (recipes, tea-party, picnic, and so on). Important lexis and syntax of stories chosen (decide upon most important lexis and syntax to be practised actively or only understood passively beforehand).

Key words

Names of favourite foods, 'I love —'.

'INSIDE-OUT'

Resources

- Packets and labels of children's favourite foods and drink, preferably brought to school by the children. The name labels are cut off and stuck on cards to be used as word cards (for reading, matching and word games).
- Word cards 'I', 'love', 'says' (plus name cards and any useful extras).

- Ingredients for cooking or food preparation.
- Two large class books (1) to record: 'I love — says Dina' (a page for each child or several children with the label or packet stuck on appropriately); (2) a book with photos to record the booking/food preparation/tea-party with the class.
- Different restaurants for socio-dramatic area.

Plan

1 The 'Good morning' song is now on a large card and one child points to the words as others sing.
2 The favourite food labels are discussed and read by children claiming them.
3 The puppets are woken up and whisper to a child what they love to eat for the other children to guess. The 'guessing game' 'Do you love —?' is played and different children are 'teacher'.
4 Sentences are made (using the sentence stand or magnet-board 'I love —.') and the guessing game (see Example 1) is played.
5 Words beginning with the same letter or having the same pattern are matched.
6 The children complete both the large class book 'I love —' and small individual books (see Example 1 above).
7 Depending upon the focus book chosen for the 'Outside-In', cooking and a tea-party take place (for example, making bread, butter and honey sandwiches if the focus is *The Hungry Giant* (Storychest) and the second large class photograph book completed.

'OUTSIDE-IN'

Resources

- Books recommended: *The Very Hungry Caterpillar* (Carle)
  The Little Red Hen (Galdone) and dual-language version
  The Hen and the Mice (Gregory and Walker)
- Other good books: *The Three Bears* (Galdone)
  The Fat Cat (Kent)
  My Five Senses (Aliki)
  The Funny Little Woman (Mosel and Lent)
  Hansel and Gretel (Browne)
  The Great Big Enormous Turnip (Tolstoy)
  The Gingerbread Man (Hunia)
  The Hungry Giant (Storychest)
  The Three Billy Goats Gruff (Brown, Galdone or Hunia)

- Songs: many can be invented (for example, 'This is the way I roll my dough', to the tune of 'Here we go round the mulberry bush').

Plan

See Example 1 above for a framework. Link with cooking and so on from the 'Inside-Out' approach.

Example 3: Illness/doctor's/accident/hospital

AIMS

Conceptual

Temperature, fever, and so on. Relationship between food hygiene and health, sleep, and so on; dental hygiene; emotions during illness; age, and so on.

Linguistic

Lexis concerned with illness and visits to the doctor's, hospital, and so on; 'I don't feel well'; 'I'm sick'; 'I've got a tummy-ache/headache' and so on; 'Dina (a puppet) is sick today'; 'I had an accident', 'I/my brother went to the doctor's/hospital'. Important lexis of books chosen.

'INSIDE-OUT'

Key words

Sick, ill, well, ambulance, accident, hospital, pill, doctor's, headache, tummy-ache, bandage, plaster, and so on.

Resources

Dressing-up clothes for hospital, hospital ward or surgery for dramatic play area, song (adapted version of 'Miss Polly had a dolly who was sick ...' to 'Poor little (name of puppet or child in class) is sick ...') plus a large version of the song with a gap for different children's names; bed for puppet, plus bandages, and so on; a large class book for photos of the sick puppets, and so on.

Plan

1   A puppet's accident is announced and described. A special hospital bed is made, tablets

administered, plaster, bandages, and so on applied.

2 The 'Poor little …' song is sung and acted out. One child is patient; another dresses up with a bag, hat, and so on.

3 Sentences are made relating to the puppets and the children (see Example 1).

4 The class book is completed and individual books are continued.

'OUTSIDE-IN'

Resources

- Recommended books: *John Brown, Rose and the Midnight Cat* (Wagner)

    I Know an Old Lady (Bonne and Mills)

- Other good books   *I Don't Feel Well* (Aliki)

    Hansel and Gretel (Hunia)

    Jack and the Beanstalk (Hunia)

    Sleeping Beauty (Hunia)

    Gangli Gauri (Gregory and Walker – dual-language versions)

Plan

See Example 1.

SUMMARY

- ◆ **Always link language learning with real experience (for example, going shopping, cooking, having a tea-party) wherever possible. Where this is not possible, structured socio-dramatic play areas to reflect different contexts, alongside songs, rhymes, stories and simply free play, and so on should always provide a starting point.**

- ◆ **Always remember families and community members as an excellent resource.**

- ◆ **Never forget the puppets who seem never to fail in getting young children to speak, read or write. They make difficult tasks easy, impossible tasks possible!**

Play, imagination, stories, songs and rhymes – as well as making things easy – link past, present and future in this book and lead us to some final words, offered by Tony, Tajul and Nicole, now fluent bilinguals, in the epilogue closing this volume.

9 Epilogue

Eve: *Would you want to bring your own children up speaking and reading different languages like yourself?*

Tajul: *Definitely, without a doubt. There's no disadvantage to it. Learning a different language is like a gift. It's learning different cultures, isn't it? I mean, it helps you integrate with different people too. I think, to be honest with you that people who don't speak another language, they don't like to see 'outside the box'. It's definitely an advantage. (Tajul, aged 24)*

Remember Tajul, whose early reading experiences figured in Part 1 of this book? We shall return to find out more from him, his classmate Tony, and Nicole from France in just one moment. First, I want very briefly to summarize the main messages I have tried to convey in this book. There could be many, but I shall take my cue from traditional stories and choose just three. The first concerns the 'simple' or 'complex' view of beginning reading; the second concerns 'difference' and the third relates to 'making sense'. The message put forward in this book is that reading is, indeed, a complex and not a simple activity, and the more so when children are learning to read in a new language. This does not mean to say that all children – or, indeed, all new language learners – will find learning to read difficult and complex, but whether they do or not depends upon a complex set of factors, including their first language itself, their level of oral understanding of the new language, their literacy level in the first language, their ability to relate positively to the activity and the text provided and whether they see people like themselves reflected positively in the text, and so on. Successful literacy learning cannot be explained through a simple system or method of teaching whereby one size fits all. Of course, teachers of large classes cannot take an approach tailored differently to each individual child. The approach put forward in Chapters 6 and 7 offers a programme that may be used with whole classes in countries where everyone (or almost everyone) is a new language learner. It is also appropriate in the many British and American schools across the world whose intake is almost entirely indigenous and non-English-speaking children. It offers ideas to educators working with groups in cities receiving many new language learners and to parents who wish to introduce young children simultaneously to a new language and its literacy. However, it is not a method but an approach, where no rules pertain and educators may take or leave whatever parts of the programme they wish.

The second message concerns 'difference'. The argument is made that learning to read in a new language is different from learning to read in a language spoken fluently. In some respects the strengths and weaknesses of new language learners are the reverse of those of a monolingual child. Monolinguals or fluent speakers of a language benefit from being able to predict words, phrases or sentences from their knowledge of the syntax or being able to relate the text to their own experiences from life. New language learners, on the other hand, often benefit from the ability to memorize lexis (words) and phonemes (sounds) easily, having an early awareness of symbolization (knowing an object can be represented as marks on a page) and knowing that the link between an object and its name is arbitrary (that is, a 'chair' may also be 'chaise' or 'Stuhl' according to the language spoken). If children are learning to become biliterate in a different script, they will have an even greater awareness of the arbitrariness of language as well as taking a finer attention to the detail of letters, characters and symbols. However, their weaknesses are in areas that are the monolinguals' strengths (see Chapter 5) and this needs to be recognized.

The third message is that learning to read in a new language is quintessentially about making 'sense' of what reading is all about; not just making sense of the words but of the activity itself and the 'world' it reflects and in which it occurs. Thus we see young children learning to read from complex texts such as the Bible, the Qur'ān, from letters, stories, songs and nursery rhymes, and so on and in a number of different scripts (Roman, Thai, Arabic, Mandarin, and so on). The children do not always 'understand' what they read in that they can explain the meaning, but they manage the task so long as it makes sense to them. In other words, they do not necessarily need a 'simple' approach that breaks words down into individual sounds and phonemes (it is but one approach amongst many) but they do need a reason and motive for reading. That motive is usually part of 'belonging' to a community, whether it is the community of readers of holy texts, letter writers or sharers of traditional rhymes and stories. Mediators of both new and heritage literacies, such as parents, siblings, grandparents and friends are, therefore, crucially important in their endeavour. Educators in formal settings need to create a similarly important community and motives for learning; motives that make sense to both children and the families in which they live and learn.

Which brings me back to Tajul, who opened this Epilogue. It is, perhaps, the dream of every researcher and educator of young children to be able to trace their students in later life. The children contributing to this book span seven countries and two decades. The oldest contributors, Tony, Tajul and Nicole are now in their early twenties. Others, like Husna and Naseema, will be in their late teens and many are still young children under 8. It was a great privilege to be able to meet Tony, Tajul and Nicole again and to be able to talk to them about their memories of learning to speak, read and write in a new language as well as their views on bilingualism and biliteracy and how this links with making their way in the world. I also asked if they could offer any hints for educators in the light of their own experiences.

So how do they remember learning to read and how does this relate to their present lives? After having had the whole of her school education in France, Nicole, at 20 the youngest of the three, has chosen to go to university in Scotland. Tony, now 24, works for the Nationwide Building Society in the same town as his school after gaining his HND (Higher National Diploma) in computing. Tajul has also stayed close to his family. After completing A levels at school, he chose not to go to university but to follow his father into the restaurant business. At 24, he owns and manages two restaurants in the town centre and, jokingly, hopes to retire at 35.

Memories of learning to read in their different languages are patchy for all three. Nicole (see Chapters 4 and 5) has most memories and can compare her experiences in French and English:

Nicole: *I don't really remember learning to read in English that much. I remember French. I remember learning the syllables first and how to recognize the letters, breaking the words up into syllables and then putting the syllables together. Like if words had four syllables, I used to clap four times. I remember having lots of books (in English) with mum and nan, but I don't remember picking up a book and thinking 'I can do it'. I can't remember how mum taught me. I suppose I just picked it up. I had loads of Ladybird books … I used to memorize things. I remember I had a big book of nursery rhymes and I used to look at the pictures and know which nursery rhyme went with it, so it looked like I was reading when I was two or so! I think I just memorized it really … Reading French at school was tortuous. It was really pushy. It was, like, 'You **will** learn to read and you'll learn by the time you leave today.' You had to say whether it was a long or short syllable. We had like pads, they weren't really books, and I used to write words in it and I had to draw a line where the syllable was and we had to put this dot or circle under it to show if it was a long or short syllable. They weren't actually books … it was more just words with different letters and short sentences … I always remember this word 'Nicholas'.*

Eve: *Did you find it hard?*
Nicole: *I don't really know if I found it hard or not. I just did it.*

Nicole feels that she held her two languages and their corresponding literacies separate:

> *I don't really think I transferred reading from one language to the other. I think I just sort of switched … used different parts of the brain, maybe. I think when I saw something in French,*

in my head, I would do the syllable thing, and when I was with mum I would use a different system. I remember we had those flash cards with the word on and they probably helped me ... I was probably more relaxed reading English ...

Besides her parents, Nicole's nan, who lives next door with her grandfather, played an important part in her English literacy:

Nanny used to spend a lot of time with me, reading with me... also playing games with me ...

In contrast, Tony and Tajul (see the introduction to Part 1 and Chapters 4, 5 and 6) have relatively vague memories of learning to read in any of their languages. Tajul reflects that he found all his reading enjoyable but has little idea of how he learned to do it in English:

Tajul: *I'm guessing now ... Was it 'A,B,C'? I learned to read Bengali at Saturday School. Then I went to the Mosque to read Arabic from five 'til seven in the evening. I learned at Bengali school until I was 11.*
Eve: *Did you enjoy reading?*
Tajul: *I must have ... I must have ... I think I enjoyed it all.*

Tajul knows he benefited from the skilled teaching of his three older sisters who sat with him for both his English and Bengali reading. A close family, Tajul 'loves his five sisters to bits'. His youngest sister is now completing her intial teacher education at the local university.

Tony, whose story opened Part 1 of this book, also has few memories of learning to read at either his English or Chinese school. As a Hakka mother-tongue speaker, he needed to learn in Cantonese at his Chinese class. Like Tajul, then, he was learning in three different languages. He attended Chinese school for one or two years and claims he has few memories of the experience. As a child, Tony lived with his grandparents, parents and younger brother. Reading is not something he particularly enjoys. *'Reading isn't my forte, really,'* he says, preferring maths and computing which he later studied.

So what about their lives, languages and reading since those early days? Nicole is in no doubt about her preferences:

I prefer reading in English now. In fact, apart from a book I had 'Winnie-the-Pooh' and 'Goosebumps' in French, I only read French books when I had to ... I just find them boring now. Just the way they're written. For some reason, even if they're written for younger people, they seem really old. I think the last time I read a French book was about four or five years ago at school ... Now I usually read in the evening, nothing classic, like comedy books. I get them from charity shops and take them back when I've finished them. I read them after I've finished studying ... It's a leisure thing ...

Tajul and Tony prefer movies now to reading, although Tajul tries to maintain his religious literacy at the Mosque whenever he can.

Like Tajul, who opened this epilogue, both Tony and Nicole were emphatically and enthusiastically in favour of the bilingualism and biliteracy in their lives. All realize that their bilingualism and biliteracy has opened doors that are likely to remain closed to their monolingual peers. Although recognizing his lack of self-confidence, Tony would like later to become an actor. He spent a year in Canada taking on smaller parts several years ago and would like to visit his grandparents in Hong Kong soon. He feels sure that his knowledge of spoken and written Chinese will stand him in good stead for future jobs and would later like his children to become biliterate too. Tajul was able to return for a year at 14 to attend school in Bangladesh – something that would have been impossible without his bilingual and biliterate abilities. Closest in age to her school days, Nicole considers her advantage in switching countries with ease to attend university:

It's handy growing up with two languages because it guarantees you're going to get a good mark in English all the time and, as well, especially English, it's a really important language to have, being one of the most widely spoken languages in the world. But it's handy having French as well because it means I can come back here one day, or even on holiday, and speak to people. Instead of thinking 'Oh God', I can speak to people, and speak to them well ...

Both Nicole and Tajul stressed their bilingual and bicultural identities:

Nicole: *I always felt more French than English since I was brought up living out here (France). Even though I was English, I'd learned the French way of life – even though I spoke the English language. When we went back to England I always felt, not out of my depth, but sort of confused. I would think 'These people are my age but they're completely different even though I'm the same because of the language'. But I still felt slightly English. Now I'm in Scotland, I still speak French and speak French a lot ... It's sort of blurring the boundaries 'cos it's been reversed really. I used to speak French at school and English at home all the time and now I speak English at Uni and French at home all the time with my friend Claire (whose mother is English and father is French). At Uni we both speak English together because our friends speak English. I still feel French because I haven't lost any of it but I'm using my English more now ... I'm enjoying Scotland. If I come back here (France), I'd like to live in a bigger place ...*

Tajul: *I identify myself as both (British and Bengali). I have lots of English friends. I see them ever day really. I was born in Britain but I am Bengali … I can't deny it. It's in my blood. It's my roots. Even though I've been brought up here, I wouldn't turn my back on it …*

Tony, however, refuses to enter this debate:

Eve: *Do you think you feel more Chinese or British or both?*
Tony: *I can't really say. I just feel I'm a human being …*

Finally, what advice might these young adults offer to those educating young new language learners during the very early stages? Their ideas are most enlightening when looking back to their reading excerpts in Part 1 of the book. Tony, whose early language and literacy skills were somehow different from those that counted in the English school, now says, *'make things easier for them (the children) to understand'.* Nicole, whose brilliance in reading English stood out, in spite of learning informally and in a relaxed way with her mother, says, *'Don't push children. A mistake is pushing them to learn 'cos you dig your heels in'.* But the last message of this book must surely come from Tajul. Tajul, whom we met in Chapter 5 taking risks (*'there's the window'* – meaning *'magnifying glass'*), questioning his teacher (*'English eat Octopus?'*), and playing with language (*'This not bread, these are finger'*) and who is now referred to as 'the crazy one' of the family by his dad because of his risk-taking in life, stresses, *'Be their friend first. Play with them and take them slowly into learning. Put things in front of them and see what they're interested in'.* For young children, learning to read in a new language is an adventurous journey. A journey that is full of hazards, where many risks need to be taken along the way. Our task as educators is to encourage children's risk-taking, to understand the uniqueness of every child's journey and to ensure success at every step.

Glossary

Additive/subtractive language learning Second language learning is referred to as 'additive' if the new language is learned without detriment to the mother tongue. It is 'subtractive' if the aim is to replace the first language with the new one.

Arbitrary nature of language The relationship between the word (or symbol) and the sound it makes is referred to as arbitrary because there is no intrinsic link between the sound sequence and the word it refers to. Young bilinguals have an early awareness of the arbitrariness of language as they know that an object can be represented by more than one word.

Assimilation (policy of) The policy which aims to absorb immigrants as quickly as possible into the language and culture of the host country.

Bibliographic knowledge The knowledge of books or written texts in the widest sense. This may be a knowledge of the layout of a book (in English left to right, top to bottom, and so on) or the knowledge that certain words and expressions 'belong' to certain texts, for example, 'Once upon a time …'.

BISC (basic interpersonal communicative skills) These communicative skills are those needed for everyday purposes, for example, playground language, and are picked up very quickly by new language learners.

Broker 'Language broker' is the term given to those who mediate a new language (and culture) to other niembers of their family. Many children in Europe and the US are language brokers for both parents and younger siblings.

CALP (cognitive academic language proficiency) The academic language that is needed as children discuss and write about texts or other academic subjects. Children may take up to 7 years to learn these in a new language.

Cohesive devices The term used to refer to words which link one sentence (or part of a sentence) to another. Some common cohesive devices are: pronominal reference, for example, 'I saw John yesterday. *He* was ill'; synonyms, for example, sick/ill; superordinates, for example, 'apples and oranges = fruit'; collocational expressions, for example, 'toast with butter and jam'. Knowledge of these can greatly assist a child in predicting a text.

Collocation Words which are habitually associated with each other, for example, cup and saucer; knife and fork. Knowledge of more complex collocations, for example, 'rancid' rather than 'rotten' butter, come through experiences in a language or can be gained through experiences with written stories, for example, 'grinding corn; sowing seeds'.

Comprehensible input Language which contains some new element in it but is nevertheless understood by the learner because of linguistic, paralinguistic or situational clues or world knowledge back-up.

Conjunction A word used to connect words or clauses, for example, but, and, because, if, although.

Cues (reading clues) Signals sent from five knowledge centres (bibliographic or book); semantic (meaning); syntactic (structure); lexical (word) and grapho-phonic (sound/symbol relationship) to assist readers in predicting a text.

Diglossia/diglossic situation Terms in sociolinguistics for the use of two or more varieties of language (one a 'high' or standard variety and one a 'low' spoken vernacular) for different purposes or functions in the same community.

European Communities Directive (1977) A Directive from the European Community which strongly supported the principle that the teaching of the mother tongue improves rather than impairs the linguistic and educational performance of bilingual children and urged all member countries to provide mother-tongue teaching.

Generative words The term used by Paolo Freire in his work with adult illiterates in Brazil during the 1960s to denote words of high personal value which also generated a variety of phonemic combinations, for example, sl- ave: c- ave; r- ave.

Grapho-phonic and phonological knowledge Knowledge which enables readers to match written symbols (graphemes) with the sounds we attach to them (phonemes).

Holophrastic stage (of language learning) The first stage of language acquisition whereby, a one word utterance can be made sense of only in the immediate situation, for example, 'doggie can mean 'Look at the doggie' or 'Doggie wants his food', and so on.

Interdependency principle The principle that a child will be able to transfer knowledge gained in one language to others.

Inter-lingual/intra-lingual miscues Inter-lingual miscues are those which arise from interference of the mother tongue, for example, 'she's' for male and female for Asian children speaking languages where gender is not marked by the relative pronoun. Intra-lingual miscues arise from the structure of the target language itself, for example, 'goed' where the past tense rule 'add -ed' is applied to irregular past tenses.

Inter-psychological/intra-psychological planes According to Vygotsky (1962), children's development appears first on the interpsychological (or social) plane in interaction with others and then on the intrapsychological (or mental) plane.

Key vocabulary The term used by Sylvia Ashton-Warner in her book *Teacher* (1963) to denote the words which are most important to children as they begin reading.

Knowledge centre According to Rummelhart's interactive theory of reading (1977), we draw upon cues (clues) sent out from four knowledge centres (semantic, syntactic, lexical, orthographic/grapho-phonic) as we set about learning to read. In this book, I add 'bibliographic knowledge' as a fifth knowledge centre.

Lexis (lexical knowledge) Lexis is the vocabulary of a language. Lexical knowledge is the knowledge of words which enables readers to predict which word might follow in a text. This may be through *collocation*, *pronominal reference*, and so on.

Lingua franca Language that is widely used as a means of communication amongst speakers of other languages.

Linguistic set A group of words linked through common association, for example, 'breakfast' words, 'school' words.

Linguistic stem The term is used here to mean 'structure'. Ben-Zeev (1977) found that bilingual children were more able than monolinguals to analyse linguistic stems when asked to ignore word meaning and sentence framing and substitute one word for another, for example, Researcher: 'If "they" means "spaghetti", how do we say "They are good children"?' (Answer: 'Spaghetti' are good children.)

Metalanguage/metalinguistic awareness A term in linguistics for language used to talk about language. Research studies show that young bilinguals have an advanced metalinguistic awareness as they are able to realise the arbitrariness of language, see word boundaries, and so on at an earlier stage than monolinguals.

Minority language submersion When minority languages are totally ignored or deliberately suppressed, we refer to the situation as one of 'minority language submersion'.

Miscue analysis A detailed analysis of the errors made by an inexperienced reader in order to ascertain which cues (clues) s/he can use as well as which may be lacking.

New language learners The term used in this book to refer to children who are learning to read in a language that they do not fluently speak. This may describe children who do not speak the host language at home or it may apply to children who are learning to read in a new language (often English) at the same time as becoming literate in their first language. They may also be learning a number of different scripts simultaneously and becoming biliterate or even pluriliterate.

Oral cloze Originally from 'close' (to complete a pattern in Gestalt theory). A cloze exercise asks children to supply missing words either orally or in writing, for example, 'Little Red Riding Hood went to the forest to pick —'.

Oronym Strings of sound that can be carved into words in different ways, for example, 'I scream' or 'ice-cream'.

Orthographic knowledge One of the five knowledge centres called upon by the reader: an awareness of spelling patterns, for example, 'scr' may begin words in English but 'hlt' may not.

Paired reading Usually used to refer to home reading schemes whereby caregiver and child share the reading. Usually the child begins reading and signs to the caregiver to continue.

Participation structure A term used to refer to the nature of turn-taking between teacher or caregiver and child as they interact during reading events.

Parts of speech A grammatical category or class of words. Traditional grammars of English generally list eight parts of speech: noun, pronoun, verb, adjective, adverb, preposition, conjunction, interjection.

Phoneme In linguistics, the smallest category of sound which can distinguish two words, for example, 'p-an', 'b-an' which comprise three phonemes 'b' or 'p', 'a' and 'n'.

Phonological knowledge The knowledge of sound patterns in a language.

Preposition One of the traditional parts of speech denoting principally time and space (at, from, through, without, up, down, under, over, in, to, and so on) but also cause and purpose (for) and agent (by, with).

Pronominal reference Where a pronoun (he, she, it, we, you, they) refers to a noun which precedes it, for example, 'I saw Mary yesterday. *She* was ill'.

Qur'ān The sacred book of Islam.

Redundancy Part(s) of a message which can be eliminated without loss of essential information.

Scaffolding The metaphor used to describe the way in which both caregivers and teachers structure young children's learning. The notion of a 'scaffold' which can be dismounted piece by piece highlights the child's growing capacity and independence.

Schema A mental model of the world which enables one to make personal sense of it.

Semantic knowledge The knowledge of the meaning of words within a culture including their denotations, orientations, implications and ambiguities.

Sense and meaning In this book, Vygotsky's (1962) definitions are used, whereby 'meaning' denotes the dictionary definition of a word, the way it is commonly understood, and 'sense' the personal meaning attached to a word which will depend upon the personal and cultural experiences an individual has made in relation to a word, for example, 'flag' may have a positive or negative 'sense' according to an individual's experience within a culture.

Signifier/signified In linguistics, the word is sometimes referred to as the 'signifier' and the object it refers to the 'signified'.

Speech event The term used by Hymes (1974) to denote an event for which certain words, phrases and linguistic 'recipes' are necessary. These will be different from one culture to another (for example, weddings, funerals).

Superordinates Terms with a wide reference, for example, *flower* and *furniture*, which will include a number of subordinates, for example, rose, daisy, table or chair.

Synonym Words which have similar meanings, for example, obedient, compliant.

Syntactic knowledge Knowledge of the grammar of a language (the way in which words combine into units such as phrase, clause and sentence).

Voiced/unvoiced (voiceless) consonants 'Voice' is the buzzing sound made in the larynx by the vibration of the vocal chords. 'Voiced' sounds are 'b, d, g, z'; 'voiceless' sounds are 'p, t, k, s' whereby 's' can be voiced if it follows a voiced sound (wugs) or voiceless if it does not (bus).

Bibliography

Adams, M.J. (1995) *Beginning to Read: Thinking and Learning about Print*. Cambridge, MA: MIT Press.

Ashton-Warner, S. (1963) *Teacher*. London: Penguin (reprinted by Virago, 1980).

Bakhtin, M. (1986) *Speech Genres and Other Late Essays*. Austin, TX: University of Texas Press.

Bateson, G. (1955) A theory of play and fantasy, in J.S. Bruner, A. Jolly and K. Sylva (eds), *Play*. London: Penguin.

Bateson, G. (1979) *Mind and Nature*. London: Wildwood House.

Ben-Zeev, S. (1977) The influence of bilingualism on cognitive strategy and cognitive development, *Child Development*, 48: 1009–18.

Bettelheim, B. (1975) *The Uses of Enchantment*. London: Thames & Hudson.

Brooker, E. (2002) *Starting School – Young Children Learning Culture*. Buckingham: Open University Press.

Bruner, J.S. (1979) From communication to language: a psychological perspective, in V. Lee (ed.), *Language Development*. London: Croom Helm.

Bruner, J.S. (1986) *Actual Minds, Possible Worlds*. Cambridge, MA: Harvard University Press.

Chall, J.S. (1979) The great debate: ten years later, with a modest proposal for reading stages, in L.B. Resnick and P.A. Weaver (eds), *Theory and Practice of Early Reading, Vol. 1*. Hillsdale, NJ: Lawrence Erlbaum Associates.

Chen, Y. and Gregory, E. (2004) 'How do I read these words?': bilingual exchange teaching between Cantonese-speaking peers, in E. Gregory, S. Long and D. Volk (eds), *Many Pathways to Literacy: Young Children Learning with Siblings, Grandparents, Peers and Communities*. New York and London: Routledge.

Chittenden, E.A., Salinger, T.S. and Bussis, A.M (2001) *Inquiry into Meaning: an Investigation of Learning to Read*. New York: Teachers College Press.

Chomsky, N. (1964) *Aspects of the Theory of Syntax*. Cambridge, MA: Institute of Technology Press.

Clay, M. (1991) *Becoming Literate: The Construction of Inner Control*. Portsmouth, NH: Heinemann.

Cochran-Smith, M. (1984) *The Making of a Reader.* Norwood, NJ: Ablex.

Cole, M. (1985) The zone of proximal development; where culture and cognition create each other, in J.V. Wertsch (ed.), *Culture, Communication and Cognition: Vygotskian Perspectives.* Cambridge: Cambridge University Press.

Cole, M. (1996) *Cultural Psychology: A Once and Future Discipline.* Cambridge, MA: Belknap Press of Harvard University Press.

Collins English Dictionary (1992) 3rd edn. London: HarperCollins.

Comrie, B. (ed.) (1987) *The World's Major Languages.* London: Routledge.

Crystal, D. (1987) *The Cambridge Encyclopedia of Language.* Cambridge: Guild Publishing.

Cummins, J. (1979) Linguistic interdependence and the educational development of bilingual children, *Review of Educational Research*, 49: 222–51.

Datta, M. (ed.) (2000) *Bilinguality and Literacy: Principles and Practice.* London: Continuum.

Dombey, H. (1983) Learning the language of books, in M. Meek (ed.), *Opening Moves.* Bedford Way Papers 17. London: Institute of Education, University of London.

Dombey, H. (1988) Partners in the telling, in M. Meek and C. Mills (eds), *Language and Literacy in the Primacy School.* Lewes: Falmer Press.

Donaldson, M. (1978) *Children's Minds.* Glasgow: Fontana.

Douglas, M. (1970) *Purity and Danger.* London: Pelican Books.

Drury, R. (2004) Samia and Sadaqat play school: early bilingual literacy at home, in E. Gregory, S. Long and D. Volk (eds), *Many Pathways to Literacy: Young Children Learning with Siblings, Grandparents, Peers and Communities.* New York and London: Routledge.

Drury, R. (2007) *Young Bilingual Learners at Home and at School.* Stoke-on-Trent: Trentham.

Dunn, J. (1989) The family as an educational environment in the pre-school years, in C.W. Desforges (ed.), *Early Childhood Education. The British Journal of Educational Psychology.* Monograph Series No. 4, Scottish Academic Press.

Duranti, A. and Ochs, E. (1995) Syncretic literacy in a Samoan American community, *Focus on Diversity*, 55(2): 1–2, Bilingual Research Centre, University of California, Santa Cruz.

Dyson, A.H. (1993) *Social Worlds of Children Learning to Write in an Urban Primary School.* New York: Teachers College Press

Eco, U. (1980) *The Name of the Rose.* London: Picador.

Edwards, V. (1995) *Reading in Multilingual Classrooms.* Reading: Reading and Language Information Centre, University of Reading.

Edwards, V. (2004) *Multilingualism in the English Speaking World.* Oxford: Blackwell.

Edwards, V. and Walker, S. (1995) *Building Bridges: Multilingual Resources for Children.* The Multilingual Resource for Children Project, University of Reading. Clevedon: Multilingual Matters.

Fitzpatrick, F. (1987) *The Open Door.* Clevedon: Multilingual Matters.

Fox, C. (1988) Poppies will make them grant, in M. Meek and C. Mills (eds), *Language and*

Literacy in The Primary School. Lewes: Falmer Press.

Freire, P. (1973) *Education: The Practice of Freedom.* London: Writers and Readers Publishing Co-op.

Garvie, E. (1990) *Story as Vehicle.* Clevedon: Multilingual Matters.

Gibbons, P. (1995) *Learning to Learn in a Second Language.* Newtown, NSW: Primary English Teaching Association.

Goelman, H., Oberg, A. and Smith, F. (eds) (1984) *Awakening to Literacy.* London: Heinemann Education.

Goethe, W., in Vygotsky, L. (1962) *Thought and Language.* Cambridge, MA: MIT Press.

González, N., Moll, L.C. and Amanti, C. (2005) *Funds of Knowledge: Theorising Practices in Households, Communities and Classrooms.* Hillsdale, NJ: Lawrence Erlbaum Associates.

Goodman, K. (1996) *On Reading: A Common-sense Look at the Nature of Language and the Science of Reading.* Portsmouth, NH: Heinemann.

Gough, P.B. and Tunmer, W.E. (1986) Decoding, reading and reading disability, *Remedial and Special Education* 7: 6–10.

Gregory, E. (1993) What counts as reading in the early years classroom? *British Journal of Educational Psychology,* 63: 213–29.

Gregory, E. (1994a) Cultural assumptions and early years pedagogy: the effect of the home culture on minority children's interpretation of reading in school, *Language, Culture and Curriculum,* 7(2): 1–14.

Gregory, E. (1994b) The National Curriculum and non-native speakers of English, in G. Blenkin and V. Kelly (eds), *The National Curriculum and Early Learning: An Evaluation.* London: Paul Chapman Publishing.

Gregory, E. (1994c) Negotiation as a criterial factor in learning to read in a second language, in D. Graddol, J. Maybin and B. Stierer (eds), *Researching Language and Literacy in Social Context.* Clevedon: Multilingual Matters.

Gregory, E. (1996) Learning from the community: a family literacy project with Bangladeshi-origin children in London, in S. Wolfendale and K.Topping (eds), *Parental Involvement in Literacy – Effective Partnerships in Education.* London: Croom Helm.

Gregory, E. and Biarnès, J. (1994) Tony and Jean François: looking for sense in the strangeness of school, in H. Dombey and M. Meek-Spencer (eds), *First Steps Together: Home–School Early Literacy in European Contexts.* Stoke-on-Trent: Trentham/IEDPE.

Gregory, E. and Kelly, C. (1992) Bilingualism and assessment, in G. Blenkin and A. Kelly (eds), *Assessment in Early Childhood Education.* London: Paul Chapman Publishing.

Gregory, E. and Williams, A. (2000) *City Literacies: Learning to Read across Generations and Cultures.* London: Routledge.

Gregory, E., Lathwell, J., Mace, J. and Rashid, N. (1993) *Literacy at Home and at School.* London: Literacy Research Group, Faculty of Education, Goldsmiths College.

Gregory, E., Long, S. and Volk, D. (eds) (2004) *Many Pathways to Literacy: Young Children Learning with Siblings, Grandparents, Peers and Communities*. New York and London: Routledge.

Grosjean, F. (1982) *Life with Two Languages: An Introduction to Bilingualism*. London: Harvard University Press.

Haight, W.L. and Carter-Black, J. (2004) 'His eye is on the sparrow': teaching and learning in an African American church, in E. Gregory, S. Long and D. Volk (eds), *Many Pathways to Literacy: Young Children Learning with Siblings, Grandparents, Peers and Communities*. New York and London: Routledge.

Hall, E.T. (1959) *The Silent Language*. New York: Doubleday

Hatch, E. (1974) Research on reading a second language, *Journal of Reading Behaviour*, 6: 53–61.

Hatch, E., Peck, S. and Wagner-Gough, J. (1979) A look at process in child second language acquisition, in E. Ochs and B. Schieffelin (eds), *Developmental Pragmatics*. New York: Academic Press.

Heath, S.B. (1982) What no bed-time story means: narrative skills at home and in school, *Language and Society*, 6: 49–76.

Heath, S.B. (1983) *Ways with Words: Language, Life and Work in Communities and Classrooms*. Cambridge: Cambridge University Press.

Helavaara Robertson, L. (2004) Multilingual flexibility and literacy learning in an Urdu community school, in E. Gregory, S. Long and D. Volk (eds), *Many Pathways to Literacy: Young Children Learning with Siblings, Grandparents, Peers and Communities*. New York and London: Routledge.

Holdaway, D. (1979) *The Foundations of Literacy*. New York: Ashton-Scholastic.

HMSO (1967) *Children and their Primary Schools* (Plowden Report). London: HMSO.

HMSO (1975) *A Language for Life* (Bullock Report). Report of the Committee of Inquiry appointed by the Secretary of State for Education and Science. London: HMSO.

HMSO (1985) *An Education for All* (Swann Report). Report of the Committee of Inquiry into Education for Children from Ethnic Minority Groups. London: HMSO.

Holscher, P. (1995) An intercultural education project in Bavaria. Paper presented to SCCA conference, 27–28 April, London.

Hong-Kingston, M. (1977) *The Woman Warrior*. London: Picador.

Howard, R. (1974) A note on S/Z, in R. Barthes *Introduction to S/Z*, trans. R. Miller. New York: Hill and Wang.

Hudak, T.J. (1987) Thai, in B. Comrie (ed.) *The World's Major Languages*. London: Routledge.

Huey, E.B. (1908) *The Psychology and Pedagogy of Reading*. New York: Macmillan.

Hymes, D. (1974) *Foundations in Sociolinguistics*. Philadelphia, PA: University of Philadelphia Press.

Ianco-Worrall, A. (1972) Bilingualism and cognitive development, *Child Development*, 43: 390–400.

Jessel, J., Gregory, E., Arju, T., Kenner, C. and Ruby, M. (2004) Children and their grandparents at home: a mutually supportive context for learning and linguistic development, *English Quarterly. Canadian Council of Teachers of English Language Arts*, 36(4): 16–23.

John-Steiner, V. (1986) The road to competence in an alien land: a Vygotskian perspective on bilingualism, in J.V. Wertsch (ed.), *Culture, Communication and Cognition: Vygotskian Perspectives*. Cambridge: Cambridge University Press.

Keller, H., Yvosi, R.D. and Voelker, S. (2002) The role of motor stimulation in parental ethnotheories, *Journal of Cross-Cultural Psychology*, 33(4): 398–414.

Kelly, G. (1955) *A Theory of Personality*. MA: The Norton Library.

Kenner, C. (2004a) Community school pupils reinterpret their knowledge of Chinese and Arabic for primary school peers, in E. Gregory, S. Long and D. Volk (eds), *Many Pathways to Literacy: Young Children Learning with Siblings, Grandparents, Peers and Communities*. New York and London: Routledge.

Kenner, C. (2004b) *Becoming Biliterate: Young Children Learning Different Writing Systems*. Stoke-on-Trent: Trentham.

Kenner, C. Arju, T., Gregory, E., Jessel, J. and Ruby, M. (2004c) The role of grandparents in childrens' learning, *Primary Practice*, 38(Autumn): 41–5.

Lambert, W.E. (1967) A social psychology of bilingualism, *Journal of Social Issues*, 23: 91–109.

Lambert, W.E. and Tucker, G.R. (1972) *Bilingual Education of Children: The St Lambert Experiment*. Rowley, MA: Newbury House.

Lloyd, S. (2003) Synthetic phonics – what is it? *Reading Reform Foundation Newsletter*, 50(Spring): 25–7.

Long, S., with Bell, D. and Brown, J. (2004) Making a place for peer interaction: Mexican American kindergartners learning language and literacy, in E. Gregory, S. Long and D. Volk (eds), *Many Pathways to Literacy: Young Children Learning with Siblings, Grandparents, Peers and Communities*. New York and London: Routledge.

Luke, A. (1993) The social construction of literacy in the primary school, in L. Unsworth (ed.), *Literacy, Learning and Teaching*. Melbourne: Macmillan.

Lüthi, M. (1970) *Once Upon a Time: On the Nature of Fairy Tales*. New York: Frederick Ungar.

Mackay, D., Thompson, B. and Schaub, P. (1978) *Breakthrough to Literacy*. London: Longman.

Meek, M. (1979) Discussion, 1 December, Institute of Education, London.

Meek, M. (1981) Handing down the magic, in P. Salmon (ed.), *Coming to Know*. London: Routledge and Kegan Paul.

Meek, M. (1982) *Learning to Read*. London: Bodley Head.

Meek, M. (1988) *How Texts Teach What Readers Learn*. London: Thimble Press.

Meek, M. (1991) *On Being Literate*. London: Bodley Head.

Michaels, S. (1986) Narrative presentations: an oral preparation for literacy with 1st graders, in J. Cook-Gumperz (ed.), *The Social Construction of Literacy*. Cambridge: Cambridge University Press.

Minns, H. (1990) *Read It To Me Now*. London: Virago Press.

Miskin, R. (2005) in *Teaching Children to Read*. Eighth Report of Session 2004–2005, House of Commons Education and Skills Committee.

Moll, L.C., Amanti, C., Neff, D. and Gonzalez, N. (1992) Funds of knowledge for teaching: using a qualitative approach to connect homes and classrooms, *Theory into Practice*, 31: 132–41.

Mor-Sommerfeld, A. (2002) Language mosaic: developing literacy in a second new language: a new perspective, *Reading Literacy and Language*, 36(3): 99–105.

National Reading Panel (2000) *Teaching Children to Read: An Evidence Based Assessment of the Scientific Research Literature on Reading and Its Implications for Reading Instruction*. National Institute of Child Health and Human Development: N.H. Pub. 00–4769.

Newson, J. and Newson, E. (1975) Intersubjectivity and the transmission of culture: on the social origins of symbolic functioning, *Bulletin of the British Psychology Society*, 218: 437–46.

Nsamenang, A.B. and Lamb, M.E. (1998) Socialisation of Nso children in the Bamenda grassfields of Northwest Cameroon, in M. Woodhead, D. Faulkner and K. Littleton (eds), *Cultural Worlds of Early Childhood*. London and New York: Routledge.

Oberhuemer, P. (1994) Stories make a difference: intercultural dialogue in the early years, *European Early Childhood Research Journal*, 2(1): 35–42.

Olgaç, C.R. (2001) Socialization, language and learning in a Somali diasporic community, in Rinkeby. *Africa and Asia*, No.1: 69-78. Department of African and Oriental Languages: Göteborg University.

Olmedo, I. (2004) Storytelling and Latino elders: what can children learn?, in E. Gregory, S. Long and D. Volk (eds), *Many Pathways to Literacy: Young Children Learning with Siblings, Grandparents, Peers and Communities*. New York and London: Routledge.

Palincsar, A.S., Brown, A. and Campione, J.C. (1993) 1st grade dialogues for knowledge acquisition and use, in E.A. Foreman, N. Minick and C.A. Stone (eds), *Contexts for Learning*. New York: Oxford University Press.

Perfetti, C.H. (1984) *Reading Ability*. New York: Oxford University Press.

Piaget, J. (1959) *The Language and Thought of the Child*. London: Routledge and Kegan Paul.

Pinker, S. (1994) *The Language Instinct: The New Science of Language and Mind*. London: Allen Lane/Penguin Press.

Robertson, L.H. (2004) Multilingual flexibility and literacy learning in an Urdu community school, in E. Gregory, S. Long and D. Volk (eds), *Many Pathways to Literacy: Young Children Learning with Siblings, Grandparents, Peer and Communities*. New York and London: Routledge.

Rogoff, B. (1990) *Apprenticeship in Thinking. Cognitive Development in Social Context*. New York: Oxford University Press.

Rogoff, B. (2003) *The Cultural Nature of Human Development.* New York: Oxford University Press.

Rogoff, B., Mosier, C., Mistry, J. and Goncu, A. (1993) Toddlers' guided participation with their caregivers in cultural activity, in E. Forman, N. Minick and C. Stone (eds), *Contexts for Learning.* New York: Oxford University Press.

Rosaldo, R. (1989) *Culture and Truth: The Remaking of Social Analysis.* Boston, MA: Beacon Press.

Rosaldo, R. (1993) *Culture and Truth: The Remaking of Social Analysis.* Boston, MA: Beacon Press.

Rose, J. (2006) *Independent Review of the Teaching of Early Reading.* March. London: DfES.

Rosen, H. (1985) *Stories and Meanings.* Sheffield: National Association for the Teaching of English (49 Broomgrove Road, Sheffield S10 2NA).

Rummelhart, D.E. (1977) Toward an interactive model of reading, in S. Dornic (ed.), *Attention and Performance.* Hillsdale, NJ: Lawrence Erlbaum Associates.

Salmon, P. (ed.) (1981) *Coming to Know.* London: Routledge and Kegan Paul.

Sapir, E. (1970) *Language, Culture and Personality.* Berkeley, CA: University of California Press.

Schieffelin, B.B. and Cochran-Smith, M. (1984) Learning to read culturally: literacy before schooling, in H. Goelmann, A. Oberg and F. Smith (eds), *Awakening to Literacy.* London: Heinemann Educational.

Schieffelin, B.B. and Ochs, E. (1998) A cultural perspective on the transition from prelinguistic to linguistic communication, in M. Woodhead, D. Faulkner and K. Littleton (eds), *Cultural Worlds of Early Childhood.* London and New York: Routledge.

Scollon, R. (1979) A real early stage: an unzippered condensation of a dissertation on child language, in E. Ochs and B. Schieffelin (eds), *Developmental Pragmatics.* New York: Academic Press.

Scollon, R. and Scollon, B.K. (1981) *Narrative, Literacy and Face in Interethnic Communication.* Norwood, NJ: Ablex.

Scribner, S. and Cole, M., (1981) *The Psychology of Literacy.* Cambridge, MA: Harvard University Press.

Singer, I.B. (1966) *Zlateh the Goat and Other Stories.* New York: HarperTrophy.

Skutnabb-Kangas, T. (1981) *Bilingualism or Not? The Education of Minorities.* Clevedon: Multilingual Matters.

Skutnabb-Kangas, T. (1984) Multilingualism and the education of minority children, in T. Skutnabb-Kangas and J. Cummins (eds), *Minority Education.* Clevedon: Multilingual Matters.

Snow. C.E. (1977) The development of conversation between mothers and babies, *Journal of Child Language*, 4: 1–22.

Steffensen, M.S., Joag-dev, C. and Anderson, C. (1980) A cross-cultural perspective on reading comprehension, *Reading Research Quarterly*, 15: 10–29.

Street, B. (1984) *Literacy in Theory and Practice.* Cambridge: Cambridge University Press.

Super, C. and Harkness, S. (1996) The cultural structuring of child development, in J.W. Berry, P.R. Dasen and T.S. Saraswathi (eds), *Handbook of Cross Cultural Psychology, Vol. 2: Basic Processes and Human Development.* Boston, MA: Allyn and Bacon.

Thwe, P.K. (2002) *From the Land of Green Ghosts.* London: HarperCollins.

Tobin, J.J., Wu, D.Y.H. and Davidson, D.H. (1989) *Pre-School in Three Cultures.* New Haven, CT: Yale University Press.

Torgerson, C.J., Brooks, G. and Hall, J. (2006) *A Systematic Review of the Research Literature on the Use of Phonics in the Teaching of Reading and Spelling.* Research Report RR711. London: DfES.

Tosi, A. (1984) *Immigration and Bilingual Education.* Oxford: Pergamon Press.

Trevarthan, C. (1998) The child's need to learn a culture, in M. Woodhead, D. Faulkner and K. Littleton (eds), *Cultural Worlds of Early Childhood.* London and New York: Routledge.

Unsworth, L. (ed.) (1993) *Literacy Learning and Teaching: Language as Social Practice in the Primary School.* Melbourne: Macmillan.

Unsworth, L. and O'Toole, M. (1993) Beginning reading with children's literature, in L. Unsworth (ed.), *Literacy Learning and Teaching: Language as Social Practice in The Primary School.* Melbourne: Macmillan.

Verhoeven, L. (1987) *Ethnic Minority Children Acquiring Literacy.* Dordrecht: Foris.

Volk, D., with de Acosta, M. (2004) Mediating networks for literacy learning: the role of Puerto Rican siblings, in E. Gregory, S. Long and D. Volk (eds), *Many Pathways to Literacy: Young Children Learning with Siblings, Grandparents, Peers and Communities.* New York and London: Routledge.

Vygotsky, L. (1962) *Thought and Language.* Cambridge, MA: MIT Press.

Vygotsky, L. (1978) *Mind in Society: The Development of Higher Psychological Processes.* Cambridge, MA: Harvard University Press.

Vygotsky, L. (1981) The genesis of higher mental functions, in J.V. Wertsch (ed.), *The Concept of Activity in Soviet Psychology.* New York: M.E. Sharpe.

Wagner, D.A., Messick, B.M. and Spratt, J. (1986) Studying literacy in Morocco, in B. Schieffelin and P. Gilmore (eds), *Ethnographic Perspectives*, Vol. 21 in the series Advance in Discourse Processes. New York: Academic Press.

Walkerdine, V. (1981) From context to text: a psychosemiotic approach to abstract thought, in B. Beveridge (ed.), *Children Thinking Through Language.* London: Edward Arnold.

Wallace, C. (1986) *Learning to Read in a Multicultural Society.* Oxford: Pergamon Press.

Wertsch, J.V. (ed.) (1985) *Culture, Communication and Cognition: Vygotskian Perspectives.* Cambridge: Cambridge University Press.

Whitehead, M. (2004) *Language and Literacy in the Early Years: An Approach for Education Students.* London: Paul Chapman Publishing.

Wong-Fillmore, L. (1982) The language learner as an individual: implications of research on individual differences for the ESL teacher, in M.A. Clarke and J. Handscombe (eds), *On TEOL '82: Pacific Perspectives on Language Learning and Teaching.* Washington, DC: TESOL.

Wood, D., Bruner, J.S. and Ross, G. (1976) The role of tutoring in problem solving, *Journal of Child Psychology and Psychiatry*, 17: 89–100.

Woodhead, M., Faulkner, D. and Littleton, K. (eds) (1998) *Cultural Worlds of Early Childhood.* London and New York: Routledge.

Children's books

(Mentioned in the text or classic children's books recommended for use in homes and classrooms for young children learning to read in English. Books by John Burningham, Eric Carle and Pat Hutchins are particularly recommended – although only a small selection is featured below.)

Ahlberg, J. and Ahlberg, A. (1977) *Each Peach, Pear, Plum.* London: Kestrel/Penguin Books.

Aliki (1963) *My Five Senses.* New York: Crowell.

Aliki (1977) *I Don't Feel Well.* London: Hamish Hamilton.

Barnett, C. (1983) *The Lion and the Mouse.* Oxford: Oxford University Press.

Bernal, M.C. et al. (1989) *La Ventafocs.* Vie: Eumo Editorial.

Bonne, R. and Mills, A. (1961) *I Know an Old Lady.* New York: Rand McNally.

Browne, A. (1976) *Bear Hunt.* London: Hamish Hamilton.

Browne, A. (1981) *Hansel and Gretel.* London: Julia McRae.

Browne, A. (1986) *Willy the Wimp.* London: Methuen.

Brown, M. (1995) *Goodnight Moon.* New York: Harper Children's Audio (story and audio-cassette)

Burningham, J. (1978) *Mr Gumpy's Outing.* London: Walker Books.

Burningham, J. (1992) *Come Away from the Water, Shirley.* London: Walker Books.

Burningham, J. (2003) *Granpa.* London: Walker Books.

Carle, E. (1969) *The Very Hungry Caterpillar.* Cleveland, OH: Collins World.

Carle, E. (1971) *Do you want to be my friend?* New York: HarperCollins.

Carle, E. (1984) *The Very Busy Spider.* New York: Philomel Books.

Carle, E. (1990) *The Very Quiet Cricket.* New York: Penguin Putnam Books.

Carle, E. (1995) *The Very Lonely Firefly.* New York: Philomel Books.

Colwell, E. (1970) *Tell Me a Story.* London: Penguin Books.

Eastman, P.D. (1962) *Are You My Mother?* London: (Collins) Beginner Books.

Foster, J. (1985) *My Very First Poetry Book.* Oxford: Oxford University Press.

Galdone, P. (1970) *The Three Little Pigs.* New York: Seabury Press.

Galdone, P. (1972) *The Three Bears.* New York: Scholastic.

Galdone, P. (1973) *The Little Red Hen.* New York: Scholastic.

Galdone, P. (1973) *The Three Billy Goats Gruff.* New York: Scholastic.

Ginsburg, M. (1972) *The Chick and the Duckling.* New York: Macmillan.

Gregory, E. and Walker, D. (1987) *The Hen and the Mice: A Tale of Laziness.* London: Hodder & Stoughton (dual-language versions in Bengali, Gujarati, Punjabi and Urdu).

Gregory, E. and Walker, D. (1987) *Gangli Gauri.* London: Hodder & Stoughton (dual-language versions in Bengali, Gujarati, Punjabi and Urdu).

Grimm, J. (1993) *Rumpelstiltskin.* Ladybird Grade II Easy Reader. London: Ladybird Books.

Hargreaves, R. (1976) *Mr Funny.* London: Thurman.

Hargreaves, R. (1976) *Mr Impossible.* London: Thurman.

Hargreaves, R. (1976) *Mr Messy.* London: Thurman.

Hargreaves, R. (1976) *Mr Nosey.* London: Thurman.

Hill, E. (1980) *The Spot Book.* London: Heinemann (series also in dual-language versions).

Hunia, F. (1993) *Red Riding Hood.* Read it Yourself. Loughborough: Ladybird Books.

Hunia, F. (1993) *The Billy Goats Gruff.* Read it Yourself. Loughborough: Ladybird Books.

Hunia, F. (1993) *Rumpelstiltskin.* Read it Yourself. Loughborough: Ladybird Books.

Hunia, F. (1993) *Jack and the Beanstalk.* Read it Yourself. Loughborough: Ladybird Books.

Hunia, F. (1993) *Hansel and Gretel.* Read it Yourself. Loughborough: Ladybird Books.

Hunia, F. (1993) *Sleeping Beauty.* Read it Yourself. Loughborough: Ladybird Books.

Hutchins, P. (1968) *Rosie's Walk.* London: Bodley Head.

Hutchins, P. (1975) *Goodnight Owl.* London: Puffin.

Hutchins, P. (1978) *Don't Forget the Bacon.* London: Puffin.

Hutchins, P. (1978) *The Wind Blew.* London: Puffin.

Hutchins, P. (1982) *I Hunter.* London: Bodley Head.

Hutchins, P. (1986) *The Very Worst Monster.* London: Puffin.

Kent, J. (1971) *The Fat Cat.* New York: Scholastic.

Kerr, J. (1968) *The Tiger who Came to Tea.* London: Collins Picture Lions.

McDermott, G. (1972) *Anansi the Spider.* New York: Holt, Rinehart & Winston.

McKee, D. (1987) *Not Now, Bernard.* London: Arrow, Random Century.

Mack, S. (1974) *Ten Bears in my Bed.* New York: Pantheon.

Mantra Books (an excellent selection of dual-language books, CD Roms and so on).

Martin, B. and Carle, E. (2007 edn) *Brown Bear.* New York: Henry Holt.

Martin, B. and Carle, E. (2007 edn) *Polar Bear.* New York: Henry Holt.

Martin, B. (1970) *Fire! Fire! said Mrs. McGuire.* New York: Holt, Rinehart & Winston.

Mosel, A. and Lent, D. (1972) *The Funny Little Woman*. Harlow: Longman Young Books.

Murphy, J. (1980) *Peace at Last*. London: Macmillan.

Nicholl, H. and Pienkowski, J. (1972) *Meg's Car*. London: Heinemann.

Nicholls, H. and Pienkowski, J. (1972) *Meg at Sea*. London: Heinemann.

Piers, H. (1979) *Mouse Looks for a House*. London: Methuen.

Jayal, A. (1974) *Bhondoo the Monkey series*. India: Thomson Press.

(1975) *My Big Book of Nursery Tales*. London: Award Publishers.

Oxford Reading Series, *Bif's Aeroplane*.

Rogers, P. (1990) *Don't Blame Me*. London: Bodley Head.

Rosen, M. (1999) *Bear Hunt*. London: Walker Books.

Ross, T. (1981) *Little Red Riding Hood*. London: Penguin.

The Fireman, London: Ladybird Books.

Sendak, M. (1970) *Where the Wild Things Are*. Gosford, NSW: Ashton-Scholastic.

Southgate, V. (1965) (retold) *The Elves and the Shoemaker*. London: Penguin Books, The Well Loved Tales.

Storychest Series, *The Hungry Giant*. Gosford, NSW: Ashton-Scholastic.

The Animal Story, *Elephant*. Thai Airlines (dual-language Thai/English text).

Tolstoy, A. (1968) *The Great Big Enormous Turnip*. New York: Franklin Watts.

Topiwalo, the Hat Maker. Plus tape. London: Harmony.

Vipont, E. (1969) *The Elephant and the Bad Baby*. London: Hamish Hamilton.

Wadsworth, O. (1986) *Over in the Meadow: A Counting Out Rhyme*. London: Puffin.

Wagner, J. (1977) *John Brown, Rose and the Midnight Cat*. Melbourne: Kestrel.

Index

Added to a page number 'f' denotes a figure.